Bring 'Em On

COMMUNICATION, MEDIA, AND POLITICS

Series Editor
Robert E. Denton, Jr., Virginia Tech

This series features a broad range of work dealing with the role and function of communication in the realm of politics, broadly defined. Including general academic books, monographs, and texts for use in graduate and advanced undergraduate courses, the series will encompass humanistic, critical, historical, and empirical studies in political communication in the United States. Primary subject areas include campaigns and elections, media, and political institutions. *Communication, Media, and Politics* books will be of interest to students, teachers, and scholars of political communication from the disciplines of communication, rhetorical studies, political science, journalism, and political sociology.

Titles in the Series

Bring 'Em On

Media and Politics in the Iraq War

Edited by Lee Artz and
Yahya R. Kamalipour

ROWMAN & LITTLEFIELD PUBLISHERS, INC.
Lanham • Boulder • New York • Toronto • Oxford

ROWMAN & LITTLEFIELD PUBLISHERS, INC.

Published in the United States of America
by Rowman & Littlefield Publishers, Inc.
A wholly owned subsidiary of The Rowman & Littlefield Publishing Group, Inc.
4501 Forbes Boulevard, Suite 200, Lanham, Maryland 20706
www.rowmanlittlefield.com

PO Box 317
Oxford
OX2 9RU, UK

British Library Cataloguing in Publication Information Available

Library of Congress Cataloging-in-Publication Data

Bring 'em on : media and politics in the Iraq War / edited by Lee Artz and
Yahya R. Kamalipour.
   p. cm. — (Communication, media, and politics)
   Includes bibliographical references and index.
   ISBN 0-7425-3688-2 (cloth : alk. paper) --ISBN 0-7425-3689-0 (pbk. : alk. paper)
   1. Iraq War, 2003—Mas media and the war. 2. Mass media and public opinion—United States.
I. Title: Media and politics
in the U.S. war on Iraq. II. Artz, Lee. III. Kamalipour, Yahya R. IV. Series.
   P96.173B75 2005
   070.4'4995670443'0973—dc22

                                                          2005013657

Contents

Foreword: The Bush Administration's March to War

Douglas Kellner

The Bush administration's Iraq policy has created tremendous ongoing controversy. Since the 9/11 terror attacks, the Bush administration's foreign policy has exhibited a marked unilateralism and militarism in which U.S. military power is used to advance U.S. interests and military hegemony. The policy was first evident in the Afghanistan intervention following the September 11, 2001, terror attacks, and informed the 2003 war against Iraq (Kellner 2003a). Here, I will sketch out the trajectory of the Bush administration's march to war and highlight the change in national security policy that legitimated the Iraq intervention. See also Scott Ritter (2003) and Chalmers Johnson (2004), who have written sharp critiques of Bush's preemptive strike policy.

In a speech to West Point cadets on June 1, 2002, George W. Bush proclaimed a new "doctrine" that the United States would strike first against enemies. It was soon apparent that this was a major shift in U.S. military policy, replacing the Cold War doctrine of containment and deterrence with a new policy of preemptive strikes, one that could be tried out in Iraq. U.S. allies were extremely upset with this shift in U.S. policy and move toward an aggressive U.S. unilateralism. In an article, "Bush to Formalize a Defense Policy of Hitting First," David E. Sanger wrote for the *New York Times* (June 17, 2002):

> The process of including America's allies has only just begun, and administration officials concede that it will be difficult at best. Leaders in Berlin, Paris and Beijing, in particular, have often warned against unilateralism. But Mr. Bush's new policy could amount to ultimate unilateralism, because it reserves the right to determine what constitutes a threat to American security and to act even if that threat is not judged imminent.

After a summer of debate on the necessity of the United States going to war against Iraq to destroy its "weapons of mass destruction," on August 26, 2002, U.S. Vice President Dick Cheney applied the new preemptive strike and unilateralist doctrine to Iraq, arguing:

> What we must not do in the face of a mortal threat is to give in to wishful think-ing or willful blindness. . . . Deliverable weapons of mass destruction in the hands of a terror network or murderous dictator or the two working together constitutes [sic] as grave a threat as can be imagined. The risks of inaction are far greater than the risks of action. (Borger, 2002)

Cheney was responding to many former generals and high-level members of the earlier Bush administration who had reservations against the sort of unilateralist U.S. attack against Iraq that hawks in the Bush administration were urging.

During the late summer and fall of 2002, leading Republican leaders and generals warned about adverse consequences of an Iraq invasion and occupa-tion that could destabilize the Middle East, create havoc in Iraq, turn signifi-cant portions of the world militantly against the United States, disrupt oil sup-plies, interfere with the war on terrorism, and drive down an unstable economy. Questions were raised concerning how the Bush administration could pay for a war in Iraq and the "war on terrorism" at the same time, and whether the U.S. military could take on so many challenges. There were wor-ries that a post-Saddam regime in Iraq might be chaotic and involve the United States in a hazardous and violent period of stabilization and recon-struction that could go catastrophically wrong.

Major figures from Bush senior's administration, including his National Se-curity Advisor Brent Scowcroft, Secretary of State James Baker, and Lawrence Eagleburger made strong arguments that it would be a disaster for the United States to go it alone in Iraq and that the United States would appear to be a rogue state without significant support from allies and the United Na-tions. The head of the U.S. NATO force in the Kosovo war, General Wesley Clark, wrote a long piece on the follies of the Bush administration's Iraq plan (see also Clark, 2003). Norman Schwarzkopf, head of U.S. forces in the Gulf War, came out against an Iraq invasion; and General Anthony Zinni, who had recently served as Bush's top envoy to the Middle East, warned against war with Iraq, saying "it would stretch U.S. forces too thin and make unwanted en-emies in the volatile region." Making a pointed attack against Bush adminis-tration officials like Dick Cheney and Richard Perle, who were lusting for war and had never served in the military, Zinni remarked, "It's pretty interesting that all the generals see it the same way, and all the others who have never fired a shot and are hot to go to war see it another way" (Salinero 2002, A1).

Dick Cheney, however, continued to beat the war drums, making belli-cose and saber-rattling speeches for war against Iraq in late August. The Cheney said that UN weapons inspectors "would provide no assurance whatsoever" of Iraqi compliance with UN disarmament resolutions and would instead in-crease the danger by providing "false comfort." Cheney was, in effect, rul-ing out any political mediation of the Iraq situation at a time when global forces were furiously attempting to get UN weapons inspectors back in Iraq to get a vigorous weapons inspection process underway. Yet in a September 1 interview with the BBC, Colin Powell stated that UN weapons inspectors should be sent back to Iraq as a "first step" to deal with the threats posed by the regime of Saddam Hussein. Commentators noted that the White House had not cleared Cheney's speech and that there was evident "disarray" in the Bush administration over Iraq policy (Borger 2002; Fineman and Lip-per 2002).

As Cheney was calling for war against Iraq, reports spread on the Internet concerning how, when Cheney was CEO at Halliburton, that corporation did more business with Iraq than any other U.S. company. A *Washington Post* story was recirculating that Halliburton had signed contracts under Cheney's leadership worth $73 million through two subsidiaries that sold Iraq oil-pro-duction equipment and spare parts when there were restrictions against U.S. corporations doing business with Iraq (Lynch 2001). Cheney denied knowl-edge of these ventures, but an investigation into his Halliburton stewardship could well reveal that he had knowledge about his company's dealings with Iraq (and if he didn't have knowledge, what kind of a CEO was he?). Indeed, the current CEO, David Lesar, has stated that Cheney "unquestionably" knew about the Iraq dealings, implying that the vice president was lying. Inquiries into Halliburton under Cheney could also unfold how the company set up dummy companies, much like Enron, to cover business losses and provide fake profits, and other questionable activities that had transpired during Ch-eney's years as CEO. Cheney was being sued on behalf of stockholders for the collapse of the company's stock value under his leadership, and investi-gation of this explosive issue could put Cheney in the same category and cell as Ken Lay. Cheney desperately needed a war against Iraq to deflect attention from his misdeeds and intensely pushed for war (Woodward 2002, 2004).

When Tony Blair arrived in the United States for a war summit on Iraq on the weekend of September 8, 2002, the Bush administration released photos of what was presented as new evidence of an Iraqi nuclear facility. Bush waved the picture and a 1998 report that Iraq was six months away from nu-clear bomb capacity at the media, as Blair stood beside him, with Bush pro-claiming, "I don't know what more evidence you need" [to demonstrate that Iraq was producing dangerous nuclear weapons] (DeYoung 2002, A10). But as ABC, NBC, and the *Washington Post* quickly reported, these pictures and reports were fraudulent evidence, suggesting that the Bush-Cheney clique was resorting to a web of lies and deception to legitimate their Iraq venture. Needless to say, Fox TV and other U.S. cable networks played stories of Iraqi arms programs and their threat to the United States and its allies all day to beat the war drums.

On September 8, 2002, Cheney and the other top warmongers of the Bush administration were all over the Sunday talk shows making their case for war against Iraq. Cheney repeated on *Meet the Press* all of the well-known crimes of Saddam Hussein, insinuated long-discredited ties between Iraq and al Qaeda, and even tried to pin the anthrax attacks on Iraq, although all evidence pointed to U.S. weapons-grade facilities. Cheney was going to have a war against Iraq no matter what the price, and it appeared that George W. Bush was equally gung ho and set on war (Suskind 2004; Clarke 2004; Woodward 2004).

Throughout the fall of 2002, the Bush administration continued to multiply claims concerning the dangers of Iraqi weapons of mass destruction. The Bush administration insinuated constantly that Iraq was allied with terrorist groups, and despite no evidence of links between the Saddam regime and al Qaeda, more than 50 percent of the U.S. population believed that the Iraqis were involved in the 9/11 attacks. Moreover, Bush and others in his circle regularly described the "war against terrorism" as World War III, while U.S. Secretary of Defense Donald Rumsfeld said that it could last as long as the Cold War and Dick Cheney, speaking like a true militarist, said it could go on for a "long, long time, perhaps indefinitely." Such an Orwellian nightmare could plunge the world into a new millennium of escalating war with unintended consequences and embroil the United States in countless wars, normalizing war as conflict resolution and creating countless new enemies for the would-be American hegemon (Kellner 2003a). Indeed, as Chambers Johnson writes in *Blowback* (2000), Empire has hidden costs. Becoming hegemon breeds resentment and hostility, and when the Empire carries out aggression it elicits anger and creates enemies, intensifying the dangers of perpetual war (Johnson 2004).

On September 20, 2002, it was apparent that the hawks' position in the Bush administration had triumphed, at least on the level of official military doctrine, when the Bush administration released a document signaling some of the most important and far-ranging shifts in U.S. foreign and military policy since the end of the Cold War. Titled "The National Security Strategy of the United States," the thirty-three-page report outlined a new doctrine of U.S. military supremacy, providing justifications for the United States to undertake unilateral and preemptive strikes in the name of "counter-proliferation." This clumsy Orwellian concept was offered as a replacement for the concept of "nonproliferation" and would legitimate the unilateral destruction of a country's presumed weapons of mass destruction. The document, in effect, renounced the global security, multilateralism, and rule by international law that had informed U.S. thinking since World War II and that appeared to be a consensus among Western nations during the era of globalization.

The Bush administration's language of "preemptive strikes," "regime change," and "anticipatory self-defense" is purely Orwellian, presenting euphemisms for raw military aggression. Critics assailed the new "Strike first, ask questions later" policy, the belligerent unilateralism, and the dangerous legitimating of preemptive strikes. Israel, Pakistan, Russia, China, and lesser powers had already used the so-called Bush doctrine and war against terrorism to legitimate attacks on domestic and external foes, and there were dangers that it could legitimate a proliferation of war and make the world more unstable and violent. As William Galston (2002) writes:

> A global strategy based on the new Bush doctrine of preemption means the end of the system of international institutions, laws and norms that we have worked to build for more than half a century. What is at stake is nothing less than a fundamental shift in America's place in the world. Rather than continuing to serve as first among equals in the postwar international system, the United States would act as a law unto itself, creating new rules of international engagement without the consent of other nations. In my judgment, this new stance would ill serve the long-term interests of the United States.

To be sure, the United States itself had engaged in countless military aggressions in the post–World War II era and often subverted international law and global institutions. Nonetheless, the Bush administration doctrine of preemptive strikes was perceived as a sharp break with previous U.S. and regnant global military doctrine, and could unleash a series of wars that would plunge the world into the sort of nightmare militarism and totalitarianism sketched out in George Orwell's *1984*. The Bush policy is highly repressive, taking the global community to a social Darwinist battleground where decades of international law were put aside in perhaps the most dangerous foreign policy doctrine that had ever appeared in U.S. history. It portends a militarist future and era of perpetual war in which an escalating militarism could generate a cycle of unending violence and retribution, such as has been evident in the Israel and Palestine conflict.

Around the same time that the Bush administration was pushing its new strategic doctrine and seeking to apply it in a war against Iraq, a 2000 report circulated titled "Rebuilding America's Defenses: Strategies, Forces and Resources for a New American Century." Drawn up by the neoconservative think tank Project for a New American Century (PNAC) for a group that now comprises the right wing of the Bush administration, including Dick Cheney, Donald Rumsfeld, and U.S. Deputy Secretary of Defense Paul Wolfowitz, the document clearly spelled out a plan for U.S. world hegemony grounded in U.S. military dominance of the world and control of the Persian Gulf region and its oil supplies ("Rebuilding America's Defenses," 2000). Its upfront goals were a "Pax Americana" and U.S. domination of the world during the new millennium. The document shows that core members of the Bush administration had longed envisaged taking military control of the Gulf region, with the PNAC text stating:

> The United States has for decades sought to play a more permanent role in Gulf regional security. While the unresolved conflict with Iraq provides the immediate justification, the need for a substantial American force presence in the Gulf transcends the issue of the regime of Saddam Hussein.

The PNAC document argues for "maintaining global U.S. preeminence, precluding the rise of a great power rival, and shaping the international security order in line with American principles and interests." The vision is long range, urging U.S. domination of the Gulf "as far into the future as possible." It is also highly militarist, calling for the United States to "fight and decisively win multiple, simultaneous major theatre wars" as a "core mission." U.S. armed forces would serve as "the cavalry on the new American frontier," with U.S. military power blocking the emergence of other countries challenging U.S. domination. It would enlist key allies such as Britain as "the most effective and efficient means of exercising American global leadership," and would put the United States, and not the UN, as leader of military interventions or peacekeeping missions. Moreover, it envisages taking on Iran after Iraq, spotlights China for "regime change," and calls for creating "U.S. Space Forces" to dominate outer space and positioning the United States to totally control cyberspace to prevent "enemies" from "using the Internet against the U.S."

The architects of the PNAC document were now key members of the Bush administration, and in early February 2003 reports circulated that U.S. attacks on Iraq were inevitable. Richard Perle, a senior adviser to Donald Rumsfeld, indicated that war with Iraq was likely even if Baghdad backed down and allowed inspectors back in to hunt for weapons of mass destruction, according to an interview in early February at a Munich security conference: "I don't think there's anything [Iraqi leader] Saddam Hussein could do that would convince [the] U.S. there's no longer any danger coming from Iraq," said Perle. He also said the only thing that would convince the United States would be a change of regime. Bush was on "a very clear path" heading toward war with Iraq, Perle added ("Attack on Iraq is Unavoidable," 2002).

Colin Powell's February 5, 2003, speech to the United Nations clearly indicated that the Bush administration was dead-set on war. Powell opened by declaring: "My colleagues, every statement I make today is backed up by sources, solid sources. These are not assertions. What we are giving you are facts and conclusions based on solid intelligence." Thirty-two times Powell thundered, "We know!" that Iraq contained this or that weapons program and actual so-called weapons of mass destruction. Supported by graphs, satellite pictures of alleged weapons facilities, presentations of intercepted Iraqi messages, statistics concerning Iraqi chemical and biological weapons programs, signs of a dangerous nuclear weapons program, and other "evidence," Powell, with CIA Director George Tenet sitting impassively behind him, made the case for war on Iraq to a global audience (Greenberg 2003).

As the hawks in the Bush administration accelerated their war talk, there was a sustained array of strong criticism of the Bush war plans from throughout the world, gigantic global peace demonstrations, and criticism from the United States's closest allies, like Canada and Germany, which usually went along with U.S. military interventions. On February 13, over 8 million people on five continents demonstrated against the planned war against Iraq. This demonstration was, according to Tariq Ali, "unprecedented in size, scope and scale. . . . The turnout in Western Europe broke all records: three million in Rome, two million in Spain, a million and a half in London, half a million in Berlin" (Ali 2003, 144). There was a fierce debate in Britain over whether Tony Blair should support Bush's adventure and an indication that Blair might lose support in his own party and possibly the next election if he went along with Bush.

An attempt to produce a compromise resolution in the UN collapsed, and it was simply a matter of when the war would begin. Whereas the explicit war aims were to shut down Iraq's "weapons of mass destruction," and thus enforce UN resolutions that mandated that Iraq eliminate its offensive weapons, there were many hidden agendas in the Bush administration offensive against Iraq. To be reelected Bush needed a major victory and symbolic triumph over terrorism in order to deflect from the failings of his regime both domestically and in the realm of foreign policy.

Moreover, ideologues within the Bush administration wanted to legitimate a policy of preemptive strikes, and a successful attack on Iraq could inaugurate and normalize this policy. Some of the same militarist unilateralists in the Bush administration envisage U.S. world hegemony, the elder Bush's "New World Order," with the United States as the reigning military power and world's policeman (Kellner 2003b). Increased control of the world's oil supplies provided a tempting prize for Bush, Cheney, Condoleezza Rice, and other former oil executives who maintain key roles in the Bush administration. Moreover, key members of the PNAC constituted a neoconservative clique in the Bush administration linked to Israel's reactionary Likud Party, who wanted to destroy Saddam Hussein's regime because he was seen as a threat to Israel. And, finally, one might note the Oedipus Tex drama, where George W. Bush's desires to conclude his father's unfinished business and simultaneously defeat Evil to constitute himself as Good helped drive Bush to war against Iraq with the fervor of a religious crusade (Clarke 2004; Woodward 2004).

With all these agendas in play, a war on Iraq appears to have been inevitable. Bush's March 6, 2003, press conference made it evident that he was ready to go to war against Iraq. His handlers told him to speak slowly and keep his big stick and Texas machismo out of view, but he constantly threatened Iraq and evoked the rhetoric of good and evil that he used to justify his crusade against bin Laden and al Qaeda. Bush repeated the words "Saddam Hussein" and "terrorism" incessantly, and mentioned Iraq as a "threat" at least sixteen times, in an attempt to link Iraq with the September 11 attacks and terrorism. He used the word "I" (as in "I believe") countless times, and talked of "my government" as if he owned it, depicting a man lost in words and self-importance, positioning himself against the "evil" that he was preparing to wage war against. Unable to make an intelligent and objective case for a war against Iraq, Bush could only invoke fear and a moralistic rhetoric, attempting to present himself as a strong nationalist leader.

Bush's rhetoric, like that of fascism, deploys a mistrust and hatred of language, reducing it to manipulative speechifying, speaking in codes, and repeating the same phrases over and over. This is grounded in anti-intellectualism and a hatred of democracy and intellectuals. It is clearly evident in Bush's press conferences, in which he gives snitty responses to questions and shows general contempt for the whole procedure. It plays to anti-intellectual proclivities and tendencies in the extreme conservative and fundamentalist Christian constituencies who support him.

But Bush's Iraq discourse failed to convince those who were not already true believers in the need to invade Iraq, and many of the United States' traditional allies were deeply angered by Bush's arrogance and were distanced and not convinced by his rhetoric. Indeed, it appears that Bush's press conference was orchestrated to shore up his base and prepare his supporters for a major political struggle rather then to marshal arguments to convince those opposed to go to war with Iraq that it was a good idea. He displayed, against his will, the complete poverty of his case to go to war against Iraq: he had no convincing arguments, had nothing new to communicate, and just repeated the same tired clichés over and over.

Bush's discourse also displayed Orwellian features of Doublespeak where war against Iraq is for peace, the occupation of Iraq is its liberation, destroying its food and water supplies enables "humanitarian" action, and the murder of countless Iraqis and destruction of the country will produce "freedom" and "democracy." In a prewar summit with Tony Blair in the Azores and in his first talk after the bombing began, Bush went on and on about the "coalition of the willing" and how many countries were supporting and participating in the "allied" effort. In fact, however, it was a Coalition of Two, with the United States and United Kingdom doing most of the fighting and with many of the countries that Bush claimed supported his war quickly backtracking and expressing reservations about the highly unpopular assault that was strongly opposed by most people and countries in the world.

The 2003 Iraq war was a major global media event constructed very differently by varying broadcasting networks in diverse parts of the world. While the U.S. networks framed the event as "Operation Iraqi Freedom" (the Pentagon concept) or "War in Iraq," the Canadian CBC used the logo "War on Iraq," and various Arab networks presented it as an "invasion" and "occupation." In the essays collected in *Bring 'Em On,* a group of distinguished media scholars from around the world dissect the various ways that the mainstream media in the United States manufactured consent for the Iraq war and how various other national or alternative media served to advance or contest the Bush administration's Iraq intervention. The essays explore interaction between media institutions, political groups, and cultural norms and practices.

Lee Artz's essay explicates a model of communication illustrated in many of the studies collected in the volume and explains why dominant mainstream media so often advance the policies of hegemonic political elites. The following essays delineate structural causes for media responses to the war in Iraq; examine specific pre-invasion media coverage and how a culture of militarism helps mobilize consent to war; explore how national security strategy plays out in mobilizing consent for war, how specific propaganda and public relation techniques are used by the Bush administration in the Second Gulf War, and how this policy was sold to the world; examine the culture of consensus and how cultural forms of patriotism and persuasion are embodied in media practices that mobilize consent for war; and explore how the media frame political events like wars and the consequences of specific framings in the Iraq war.

These studies all deploy fresh scholarship and illuminating analysis to engage an issue of ongoing public importance. As the Iraq intervention spins out of control with growing insurgency against the U.S. occupation and scandals such as the Iraqi prisoner abuse and torture that came to light in April and May 2004 circulating through global media, questions are being raised concerning how the Bush administration's Iraq invasion came about and the responsibility of various groups and institutions like the media. This book shows how the U.S. corporate media enabled the Bush administration's policy and raises serious questions concerning the role of the media in a democracy—and the need for the media to play more critical and democratic roles in debating issues of war and peace and national security. As the Iraq debate intensifies, this volume should contribute to dialogue and understanding on some of the most important political issues of our time.

REFERENCES

Ali, T. (2003). *Bush in Babylon: The reconstruction of Iraq*. London: Verso.

Attack on Iraq is unavoidable: U.S. official's warning. (2002, February 5). [Electronic version]. *Dawn*. Retrieved May 2, 2004, from www.dawn.com/2002/02/05/int2.htm

Borger, J. (2002, September 2). White House in disarray over Cheney speech. *Guardian*, A1.

Clark, W. (2003). *Winning modern wars: Iraq, terrorism, and the American empire*. Washington, DC: Public Affairs Books.

Clarke, R. A. (2004). *Against all enemies*. New York: Context Books.

DeYoung, K. (2002, September 8). Bush, Blair decry Hussein. *Washington Post*, A1.

Fineman, H., & Lipper, T. (2002, September 9). Same as he ever was. *MSNBC*. Retrieved May 6, 2004, from http://msnbc.msn.com/id/3068035/

Galston, W. (2002, September 23). Perils of preemptive war. [Electronic version]. *American Prospect*. Retrieved May 2, 2004, from www.prospect.org/print/V13/17/galston-w.html

Greenberg, R. (Producer/Director). (2003). *Uncovered* [Videocassette]. Culver City, CA: Carolina Productions.

Johnson, C. (2000). *Blowback: The costs and consequences of American empire*. New York: Henry Holt.

———. (2004). *The sorrows of empire: Militarism, secrecy, and the end of the republic*. New York: Henry Holt.

Kellner, D. (2003a). *From 9/11 to terror war: Dangers of the Bush legacy*. Lanham, MD: Rowman & Littlefield.

——— (2003b). Postmodern military and permanent wars. In C. Boggs (Ed.), *Masters of war: Militarism and blowback in the era of American Empire* (pp. 229–244). New York: Routledge.

Lynch, C. (2001, June 23). Firm's Iraq deals greater than Cheney has said; affiliates had $73 million in contracts. *Washington Post*, A1.

Rebuilding America's defenses: Strategies, forces and resources for a new American century. 2000. Retrieved April 24, 2004 from www.newamericancentury.org/RebuildingAmericasDefenses.pdf

Ritter, S. (2003). *Frontier justice: Weapons of mass destruction and the Bushwhacking of America*. New York: Context Books.

Salinero, M. (2002, August 24). Gen. Zinni says war with Iraq is unwise. *Tampa Tribune*, A1.

Suskind, R. (2004). *The price of loyalty: George W. Bush, the White House, and the education of Paul O'Neill*. New York: Simon & Schuster.

Woodward, B. (2002). *Bush at war*. New York: Simon & Schuster.

———. (2004). *Plan of attack*. New York: Simon & Schuster.

Acknowledgments

In completing this book project, we have benefited from the kind support and cooperation of many people: colleagues, reviewers, students, and assistants. We especially would like to offer our deepest gratitude to the contributing authors of this book, for without their genuine interest, hard work, and support, this project could not have materialized. Also, we would like to thank the authors' colleges/universities and organizations for providing financial, research, administrative, and secretarial support to them during the course of this project.

Furthermore, we are indebted to the following individuals for their valuable support and encouragement throughout this project. We thank Heather Cook and Vanessa Laterneau at Purdue University Calumet for their copyediting, transcription, and organizational and administrative assistance. We are also grateful to Nabil Ibrahim, vice chancellor for academic affairs, and Dan Dunn, dean of the School of Liberal Arts and Social Sciences, at Purdue University Calumet.

At Rowman & Littlefield, we appreciate the support and encouragement of Brenda Hadenfeldt and the professional assistance of the editorial, production, and marketing staffs and everyone else involved in the various stages of this project.

Of course, we are indebted to our respective families for their unconditional love, emotional support, and understanding.

Introduction

Yahya R. Kamalipour

A military operation involves deception. Even though you are competent, appear to be incompetent. Though effective, appear to be ineffective.

Sun-tzu (~400 B.C.)

Politics is the art of looking for trouble, finding it whether it exists or not, diagnosing it incorrectly, and applying the wrong remedy.

Ernest Benn

Patriotism is the willingness to kill and be killed for trivial reasons.

Bertrand Russell (1872–1970)

One is left with the horrible feeling now that war settles nothing; that to win a war is as disastrous as to lose one.

Agatha Christie (1890–1976)

Although media practices in general reflect and reinforce identifiable cultural norms and public expectations, at times of crisis, political agents and media gatekeepers modify their communication practices to protect or implement dominant political interests and goals.

In the case of Iraq, the George W. Bush administration sought domestic public approval for a "preemptive" war by campaigning on several themes, including the threat of "weapons of mass destruction," the gruesome nature of Saddam Hussein's regime, the possible links between Iraq and the terrorist group al Qaeda, and finally the patriotic duty of Americans to support their troops. In contrast to the independent media, alternative press, and most media around the world, the U.S. elite media deemed the Bush administration's rhetorical appeals newsworthy and legitimate. Hence, the media provide favorable coverage and promotion, often by dramatizing the same copy points emphasized by government speakers. From President Bush's announcement of the "axis of evil," the September 2002 launch of the Iraq crisis, the United Nations' Resolution 1440 on Iraq, Colin Powell's UN speech justifying intervention, and the international diplomatic negotiations among UN Security Council, the European Union, and Arab League members to the refusal of France, Russia, Germany, China, and Turkey to support military action; the international antiwar protests of millions; and the buildup to military intervention, U.S. elite media coverage acted and reacted to the ongoing struggle for international power with noticeable allegiance to the American administration's pronouncements. Yet the complex interactions among Pentagon and White House strategists, UN officials, administration publicists, military experts, journalists, talk show hosts, and international publics cannot be summarized as simply the outcome of standard journalistic practice or castigated as media manipulation. To unravel and fully analyze the development of U.S. public support for the war, the process must be understood in a larger politico-historical and cultural context.

This collection of essays highlights the complex links between media and politics by providing appraisals of communication activities as the result of institutional power and cultural norms. Individual chapters consider major communication events that politically and culturally prepared the world for the U.S. and U.K. military actions. Other books have recounted the political process leading to the 2003 war on Iraq, and some have even assessed and critiqued media coverage before and during the war and occupation. However, this book attempts, for the first time, to provide a more organic, holistic explanation of the intimate connections among dominant cultural norms, political agent activities, and media practices—connections essential to the construction of the necessary public support for the first "preemptive" and yet preventive war of the modern age.

FOCUS

In his opening essay, my coeditor Lee Artz explains how and why this volume focuses on investigating the interactions between media, political elites, and cultural norms and practices. A model of communication and institutional interaction is presented that identifies the marginalizing of public participation in political discourse:

1. Elites own and control media that create spectators.
2. Elites influence and control government agencies and political parties that only infrequently allow secondary public participation through opinion polls or electoral contests.
3. Elites direct cultural institutions (from entertainment media to public schools) that encourage consumer spectatorship rather than citizen involvement.

Thus, political and cultural leaderships act not with undeterred power and not as the result of sinister manipulation, but rather with considerable public consent arising from the "common sense" of ingrained, institutionalized political practices and cultural expectations. Accordingly, media and government power so configured facilitates popular decisions at odds with public interest.

STRUCTURE AND SCOPE

To provide a thorough and international overview of how media practices, government power, and cultural expectations influence public mobilization for war, the book consists of fifteen essays and a foreword. Each chapter focuses on a specific aspect of institutional structure, political ideology, or cultural and media practices.

This volume is intended to generate meaningful and, hopefully, fruitful conversation about the interplay of media, war, and politics. In a nutshell, the main topics analyzed and discussed, by a diverse group of researchers and scholars, include the following:

- Policy-making centralization, business imperatives of media institutions, and the institutional efficacy of international civil society.
- Media participation and government-media relations during the war and occupation.
- Media reliance on selected political leaders offered little difference of opinion and hence a limited range of perspectives for public consideration.
- Politically sympathetic news coverage of U.S. and U.K. military activities in Iraq rested on the more subtle cultural effects of promilitary themes.
- The shift in security strategy doctrine articulated by the Bush administration following September 11, 2001—a shift from deterrence to preemptive offensive military action.

- The role of public diplomacy in the failed marketing effort to "sell" the U.S. culture to the Middle East and the world.
- The journalistic claim to the importance of political neutrality, and the typical U.S. claim to the nobility of patriotism.
- A model of thirteen persuasive metaphors used by American editorial cartoonists to dehumanize an enemy and justify war.
- Australian media and its prewar orientation to a range of issues—terrorism, Iraq, and Islam.
- An assessment of the impact of the "Fox effect" and the "mirage of objectivity" on public opinion in the United States.
- The role of the mass media, particularly in times of social unrest, in silencing voices of dissent.
- Connections between media choices and government declarations that suggest media links to those political and economic institutions that desired military action in Iraq.
- The military and political rationale behind assigning journalists to military units during the Iraq war.
- Antiglobalization and antiwar movements worldwide.

In addition, we hope this book will be a valuable resource to the following audiences:

- Mass media, international, intercultural, and political communication scholars, researchers, and students—graduate and undergraduate.
- Middle East studies, policy studies, and development studies scholars, researchers, and students.
- Policymakers and stakeholders concerned with media, democracy, political persuasion, and cultural norms, including UNESCO, the AFL-CIO, AID, the IMF, and the WTO.
- Broadcast and print media professionals, educators, and students.
- U.S. and international developmental agencies, departments, and professionals.
- Universities in Europe, Asia, Latin America, and Africa, as well as the United States.
- Internationally concerned independent writers, critics, researchers, and readers.
- Members of cultural groups and organizations, and those interested in international, cross-cultural communication, especially mediated communication.

PAVED WITH GOOD INTENTIONS

In the fourth year of the third millennium, it has become quite apparent that we, as human beings, have made no progress toward elevating humanity to its potential level of civility. In fact, the current atmosphere of world affairs attests to a total breakdown in communication, trust, civility, international law, human rights, and freedom, and a lack of progress in terms of humanity and social/global justice. This volume is paved with good intentions, and in this respect it is intended to challenge our mindsets, senses, and intellects vis-à-vis war, media, and politics. I started this introduction with a few thought-provoking quotations and would like to punctuate it by the words of Mahatma Gandhi:

> What difference does it make to the dead, the orphans and the homeless, whether the mad destruction is wrought under the name of totalitarianism or the holy name of liberty or democracy?

Political Legitimacy, Cultural Leadership, and Public Action

Lee Artz

FROM GAMES TO GUNS

Throw away all the video games! Even if only a symbolic gesture, the disappearance of video games would make a startling political statement about commodity culture, industrial technology, human interaction, and public action. Video games (although not the culprit here) represent the interplay of many of the same forces active and the same forces missing from the drive to U.S. war in Iraq. With video games, technology appears as a source of corporate profit based on individual consumption. With video games, citizens become actively passive (or passively active) participants in their own withdrawal from collective interaction. Individual entertainment, even when configured as Internet interactivity, predominates over creativity, the nonvirtual world, and human solidarity. With video games, diversion reaches new dimensions. Gratification is immediate—any mistake simply disappears with a reset button. Virtual death? "Do over!" Although some have argued that video games and other media technology applications have psychological and cognitive effects and can cultivate certain tendencies (e.g., the U.S. Army has found video games and their cultural sites to be a useful means for recruiting), video games do not cause wars. Rather, video games and their ubiquitous popularity indicate the centrality of media entertainment to contemporary popular culture—a culture primarily of reception, not production; a culture of corporate-guided participation; a culture of active spectators prepared and equipped for decision making in the same way that video gamers are prepared and equipped for geopolitical discourse on war and revolution. Spectator culture (of which video games are only a small part) provides fertile ground for public relations and propaganda campaigns.

Media practices in general reflect and reinforce identifiable cultural norms, individual behavior, and public expectations. This is most apparent at times of unexpected or anticipated crises, when political agents and media gatekeepers modify their communication practices to protect or implement dominant political interests and goals. In the case of Iraq, the Bush administration sought domestic public approval for a "preemptive" war by campaigning on several themes, including the threat of "weapons of mass destruction," the evil of Iraqi President Saddam Hussein, Hussein's alleged ties with al Qaeda, and finally the duty of all Americans to support troops once the war began. In contrast to the independent, alternative press and most media around the world, the U.S. corporate media deemed the administration's rhetorical appeals newsworthy and legitimate, accordingly giving them favorable consideration and promotion, and often dramatizing the same copy points emphasized by government speakers. From President Bush's announcement of the "axis of evil," the September 2002 launch of the Iraq crisis, the United Nation's Resolution 1440 on Iraq, Colin Powell's UN speech justifying intervention, and the international diplomatic negotiations among UN Security Council, European Union, and Arab League members to the refusal of France, Russia, Germany, China, and Turkey to support military action; the international antiwar protests of millions; and the buildup to the invasion, U.S. elite media coverage acted and reacted to the ongoing struggle for international power with noticeable allegiance to administration pronouncements. Yet the complex interactions among Pentagon and White House strategists, UN officials, administration publicists, military experts, journalists, talk show hosts, and international publics cannot be summarized as simply the outcome of standard journalistic practice or castigated as media manipulation. To unravel and fully analyze the development of U.S. public support for the war, the process must be understood in its politico-historical and cultural context.

Others (Rutherford 2004; Woodward 2004) have reported on the political process leading to the 2003 war on Iraq. Some (Rampton and Stauber 2003; Solomon 2003; Weiner 2003) have assessed and critiqued media coverage of the war and the subsequent occupation. Combining assessments of institutional actions and political agents' reasoning with accounts of media coverage of government pronouncements would begin unearthing the war buildup process, but it would still be incomplete. A more organic, holistic explanation is needed because of the intimate, complex connections that both political agent activities and media practices have with dominant cultural norms—connections that were essential to the construction of the necessary public support for the first "preventive" war of the twenty-first century.

THE TRIANGLE OF POWER

Including popular culture changes how one would see the organization and promotion of the U.S. war on Iraq. Public support was not simply, or even primarily, the outcome of a particular government administration or even specific corporate media practices—understood by numerous analysts as lies, deceptions, failed journalistic norms, or simply hubris (e.g., see Fairness and Accuracy in Reporting [FAIR] 2004, www.fair.org/international/iraq.html). Of course, lies and manipulations of such magnitude could not have been distributed without the full use of the institutional and organizational controls available. However, and just as importantly, the effective power of government and media action depended on an energetic, receptive (yet politically passive) popular culture. Given its significant diversity, the public did not respond to administration and media justifications for war with a singular reaction. Rather, various publics wholeheartedly agreed, acquiesced, or were marginalized, but in all cases were denied participation in meaningful political discourse. Popular culture prepared the public for this nonparticipation. A culture of consumption and spectatorship encourages a reflectively passive citizenry, which may be aroused for patriotic purposes as needed.

If political decisions in the United States are reached under the following conditions: (1) elites influence and control government agencies and political parties that only infrequently allow secondary public participation through opinion polls or electoral contests; (2) elites own and control media that create spectators and consumers more than informed citizens; and (3) elites direct cultural institutions (from entertainment media to public schools) that encourage consumerism and spectatorship rather than citizen involvement, then we are likely to find millions of non-elite citizens—working class in our majority—socialized to accept authority, political impotency, and life in isolated worlds of narrowcast entertainment. In other words, political and cultural leaderships act neither with unlimited power nor simply through manipulation, but rather with widespread consent arising from the "common sense" of everyday life that has been institutionally organized. Accordingly, media and government power so configured facilitates popular decisions at odds with public interests.

It was not always thus, nor is it so in other lands from Britain, Germany, Spain, and France to Venezuela, Indonesia, and Cuba. Rather, the prerequisite conditions for public support for the invasion and occupation of Iraq appeared at a time when the political economy of the media parallels the political centralization of the U.S. government apparatus, both of which occur at a time of a historic U.S. international debt, intense expansion of U.S. corporate investment and its commercial model, overwhelming U.S. world military dominance, and considerable political disarray among working classes and social movements that might offer alternative visions for humanity. I make these observations without any pretension toward a conclusion, but for the sake of moving any understanding of public support for the U.S. war to its concrete, historical context.

To triangulate the investigation of popular consent for the U.S. war within the historically specific space constructed by government propaganda, corporate media, and popular culture enriches our critique. It might keep the United States from getting bogged down in the individual personality details of Secretary of Defense Donald Rumsfeld's ruminations, or President George Bush's prayer meetings, or Fox network Chairman Robert Ailes's prowar ravings at staff meetings. Instead, this media–government–popular culture model encourages the United States to understand individual actions as they institutionally and culturally played out in the daily lives of working Americans as citizens, students, and soldiers. More dramatically, this model posits that our contemporary culture of spectatorship grounds the legitimacy of government actions and "our way of life," builds palpable public consent for corporate and government actions, and discourages democratic discourse and conscious, critical reflection—not quite Walter Lippmann's (1922) ideal for elite control of the "bewildered herd," but more accurate for our mercenary times.

Government machinations for war included baseless assertions about weapons and terrorism, and outrageous activities (e.g., wiretapping the United Nations Security Council, publicly threatening and bribing nations from France and Mexico to Turkey and Spain, and allying with the nuclear-proliferating Musharraf dictatorship in Pakistan). Media acquiescence to government propaganda not only included agenda setting and framing of news coverage, but also in many instances ascended to the promotion of jingoistic patriotism (from Dan Rather and CNN to Geraldo Rivera and the Fox network). The war drive was consciously organized by these two dominating institutions: the federal government, especially the White House administration and Pentagon; and the corporate media, especially its news departments. But the success of this joint operation was predicated on two conditions: near-complete control of government and media, and a compliant, disoriented populace.

GOVERNMENT AGENTS

The administration misled the public. One account says Bush lied. Cheney lied. Rumsfeld lied. Powell was uninformed? Another story line cites faulty intelligence (of the investigatory type), so Bush told the truth as he knew it or understood it. Too bad, but hey! Once started, a war must be finished. . . . Yet, troops kill, troops die. At what point did the Bush administration transcend the actions of previous presidencies? Forget Monica; Clinton lied about Iraq, about Sudan, about Kosovo. . . . Bush Sr. lied about Iran and Nicaragua. Reagan lied about Nicaragua, Guatemala, El Salvador, and Chile. Pick another country. Nixon, anyone? LBJ lied about Vietnam, Santo Domingo. . . . Truman lied about Hiroshima and Nagasaki; he had Japan's surrender in hand when he dropped the bomb. Bush has gone unilateral, preemptive, violating the international rule of law! Tell that to Grenada, Panama, Nicaragua, and dozens of other countries that have experienced unilateral, preventive invasions by the United States over the years. Arguably, the Iraq war was promoted more obnoxiously and with less regard for international diplomacy than previous U.S. wars, but that is a matter of degree, not direction. Bush may have improved executive control over public information. He had his Office of Global Communications, but Clinton had an international information agency, and Reagan had an Office of Public Diplomacy. Karl Rove, Andrew Card, and Victoria Clarke counseled the Bush administration on the finer points of marketing, from when to launch a war to how to appropriate journalists or embed them. The George W. Bush administration's PR people may have been more effective than Hill & Knowlton, the PR firm for the first Bush administration that fabricated a story of Iraqi soldiers toppling incubators and killing babies during the invasion of Kuwait in 1990. In 2003, Bush went to war without needing a tragedy or incident such as the *USS Maine* (Spanish-American War 1898), the *Lusitania* (World War I), Pearl Harbor (World War II), the Gulf of Tonkin (Vietnam), or Russian planes in a box (U.S. contra war in Nicaragua). Bush simply conjectured a potential tragic incident by referring to a disconnected but frightening recent tragic event: the September 11, 2001, attack. Meanwhile, the U.S. Congress, Democrats and Republicans alike, rushed to vote for the invasion and occupation. Even as the administration's assertions toppled one by one, legislators continued to support the war, its economic cost, and its cost in lives.

CORPORATE MEDIA

In another corner, the media were at the very least complicit in making war (FAIR 2004; Rampton & Stauber 2003; Schecter 2003). There were no weapons of mass destruction in Iraq. Before the war, United Nations investigators had indicated as much; several outspoken critics like former UN arms inspector Scott Ritter had insisted that U.S. claims were unfounded (Pitt & Ritter 2002). Yet the corporate media didn't challenge even the most spurious

U.S. assertions (e.g., "We know where they are," said Vice President Dick Cheney). There was no evidence of al Qaeda in Iraq. Did the media ask for any? There was no war on terror; there was no war of liberation for Iraq; the media didn't challenge White House talking points. When the administration's PR copy was weak, the media offered their own taglines, from the *New York Times'* special daily section, "America at War," to the Fox network's news logo, "Operation Iraqi Freedom," replete with drumbeat martial music. Many now lament the poor performance of the U.S. corporate media, especially compared with the news accounts provided by much of the European, Middle Eastern, and independent media. In May 2004, after media misdeeds during the U.S. war drive became apparent to many, *Nation* correspondent William Greider wrote a typical melancholy summary:

> It is a pity the major news media have not convened a commission of inquiry to examine their own mistakes and derelictions concerning the war in Iraq. Wouldn't it be instructive to go back now and reexamine the "documents" the press and television provided Americans to understand why the United States must invade and conquer? Many of the news stories would sound quite naïve and gullible (also hysterical) in light of present events. The patriotic banners that accompanied TV news reports would look irresponsibly biased. Remember those investigative reporters uncovering Saddam's secret weapons like bomb-sniffing dogs? Remember the bellicose columnists and editorial writers who called for the war with grotesque self-confidence? (Greider 2004, 5)

But media performance can only be considered a "dereliction" of duty, if one expects them to practice ethical journalistic standards suitable for participatory democracy and citizen action, or at a minimum be the watchdog for public interest. However, if media monopolies are understood to be corporate driven and thus politically integrated and ideologically connected to government actions on behalf of market imperatives, then U.S. media behavior during the U.S. invasion and occupation is exemplary. My own content analysis of that standard bearer of journalistic objectivity, the *New York Times*, found that during the first two weeks of the war, photographs visually and persuasively supported administration justification and spin (Artz 2004). Analyses of other media and their war-related activities are similarly revealing. Included in this volume are two such studies: Adel Iskander's look at Murdoch's Fox network, and Matthew Killmeier's account of radio giant Clear Channel's boycott of the Dixie Chicks.

Of course, many more accounts document some of the complex and convoluted workings of political and media elites. From Richard Clarke (2004) and Bob Woodward (2004) to Kavotsky and Carlson (2003), Schecter (2003), and Kamalipour and Snow (2004), the exposés and appraisals of executive decisions and corporate media promiscuity have been published or forthcoming. But in sum total, what do they teach the United States about propaganda and persuasion? As one observer described Vatican television, there is an advantage to owning a media operation: "They can put their own spin on anything they produce. If you give them the cameras and give them access, they are in control" (in Ritzer 1993, 117).

THE CULTURE OF CONSENT

Consider a similar war drive with suspect motivation under different social and political conditions. In Britain, Tony Blair's charismatic but specious arguments for war (many borrowed from George Bush) were roundly ridiculed and rejected in most quarters, including political debates, because the Labor Party (which still has some organizational connection to the trade unions and working classes) refused to be a loyal opposition. Additionally, the British corporate media held no monopoly: the BBC, the *Guardian*, the *Independent*, and dozens of other media exposed the lies and contradictions early on, bolstering the antiwar movement. Elite control over government and media in Britain might be judged to be predominant but tenuous, at best. More importantly, political action in Britain is part of a popular culture not fully divorced from class awareness.

Spain provides another example. Although media accounts in the United States often depicted Spain as a U.S. ally in the Iraq operation, support for the U.S. invasion was largely confined to Spanish Prime Minister José Maria Aznar, a leader politically isolated outside his own Popular Party for his support to the war. Aznar controlled the state TV and thus could readily distribute U.S.-inspired arguments for the Iraqi war. He could also count on influential corporate media, such as *El Mundo*, *El Rázon*, and the Cope radio network for support. However, newspapers such as *El País* and *El Periódico* and radio stations such as SER more accurately expressed Spanish opposition to intervention. Additionally, and crucially, the political culture of Spain was vibrant, critically reflective, and active. At the time of parliamentary elections in March 2004, which coincided with a bombing of a train station and a government disinformation campaign, Spanish working people (who rely on communications technology for daily activities) were transmitting their opinions via e-mail, Internet chat rooms, and cell phones:

> There were millions of text messages. . . . An effective anti-lie and counterinformation network was established, mobilizing hundreds of thousands of people whose votes assured the victory of the Socialist Worker's Party and its candidate for prime minister, José Luis Rodríguez Zapatero. (Ramonet 2004, 1)

In the United States, in contrast, government publicists and corporate media directors did not have to work the ground very hard to turn consent into cheerleading for the invasion. Citizens here are immersed in an enjoyable, gratifying, diversionary culture that discourages political critique and public action.

We live in a "sea of communication" (Rutherford 2004, 111) filled with narratives, images, and vocabularies provided by mass entertainment and public education. Disney, *Drew Carey*, *Law & Order*, *The Shield*, and Jerry Springer express a common worldview about authority, morality, and responsibility. Whether we laugh, cry, or cheer, decisions are made by authorized persons—the sultan, the store manager, the judge, the vigilante cop, or the program host. Whether it is the law of the jungle, store rules, legal statutes, vigilante justice, or social norms, "doing the right thing" means following the rules already in place. Likewise, violators of any existing code will be punished accordingly. And, as viewers, we are cued to actively respond appropriately to the humor, drama, or tragedy by all of the programmers' creative wizardry, behaviorally encouraged to be satisfied with others acting out our predilections and preferences. They act, they act right; we watch, we applaud at the right moments.

Where in popular culture is this not true? Sport has become a spectacle for most Americans, not an activity. Basketball, baseball, soccer, golf, football, and hockey . . . easily commodified and packaged for the programmers' desired demographic, whether in the stadium or on the screen. If we miss the whole game, we can catch *ESPN Sports Center*, or the local news, and see the important parts—the dunks, the homeruns, the scores, the putts, the touchdowns—all sound bites of spectacle, packaged for resale to advertisers seeking audiences. Game shows are likewise ready-made for capitalism— simple, made-for-TV rules, celebrity and trivia knowledge, good humor, bright lights, fast pace, and luck. Good fortune is easy in the land of bounty! You, too, can be a winner of commodities now on sale! Television soap operas, situation comedies, talk shows, "reality" programming, and other television genres churn out similar small pleasures for viewers needing an immediate, quick dose of diversion. More farsighted (and more financially resourced) spectators plan ahead for Hollywood movies, major sporting events, music concerts, or packaged tours, cruises, and vacations—in most cases, finding carefully scripted entertainment needing minimal effort (with the possible exception of some extreme sport or adventure camps, which are still carefully orchestrated experiences). Outside its most creative moments, which are invariably artistically independent of corporate planning, popular culture appears as little more than a marketing exercise for diverse consumer audiences. Ariel Dorfman (1983) has decried this consumerist popular culture as the marketing of infantilism:

The culture industry, tailored to answer the simultaneous needs of immense groups of people, levels off its messages at the so-called lowest common denominator, creating only that which everybody can understand effortlessly . . . the median, quintessential North American common man, who has undergone secular canonization as the universal measure for humanity. What has not been so clearly stated is this: When that man is reduced to his average, shaved of his adult faculties and conflicting experiences, handed solutions that suckle and comfort him, robbed of his future, what is left is a babe, a decreased human being. Perhaps it is inevitable that the consumer should be treated as an infant, helpless and demanding, in societies such as ours. As a member of a democratic system, he has the right to vote and even more important the right and obligation to consume; but at the same time he is not really participating in the determination of his future or that of the world. People can be treated as children because they do not, in effect, control their own destiny. Even if they feel themselves to be utterly free, they are objectively vulnerable and dependent, passive in a world commandeered by others, a world where messages they swallow have originated in other people's minds. (199–200)

Spiderman, Batman, Superman, *Charlie's Angels*, *Star Wars*, *Harry Potter*, and *Lord of the Rings* (or, for that matter, R-rated thrillers, *Van Helsing*, and the WWF Smackdown!) each preserves our innocence. We are dependent on the messages of others who create magical dream worlds. From gentle to horrifying, these fairy tales build bunkers against our everyday lives. And we like it! The hero always wins. Where else do working people have such success? In one industry after another, workers do little more than operate and maintain technologies that replace skilled crafts. Globalization is only the most recent catchword for the process of decision making that belongs to the capitalist class at the expense of working- and middle-class livelihood and control. In popular culture narratives, whatever the difficulty, the honorable always triumph. Where else do hard work and honesty find reward? Bad guys get pummeled on cop shows; they evaporate in animated features and sci-fi. Interracial harmony reigns. Where else does injustice get its due? Movies, music, radio, television, comics, romance novels, championship sports . . . popular culture may have replaced religion as the opiate of the people.

Mass cultural forms have colonized the leisure activities of youth so completely that giving up, through analysis, the pleasure one gets from them may be painful. . . . To give up the "pleasure" of the mass cultural product is tantamount to giving up almost everything that gives a respite from alienated activity. . . . When the safety valves of mass culture have been removed, ordinary existence may be truly intolerable. (Aronowitz 1987, 470)

Mass popular culture provides pleasure for millions, but at a cost to their political awareness, because mass culture is organized and produced according to the market imperative that needs eager, nonreflective consumers who believe that products solve problems and bring happiness (Jhally 1988). This is not to say that consumers or spectators are inactive. Americans are well aware of the multitude of choices they decide everyday; they are simply not fully aware of the structures that provide the menu from which choices are made (Storey 1999). Consumer-citizens are not passive recipients of cultural practices, but participants actively involved within the constraints of the system, reproducing the general features of the capitalist political and social system (Giddens 1984).

One might think that mass-produced commodity culture would be mitigated by mass public education. After all, even if we watch television four or five hours a day, we are in school six or seven hours a day until we are eighteen. Schools prepare citizens. Students gain knowledge, learn to reason, and practice life skills. John Dewey and other progressive educators believed that schools could even be a social leveler—through education, children from any social class would find the opportunity for success and improvement—a myth still held as "common sense" today. A more accurate description of schooling in capitalist America is provided by Bowles and Gintis (1976, 2004) who write, "Schools prepare people for adult work rules, by socializing people to function well (and without complaint) in the hierarchical structure of the modern corporation . . . structuring social interactions and individual rewards to replicate the environment of the workplace" (2004, 1). Their findings are echoed and expanded by the elite think tank, Trilateral Commission, which sees schools as institutions for the "indoctrination of the young" (in Chomsky 2000, 23) and, as Noam Chomsky (2000) adds, "imposing obedience" (16).

Long before the No Child Left Behind Act of 2001, the Bush education policy that rewards and punishes schools for achievement results on mandatory skills tests, public schools were "based on [an] instrumental skills-banking approach that often prevents the development of the kind of thinking that enables one to 'read the world' critically and to understand the reasons and linkages behind the facts . . . characterized by mindless, meaningless drill and exercises" given in preparation for multiple-choice exams (Macedo 2000, 3–4). Investigating the typical curriculum, texts, and pedagogy of public school education would be helpful in identifying the socialization process (Bowles & Gintis 1976, 2004; Apple & Christian-Smith 1994), with the central place accorded to nationalism and patriotism particularly illustrative.

Perhaps one example will unearth some revelation: before beginning their daily ideological lessons in democracy, freedom, the free market, and other recognized attributes of Western civilization, students must recite the pledge of allegiance, standing erect, hands over hearts. Breaking into the grim day for some 8 million students, Channel One, the in-school television network, provides more ideological messages, this time with rock music, scantily clad teens, and enticing visuals: twelve minutes of dumbed-down happy news about the war and upbeat commercials for candy, soda, and face cream—essential for teen consumers (Hoynes 1997; Miller 1997). To end the week, student fans may take in a high school sports contest, where once again they stand, hats in hand, for the mandatory national anthem.

As Göran Therborn (1980) observes, ideology is socially organized. Belief and behavior are structured discursively and nondiscursively. The ritual of the pledge of allegiance and the national anthem are publicly enacted discursive affirmations of the good, clean, wholesome, benevolent empire of innocence that Dorfman (1983) recognized in our more mediated culture. While the affirmations of "liberty and justice for all" are repeated daily for a decade or more, alternative discourses are restricted or excluded from the public schools. The rituals of the pledge and the anthem also have a complementary nondiscursive dimension: one can be reprimanded by teachers, ridiculed by higher authorities and peers, and ultimately expelled from the group and the school for noncompliance.

The pledge and anthem became flash points for many as the United States turned belligerent toward Iraq. For instance, the principal in my sons' elementary school insisted on daily recitations by students. Teacher forgetfulness or noncompliance merited authoritative reminders and administrative surveillance. Finally, to guarantee compliance with less oversight, he instituted the daily ritual over the sound system led by selected students. Athletes at the University of Virginia and other colleges who expressed opposition to the U.S. war were threatened with the loss of scholarship to keep their opinions off the court—so the national anthem could be performed without question. Likewise, professional athletes not wearing American flags on their uniforms or not exhibiting proper decorum during the national anthem were reprimanded, fined, and threatened with job loss. Sports, politics, and education intersect at accepted ideological expressions.

Nor could refuge be found in religious education or Sunday school. Following the lead of national and local politicians and red-white-and-blue bumper stickers, "God Bless America" became the hymn of choice, the phrase appearing frequently on church signs. In the drive to war, in the turn to prayer for loved ones, one wonders what happened to "Jesus loves the little children, red and yellow, black and white, they are precious in his sight." In the midst of the cultural slide to warring on Iraq, it seems that Caesar received his due.

Without coercion, rulers are obeyed because they are seen as ruling on behalf of the ruled (Gramsci 1971). It may be that the ruled identify with the ruler as the personification of themselves. America is under attack. Americans defend themselves. Bush acts as they would. They find that the ruler represents their interests. Or it may be deference: Bush is privy to more information, so he legitimately acts on their behalf. He knows more; he knows best. Possibly, the ruled feel resigned, that there is no alternative; Bush rules by default. Finally, opposition may make accommodations to the ruler. Sixty percent of Americans opposed the war without United Nations approval. After Powell and Bush performed a pseudo-request, many felt their objections had been answered. Each of these noncoercive conditions suggests that rulers can achieve obedience through citizen choice (Therborn 1980). Each also indicates that legitimacy is contradictory, uneasy, and open to disruption, which is why the contours of popular culture are so important to political power. Rulers need consensus for their legitimacy, but not through the force of logic: democracy, freedom, and liberation are all fairly meaningless terms, especially as used by government agents and media gatekeepers. The power of the information comes from outside its accuracy; its power is a manifestation of the "delegated power" held by authorized speakers, viewed as legitimate "official policy" by the public (Bourdieu 1991, 107). More importantly, lacking an alternative, a culture of abundance or even sustenance girds consent for the status quo. Bush, or any ruler, can win (at least temporary) support even if knowledge about justifications for war is partial, incomplete, or contradictory, as long as the mass culture has the means to withstand silence, disaffection, skepticism, and independent political organization. As Stanley Deetz (1992) has observed, "The greatest censorship comes in what is never thought of, and in the forces that make some things unthinkable" (49). Laugh tracks, mandatory pledges, nihilism, apathy, relativism, narrowcasting, subculture self-centeredness, and an abundance of distraction may suffice, because there is no crisis of legitimacy, if there is no alternative vision that can organize resistance. The routines of culture—media entertainment, public schooling, and everyday consumption—establish information gathering and thought formation outside public formations (Deetz 1992). Lacking political experiences or cultural narratives, working classes and citizens in general are handicapped in imagining possible alternatives, including alternative forms of public discourse and public action. The examples of mass action in Europe and elsewhere underscore the crucial importance of political organization and cultural opportunity for participatory communication, media access, and social movement campaigns.

ORGANIZING HABITS

Government deceit, capitalist belief, corporate control, media complicity, media ideology, and media control—however deep, however wide, however powerful—ultimately depend on the consent of the majority. Generals do not fight wars. From pilots to cooks, from munitions workers to drivers, from soldiers to radio assemblers, working people fight the wars, support the wars, and pay for the wars. Bush knows. Murdoch knows. We need to know what Edward Bernays, the father of public relations, wrote more than five decades ago about the "engineering of consent": "The astounding success of propaganda during the war opened the eyes of the intelligent few in all departments of life to the possibilities of regimenting the public mind"; the task of government, corporate, and media leaders is "the conscious and intelligent manipulation of the organized habits and opinions of the masses" (in Chomsky 2000, 137). The manipulation of organized habits has the force of government regulation in everything from housing to public assembly, school curriculum, and workday schedules. The manipulation of the opinions of the masses has the expertise of thousands of publicists trained in the Bernays tradition serving the interests of corporations, government institutions, and media monopolies. Yet the effects of government control and media spin travel only as far as consciousness and independent political organization allows.

Our commercial culture encourages reflection for about three seconds, the average duration of an image in a televised ad. Our political culture relegates decision making to a choice between two similarities every four years. Consumer-citizens expect quick answers, quick fixes, "do-overs," and super-sized McNuggets of information for easy digestion. In this land of everything for sale, the distracting mantra of immediate individual gratification drowns out the background hum of debt and despair. But this popular culture is a very unstable support for capitalist hegemony, because consent is less about free choice and more about suppressed contradiction and conflict (Deetz 1992, 57). We may get information about the Iraq war and other topics without any insight, analysis, or explanation of context or relationships, but reality has a way of revealing contradiction, hypocrisy, and deceit. Tacit agreement often hides an underlying irrational rage, and without sufficient material benefit, consent is fragile (Artz 2000). Ignorance may be bliss. Faith in authority may be reassuring. Infantilism may be comforting. But childlike dissatisfaction often ends with temper tantrums, never with conscious, constructive solutions.

Maybe it isn't such a bad idea to throw away the video games—unless and until we can build our own. We need a culture: a society of conversation, cooperation, and meaningful exchange about how to realize human needs in a land of abundance. It is possible to develop new habits, new opinions, more conducive to democratic life—if we work toward a popular culture of citizen participation, a public education of pedagogic inquiry, and a media of community and public access, artistic integrity, and creative energy. The essays assembled in this volume illustrate the inadequacies and dangers for humanity if the current practices and structures of government, media, and culture remain. Hopefully, the insights will inspire creative impulses for the political legitimacy, cultural leadership, and public action of working people in the United States and around the world. To end the U.S. occupation of Iraq and avoid further military onslaughts elsewhere, ideas, organizations, and movements for a new world order need to be on the agenda. Bring 'em on!

REFERENCES

Apple, M., & Christian-Smith, L. (Eds.). (1994). *The politics of the textbook*. London: Routledge.

Aronowitz, S. (1987). Mass culture and the eclipse of reason: The implications for pedagogy. In D. Lazere (Ed.), *American media and mass culture* (pp. 465–471). Berkeley: University of California Press.

Artz, L. (2004). War as promotional "photo-op": The *New York Times'* visual coverage of the U.S. invasion of Iraq. In N. Snow & Y. Kamalipour (Eds.), *War, Media, and Propaganda*. Lanham, MD: Rowman & Littlefield.

Artz, L., & Murphy, B. (2000). *Cultural hegemony in the United States*. Thousand Oaks, CA: Sage.

Bourdieu, P. (1991). *Language and symbolic power*. Cambridge, MA: Harvard University Press.

Bowles, S., & Gintis, H. (1976). *Schooling in capitalist America: Educational reform and the contradictions of economic life*. New York: Basic Books.

———. (2004). Schooling in capitalist America: Revisited. Retrieved March 10, 2004, from http://64.233.167.104/search?q=cache:yMTL65sSf_MJ:www.santafe.edu/~bowles/schooling_revisited.pdf+schooling+in+capitalist+america&hl=en

Chomsky, N. (2000). *Chomsky on miseducation*. Lanham, MD: Rowman & Littlefield.

Clarke, R. (2004). *Against all enemies: Inside America's war on terror*. New York: Free Press.

Deetz, S. A. (1992). *Democracy in an age of corporate colonization: Developments in communication and the politics of everyday life*. Albany: State University of New York Press.

Dorfman, A. (1983). *The empire's old clothes: What the Lone Ranger, Babar, and other innocent heroes do to our minds*. New York: Pantheon.

Fairness and Accuracy in Reporting (FAIR). (2004). Iraq and the media. Retrieved March 30, 2004, from www.fair.org/international/iraq.html

Giddens, A. (1984). *The constitution of society*. Cambridge, MA: Polity.

Gramsci, A. (1971). *Selections from prison notebooks* (Q. Hoare & G. N. Smith, Trans.). New York: International Publishers.

Greider, W. (2004, May 3). Iraq as Vietnam. *Nation*, 5.

Hoynes, W. (1997, May). News for a captive audience: An analysis of Channel One. *Extra!* Retrieved April 2, 2004, from www.fair.org/extra/9705/ch1-hoynes.html

Jhally, S. (Producer/Director). (1988). *Advertising and the end of the world* [Video-cassette]. Amherst, MA: Media Education Foundation.

Kamalipour, Y. R. & Snow, N. (2004). *War, media, and propaganda: A global perspective.* Lanham, MD: Rowman & Littlefield.

Kavotsky, B., & Carlson, T. (2003). *Embedded: The media at war in Iraq.* Lyons Press.

Lippmann, W. (1922). *Public opinion.* New York: Free Press.

Macedo, D. (2000). Introduction. In N. Chomsky, *Chomsky on miseducation* (pp. 1–14). Lanham, MD: Rowman & Littlefield.

Miller, M. C. (1997, May). How to be stupid: The lessons of Channel One. *Extra!* Retrieved April 2, 2004, from www.fair.org/extra/9705/ch1-miller.html

Pitt, W. R., & Ritter, S. (2002). *War on Iraq: What team Bush doesn't want you to know.* New York: Context Books.

Ramonet, I. (2004, April). Spanish lies. *Le Monde Diplomatique,* 1.

Rampton, S., & Stauber, J. D. (2003). *Weapons of mass deception: The uses of propaganda in Bush's war on Iraq.* Los Angeles: J. P. Tarcher.

Ritzer, G. (1993). *The McDonaldization of society.* Thousand Oaks, CA: Pine Forge Press.

Rutherford, P. (2004). *Weapons of mass persuasion: Marketing the war against Iraq.* Toronto: University of Toronto Press.

Schecter, D. (2003). *Weapons of mass deception: How the media failed to cover the war on Iraq.* Amherst, NY: Prometheus.

Solomon, N. (2003). *Target Iraq: What the news media didn't tell you.* New York: Context Books.

Storey, J. (1999). *Cultural consumption and everyday life.* London: Arnold.

Therborn, G. (1980). *The ideology of power and the power of ideology.* London: Verso.

Weiner, R. (2003). *Live from Baghdad: Making journalism from behind enemy lines.* New York: St. Martin's Press.

Woodward, B. (2004). *Plan of attack.* New York: Simon & Schuster.

2

Banal Militarism and the Culture of War

Tanja Thomas and Fabian Virchow

After the terrorist attacks of 9/11, the U.S.-led war against Afghanistan found wide political and military support. This broad alliance to which Germany's political class declared its support dispersed, though, when the U.S. government announced its intention to disarm and topple the Iraqi regime, by force of arms if necessary. Not only had there been millions of antiwar protesters around the globe, but furthermore, some governments of European NATO states as well as the authorities of Russia and China raised serious objections. In Germany, the ruling coalition of social-democrats and the Greens referred to the nonexisting UN mandate and demanded further proofs of Saddam Hussein's connections with al Qaeda and evidence of Iraqi possession of weapons of mass destruction (WMD) and the threat to Europe.

As a consequence, the U.S. leadership claimed, "France is a problem, Germany is a problem," and U.S. Secretary of Defense Donald Rumsfeld labeled those European countries opposing the war as the "old Europe." Thereupon French and German intellectuals, amongst them Jacques Derrida and Jürgen Habermas, urged for forcing "European unification" on the basis of those "American ideals of the 18th century" that led to the spirit of the "Universal Declaration of Human Rights and the Human Rights policy of the United Nations . . . that find more following in today's Europe than in the quite old looking New World" (*Antworten aus* 2003). Whilst the refusal of France, Germany, and Russia to warrant the war against Iraq and to support it by deploying combat troops became a point of reference for many people, the reasons underlying these positions derive from a constellation of rivalry in world politics and the aim of European governments to be in charge of the use of military force sovereignly when pushing through what is called national interest.

In the case of Germany, which had been demilitarized nearly completely after the defeat of National Socialism (Nazism) in 1945, there has been a process of remilitarization during the second half of the twentieth century. This development not only included the rearmament in the 1950s, but also finally saw the participation of the German Armed Forces (Bundeswehr) in military missions abroad and the development of several linkages between the military and several societal spheres.

Against the background of the stages and conflicts of the process of remilitarization, we will show how the requirements and justifications of the participation of German Armed Forces in future wars are produced in a discourse oscillating between phenomena of banal militarism, the accelerated transformation of the Bundeswehr into an army for worldwide intervention, and the "no war" rhetoric of the German government in the Iraqi case, the latter not constituting a contradiction to the general trend of a growing significance of military thinking in German foreign policy.

However, in a certain political situation, the political protagonists do not act independently but are part of complex interactions with other political forces in domestic policy, with governments from other nation-states, and in relation to supranational organizations. Finally, the omnipresence of the media has to be considered. Besides referring to basic narratives of the political culture in Germany and pointing to phenomena of a banal militarism, we will make use of an exploratory qualitative media analysis of German newspapers circulating nationwide.

Against this background, it becomes clear that the dissociation of the German government from the U.S. policy of war had not been sheer election campaigning but was derived from an amalgamation of economic considerations, power politics, and military reflections that has as its goal to make Germany a relevant force in world affairs again. This aim not only needs the definite possibility of deploying armed forces the same way that other powers, France and Great Britain at least, are doing it, but also is dependent on a change of cultural norms. In case of the war in Iraq, the German government had been successful in combining the frame "not to that war" with arguing for the strengthening of European armed forces.

GERMANY: REMILITARIZED

Without doubt militarism marks a significant strand in German history, from the Prussian Empire in 1871 to the prominence of the German military in making World War I and World War II. As Michael Geyer (1986) has shown, German history in the first half of the twentieth century can be read as the increasing interweaving of the society in its entirety by belligerent and violent habitus and actions. These found their most extreme expression in the genocidal crimes against the Jews and the gypsies that came to a halt only after the suppression of German fascism by the Allies in 1945. This was followed by a far-reaching demilitarization that even included the ban of the production and distribution of war toys as well as the making of model airplanes, which had been a favorite activity of the Hitler Youth. Organized militarists, at least for some time, lost their infrastructure and official financial and PR resources. In their place, an antiwar culture developed, characterized by the popularity of the slogan "Never Again War!" which was later intensified to "Never Again Armed Forces!" Accordingly, in the early 1950s nearly three-quarters of the population of the Federal Republic of Germany rejected rearmament and they themselves or one of their relatives becoming a soldier (Jakobsen 1975, 63). Berger (1998) even speaks of a "culture of antimilitarism" in postwar Germany (and Japan); Kühne (2000) is of the opinion that German society will turn to a "peace culture" in the longer historical perspective.

Sociologist Thomas Herz (Herz & Schwab-Trapp 1997), speaking at the conference of the German Sociological Association in 1995, emphasized the historical and proceeding nature of political culture and suggested a conceptionalization of political culture that assumes political culture as consisting of collectively shared interpretations that are mainly produced by political and cultural elites. Changes in political culture, he argues, can most strikingly be analyzed by looking at the political conflicts held in a society. Those conflicts relevant for the political culture in (West) Germany always show explicit or implicit references to the Nazi past. This is true also for the period of the first half of the 1950s, when the building of the Bundeswehr and the rearmament of the German state had been pushed through against widespread opposition of trade unions and the political left. This had been a first step of remilitarizing political culture in a sense that, first of all, the *existence* of armed forces in the Federal Republic of Germany once again were to become granted, this time without the old Prussian militaristic splendor; without the exhibitionism of kettledrums, trumpets and medals; and without restoring the outstanding societal position of the German regular officer. Subsequently, during the 1950s, at the height of anticommunism, the Adenauer government and Bundeswehr called for nuclear defense against the USSR. And, by the late 1960s, no relevant political group or societal force challenged the Bundeswehr (von Friedeburg 1968, 174).

When the policy of détente made the military deployment of the Bundeswehr against the Warsaw Pact all the more unlikely, the German political class as well as high-ranking officers step-by-step went public to refocus the purpose of the German Armed Forces, arguing that the international community expects

Germany to assume a stronger role in world politics (see Bundesministerium 1999, 5). The collapse of the GDR and the disintegration of the noncapitalist societies in Eastern Europe accelerated this evolving enormously. During the 1990s, the *Verteidigungspolitischen Richtlinien* (Guidelines of Defense Policy) from 1992 has been quasi valid as the document that fixed the "national interests" of Germany (see Reschke 1999, 2). Whilst the deployments of the German Armed Forces at first focused on logistics (e.g., in Somalia), meanwhile the whole range of military activities is covered. By covering up the first deployments abroad as being "humanitarian missions" and then changing their character to fighting missions bit by bit, the political and military leadership of the Bundeswehr succeeded in securing a far-reaching acceptance of the participation of the German Armed Forces in the wars in Yugoslavia and Afghanistan, although they had nothing to do with the defense of the territory of Germany. Meanwhile, decisions by political parties and the national parliament to send troops abroad or prolong already-existing missions are becoming routine procedures that sometimes go forward nearly unnoticed by the public. For the most part, there are only small articles or announcements on it in the media. This restrained media coverage may find further stimulation in case the so-called deployment law (*Entsendegesetz*) will find a majority in the national parliament; this law will give the government more decision-making powers and reduces the necessity to organize a parliamentary vote each time soldiers are to be sent abroad.

Parallel to the deployments of Bundeswehr units abroad, which include the possibility of the death of soldiers and thereby may show the "ugly face of war," there are multiple activities and events by which standards of military thinking, military points of view, and behavior of the military shall become familiar or attractive to (young) people in a very subtle way. These activities aim not only at attracting the youth to serve but also equally give further legitimacy to the apparatus of state forces. We call all those activities such as recruitment campaigns by the army, military soaps, documentary films on military topics, war games on computers, and so on by which military habitus, in Bourdieu's sense, penetrates into the pores of nonmilitary parts of the society "banal militarism."

BANAL MILITARISM

Using the term "militarism" gives rise to the picture of Prussia with its extraordinary position of military matters in affairs of state and the example of the officer as a social type. In this sense, militarism is only marginal in present-day Germany. Nevertheless, military affairs, the deployment of troops abroad, and preparations for future wars consume a relevant share of the national budget, and the Bundeswehr can rely on a substantial amount of appreciation on the part of the population that results from the army's operation in the case of the flood disaster in Eastern Germany as well as from such activities as displaying armament to the public, presenting the Bundeswehr at book fairs, and organizing a music competition for young people (*bw-musix* n.d.). However, a term is missing that gets to the heart of such phenomena that are making the military habitus an everyday and ordinary matter. As social scientist Michael Billig (1995) had emphasized, "Gaps in language are rarely innocent" (6). Following his considerations to use the term "banal nationalism" for the "whole complex of beliefs, assumptions, habits, representations and practices" by which established nations are reproduced as nations in "a banally mundane way," we introduce the term "banal militarism" to point to the comparable mechanisms and procedures by which the military, its necessity, and its demands for financial assets are (re)produced in a society. That "banal" does not necessarily mean innocuous or without consequences has been already shown by Hannah Arendt (1963).

Media industry, entertainment companies, and artists give their contribution to the wide range of phenomena that constitute banal militarism: from books and booklets on armament available at kiosks at railway stations to a wide selection of war toys in department stores and numerous video games in which players perform "virtual" role play as soldiers, military strategists, special agents, fighters, or killers. These entertainment activities and cultural practices indicate the acceptance and even internalization of the values of a cultural leadership intent on militarizing society—a hegemonic dominance developed with the consent of a participatory mass public (Artz 2000). In capitalist societies, hegemonic ideas spread more effectively and self-sustainingly the more they are shaped as an offer of emotionalizing experience and transformed into products that circulate on the marketplace for news, games, music, arts, and literature (Luckham 1984). The following examples give a lucid idea of phenomena of banal militarism as they can be found in the United States as well as in Germany.

BANAL MILITARISM AND THE FILM INDUSTRY

There is a long tradition of dual-use products resulting from the cooperation between the military and the film industry. This collaboration got a further boost after 9/11, but already the making of *Top Gun* (1986) and *Air Force One* (1997) saw relevant support and influence by U.S. Navy and U.S. Air Force authorities. When *Top Gun* had its premiere, the U.S. Navy tried to recruit soldiers directly in the lobby of some of the huger cinemas. Director Jerry Bruckheimer's *Black Hawk Down* also found support of the U.S. Department of Defense (DoD); the film tries to make sense of the mission of U.S. armed forces in Somalia by drawing a picture of masculine heroism that accepts death in battle as part of the mission against what is portrayed as uncivilized gangs and unappreciative mass populations.

But improving the image of the military and enlisting soldiers may be even cheaper and in closer connection to recent developments with the "military soaps" produced by Bruckheimer and Bertram van Munster under the title *Profiles from the Front Line*. Set in Afghanistan, *Profiles* presents a sanitized version of war, an entertaining reality TV show for the whole family. The VH1 network airs a similar show called *Military Diaries*, which is also supported by the DoD. Some sixty GIs have been equipped with digital video cameras they are using to document how they fulfill their patriotic duty. The clips are available via the Internet with just a few mouse clicks at www.vh1 .com/shows/dyn/military_diaries/series.jhtml (VH1.com 2003).

Meanwhile, actors playing German soldiers make an entrance into German film productions too. Until the early 1990s these roles had been very scarce, but in 1994 public service television launched a serial that looked into the life of members of the German navy, and 1997 saw the start of another fifty-part TV serial, this time about the air rescue service. The German Armed Forces gave support by supplying helicopters, pilots, and advice. When the war against Yugoslavia started and German military aircraft made their contribution to the air raids, a private TV company transmitted a serial about fighter pilots called *Jets—Living at the Limit*. Therein soldierly virtues, hard training, loyal friendship between men, as well as the "eroticism" of fighter planes had been combined with pithy talk of young fighter pilots.

The positive response that such serials got from many viewers contributed significantly to the judgment of Bundeswehr officials that the German Armed Forces have become socially acceptable in the media (Lilienthal 2000). Docu-soaps are continuing to normalize the military; the film *Women at the Helm* portrays four female officer cadets in their first year of training on board of the training ship *Gorch Fock*. The film production *Field Diary— Alone amongst Men*, about the training of women in a unit of armored infantryman, came under criticism by the Bundeswehr because of some training methods documented in it (see Renz 2003). After exchanging some scenes of the film and shortening it in general, the film should be relaunched under the title *Attack! Women to Arms*.

In 2001, *Soldiers Luck and God's Blessing* became the first full-length documentation about the deployment of German troops in Kosovo. The audience can watch KFOR soldiers playing skat and cleaning their boots. The main message of the film is to give the impression of ordinariness and of calcula- ble risks. In a similar way, the documentary *Good Morning Kabul* tells us the tiring story of daily live in Camp "Warehouse" on the outskirts of Kabul. And during the latest war against Iraq, *Twenty Minutes to Baghdad—On Board of the Aircraft Carrier Abraham Lincoln*, a coproduction of BBC and a regional PBS station in Germany, highlighted the dedication and commitment of U.S. soldiers to their mission in Iraq.

BANAL MILITARISM AND THE MUSIC INDUSTRY

Entertainment for the troops surely is one of the most developed, and may be even the genuine form of, "militainment." Militainment of this kind con- tributes not only to the reputation of the armed forces and supports recruit- ment but also, as a form of cooperation between the military on the one hand and protagonists from the cultural sector on the other, has repercussions on the political culture of a country or society. Prominent artists visiting the troops deployed abroad have a long tradition; the more relevant and extensive the conflict had been and the more nationally charged it was, the more famous were the actors and artists who made their visit to the troops. The U.S. armed forces have specialized branches called *USO* and *Armed Forces Entertain- ment* that organize entertaining the soldiers. Often there is cooperation with and sponsoring by industrial enterprises. NATO, too, has a special budget for what is called "Morale and Welfare Activities."

In the Federal Republic of Germany, this kind of activity has been limited to low-level entertainment in the barracks for a long time. Only since larger contingents of the Bundeswehr have been deployed in the Balkans, in Afghanistan, and in Africa can a growth and diversification of measures be found. Entertainment for the German military units abroad nowadays covers satellite TV, movie theater, sports equipment, telephone links to Germany, and special radio programs by the German Army's own radio station. Whilst these are permanent offers, visits and performances by artists and actors constitute a very special event for the soldiers. DJ Bobo, the rock band Asshole, the Berlin Thunder Cheerleaders, or the Bremer Musical Company—there is a broad range of styles. Some of the artists, like the well-known country singer Gunter Gabriel or the Heart & Soul Blues Brother Cover Band, have visited the troops several times. When the Cover Band did their gig in Pristina in April 2003, German Secretary of Defense Peter Struck took a microphone and performed as one of the Blues Brothers, wearing a black hat and sunglasses.

"What Gerri Harriwell and Britney Spears can do, I can do easily," de- clared young radio presenter Friederike "Freddy" Lippold from Leipzig when the Bundeswehr invited her to visit German soldiers in Kosovo. "This is service to my country," the twenty-three-year-old woman explained regarding her motivation to step onto the stage in front of the soldiers in Raijlovac and to present the celebration that each contingent is having before returning to Germany. The looks of the soldiers had been "well, quite masculine, um, very animal," she admits, but she still keeps contacts with the army (Lippold, personal communication, September 11, 2002).

The military leadership is well aware of the value of these kinds of cultural activities. Thus, Bundeswehr edits its own publications and media releases, including features of celebrity visits, interviews with artists and singers, and favorable comments from soldiers. At the same time, the cultural protagonists use their concerts and performances as a method of image building. In this sense, Freddy Lippold looks at her visit in Raijlovac as a "service to the listeners" of the radio station she is working for. Gunter Gabriel likes to appreciate the work of the German soldiers by giving some concerts in front of them. A song of Gabriel titled "There Is a House in Kosovo" (to the tune of "House of the Rising Sun"), which he says he had composed during one of his visits in Kosovo, is a regular part of the concerts he gives in Germany. This way, songs written for soldiers infiltrate the society.

The Bundeswehr tries hard to deepen relations to musicians. Therefore, a nationwide contest called BW-Musix '03 had been organized in autumn 2003 to attract young people (*bw-musix* n.d.). More than 2,000 DJs, music bands, and youth orchestras took part in order to win one of the prizes ranging from the production of a CD to concerts with the German Army's big band. The Bundeswehr invited several radio presenters and journalists to join the jury, not least in order to get an affirmative media coverage.

BANAL MILITARISM AND THE GAMES INDUSTRY

Computer games are one of the most popular leisure activities in many countries, and war games have a significant share of the market. Companies doing their business in this market segment try hard to make their games, the shaping of the theaters of war (desert, jungle, and so on), the availability and the use of weaponry, as well as the missions the players have to meet as realistic as possible. In addition, they often try to put new games on the market that reflect wars only recently fought in reality. Accordingly, the company Kuma Reality Games announced a new episodic game in February 2004 that incorporates scenes from films of real war in Afghanistan, Iraq, and Liberia in order to enhance authenticity. Even the killing of the sons of Saddam Hussein can be copied virtually using the same kind of ammunition that the U.S. forces used in reality.

As in many other cases, military veterans gave advice to the development of this game. The armed forces of the United States systematically make use of computer games and have entered into several cooperative agreements with computer games companies and university departments. The Naval Post-graduate School of the U.S. Navy runs the research institute Modeling, Virtual Environments and Simulation; and the U.S. Army from 1999 onward financed the Institute of Creative Technologies at the University of Southern California, where games such as *Soldiers* or *Operations* have been developed. The ego-shooter *Operations*, of which 1.2 million copies had been distributed for free, is not the only game the U.S. Armed Forces uses for recruitment. *America's Army* is downloadable from the Internet free of charge, but the U.S. Army is able to register all users by username and by e-mail address and to track the progress a player makes in the career training that he or she has chosen. One of the main matters of concern of the game is the training of obedience. To fire is allowed at command only. The violator of this rule is threatened with detention.

The growing relevance of computer games for the military goes back to the rising status of simulation as part of training exercises since the mid-1980s. Games like *Counterstrike*, which is played by more than 10 million players around the world, lead to a heightened level of visual attentiveness, as neuroscientific research has shown (Green & Bavelier 2003). Even newcomers are able to perceive various objects on the screen simultaneously after just ten days of playing the game. Of course, this is interesting for Special Forces that are trained with action videos in order to enhance their capability to scan unknown territory very quickly.

Many of the computer war games are about the battles of World War II. *Medal of Honor* and *Battlefield 1942*, to name just two of them, are regularly updated and promoted as "a must for every front-line soldier." Amongst these "front-line soldiers" are, not surprisingly, numerous far rightists. The possibility to experience World War II battles virtually in the form of an officer of the Wehrmacht or of the Waffen SS attracts them. As one can see from the German-speaking fan page (www.bf42.de n.d.), they share enthusiasm for weaponry and soldiership with militarists and nonpolitical players. The real-time computer game *Sudden Strike 2* simulates the attack of the Waffen SS on the Russian city of Charkov, which had been the place of the murder of 20,000 Jews in mid-December 1941 by members of the Wehrmacht and the Waffen SS. In the game, the soldiers of the Waffen SS are depicted as courageous fighters with soldierly virtues such as honor, patriotism, pluck, and propriety. Because *Sudden Strike 2* had been such a commercial success, the producing company CDV-Verlag launched *Blitzkrieg* as its successor. These games in general leave it to chance if players are more likely to identify with the Waffen SS or their Allied counterparts, just as if it is only a matter of taste similar to the preference for a certain baseball club.

In recent times, the German Armed Forces tried to profit from the popularity of computer games and the Internet too. On its Internet page, www .treff.bundeswehr.de, the German army offers a wide range of animated film sequences. The main target group is young people aged fourteen to seventeen: "The whole assortment is designed in a juvenile and playing way" (Henke 2003). Here, once again, the aim is to make (young) people familiar with the situation of soldiers in situations of training and battle, to lead the viewers to get involved in military thinking and behavior, and to lose distance from weapons and the force of arms.

TOWARD A CULTURE OF WAR?

At first glance, the German government held a consistent stance of rejecting the war against Iraq. Reacting to the ultimatum George Bush gave Saddam Hussein in mid-March 2003, German Chancellor Gerhard Schröder spoke to the nation via TV and justified the refusal by pointing to the missing proofs of WMDs, emphasized the prominent role that the UN should have in solving conflicts, and pleaded for the continuation of the UN weapons inspectors instead of toppling the Iraqi regime by force. Simultaneously, he rejected fundamental pacifism sharply. In an unusual step he appeared on the screen again only two days later, stressing that Germany would not stand aside if help for refugees or wounded soldiers should be necessary. This had been an offer for support of the nations going to war, the United Kingdom and the United States.

Although Germany's refusal to support the war in Iraq was deemed political maneuvering or electioneering by many in the U.S. and German media, the position of the German government corresponded to the widespread antiwar sentiment of the German population. In January 2003, more than two-thirds of it supported the refusal of the government to deploy soldiers in support of the U.S. and UK military actions against Iraq (EMNID 2003). Three months later, another 80 percent of the population stated that they saw no justification for the U.S.-led war against Iraq. In a survey conducted by the German Marshall Fund in June 2003, one out of two Germans no longer holds a strong leadership position of the United States as desirable; but 70 percent of the interviewees approved of the European Union becoming a superpower (Transatlantic Trends 2003).

As the most numerous opposition in the national parliament, Germany's conservative party accused the government of damaging, even destroying, the outstanding relationship between Germany and the United States, but had been ambiguous in their comments on the war itself, not least because of diverging opinions at the grassroots level of the party. Outstanding in her support for the Bush administration's politics had been Christian Democratic Party leader Angela Merkel, who believes that German "national interests" would best be served in a close coalition with the United States. Friedrich Merz, deputy party leader after Merkel, spoke of some kind of a "bunker mentality" in the United States; and Edmund Stoiber, head of the Christian Social Union (CSU) and leader of the Federal German state of Bavaria, on the one hand distanced himself from U.S. politics during his visit to China, but on the other hand held the war as justifiable according to international law and claimed he sides with the United States ("CDU und CSU" 2003; Levine 2003). In general, the question of the war's legality in terms of international law was largely overlooked by the major political parties. And although the Social Democrat government criticized U.S. policies, it never referred to the U.S. invasion as an act of aggression, ostensibly because that would legitimate Iraq's right to defense, placing German soldiers stationed in Kuwait and the region in harm's way (Müller 2003).

Whilst liberal daily newspapers gave experts on international law critical of the U.S. and U.K. war a chance to speak (see interview with Michael Bothe 2003), the conservative newspapers repeated the U.S. government's statements at length, portrayed U.S. military leaders positively (Schmitt 2003; Kielinger 2003), and attacked the German government directly. Main topics of criticism had been that order in world affairs can only be reached in close cooperation with the United States, that to side with France only encourages the longstanding anti-American attitudes of French politics, and that Europe alone will not be able to cope with global unsecurities and terrorist dangers. Instead of trying to "contain America with energy that hitherto has been mobilized only for the enclosement of the Soviet Union" (Kohler 2003b), German politics should try to influence U.S. politics according to German interest. No longer should gratitude or historically grown loyalty be the basis of a partnership with the United States (Inacker 2003).

Actually, there is one continuous topic that runs through liberal as well as conservative newspapers. This is about a unified European military force to act independently from the United States. Several articles and commentaries appreciate a stronger role of Germany in world politics and insist on using the EU as a "reinforcement of German power" (Kohler 2003a) whereby cooperation with France should mainly serve "the re-approaching to the strategic thinking of the British and of the Americans" (Kühnhardt 2003). Numerous are the appeals and exhortations that only the provision of additional financial resources for military purposes and the rapid change of the structure of the armed forces will give Europe, and Germany as the greatest EU member state (see Nonnenmacher 2003), more weight in a "renewed Atlantic Alliance" (Stürmer 2003). Asks, for example, the *Berliner Zeitung*,

> Why do not learn the Europeans from the Chinese? Who ever wants to have influence has to have power. Before the Europeans are able to challenge hegemonic America they first of all have to find to their own strength, politically and militaristically. (Schröder 2003)

And the influential weekly *Die Zeit* summarized that "only both contradicting decisions taken together—the willingness to go to war [in the case of Kosovo] and the refusal today [in the case of Iraq]—make up the sovereignty that have been missed especially from the conservatives that long" (Geis 2003).

The *open* refusal of the German government to support the U.S. and UK war against Iraq marks a significant change in the relationship between Germany and the United States, since Germany claims a relevant role in international politics with different priorities and aims than those of its transatlantic counterpart. Part of the historic change has been the participation of the Bundeswehr in several wars since the early 1990s, a fact that led Richard Holbrooke, former U.S. ambassador in Germany, to point out that

> Germany is not old Europe. It is the heart of Europe. . . . The Germans have been involved in the other three major interventions of the last—Bosnia, Kosovo and Afghanistan. The deployment of troops abroad has been a historic change for Germany. Three out of four is not bad. ("Interview" 2003)

This development has been widely discussed in Germany as a move to *normalcy*, which means that "the German past loses its relevance for current politics. The wars of aggression, the war crimes of the Wehrmacht, and the murder of millions of European Jews especially . . . hardly have an effect on everyday life any longer" (Beste, Bornhöft, Reuter, Schumann, & Steingart 2003). Thereby, the lesson "War never again" heralded after World War II sinks into oblivion, and a culture of war according to which war and military actions are more and more looked upon as a necessary and effective way of problem solving by the government, political parties, and growing parts of the general public gains ground.

Under these circumstances, it may not even be unlikely that in the run-up to the next war in which German troops will participate, the German government at that time will point to the refusal of the present government, thereby getting higher credibility as well as support from the population. This will probably not get the form of "hurrah patriotism," but is the banal continuation of a policy that has removed the taboos in Germany from waging war.

The present cultural hegemony of banal militarism is not simply the result of the power of the government and its maneuvering or of simple manipulation by the media, but is the outcome of a decades-long process of re-embedding the military into German society. Even if there has been disagreement between political parties and amongst the media about the war in Iraq, the widespread correspondence about the relevance and the usefulness of the military as such is (re)produced in political discourses as well as in cultural and media representations of soldiers and armament, the military, and war—lots of them offering the performance of military thinking and behavior. But, it must be remembered, banal does not necessarily mean innocuous.

REFERENCES

Antworten aus dem alten Europa: Reaktionen französischer und deutscher Intellektueller auf eine amerikanische Provokation. (2003, January 27). Retrieved February 2, 2004, from www.uni-kassel.de/fb10/frieden/themen/Europa/alteseuropa.htm

Arendt, H. (1963). *Eichmann in Jerusalem: A report on the banality of evil.* New York: Viking Press.

Artz, L. (2000). *Cultural hegemony in the United States.* Thousand Oaks, CA: Sage.

Berger, T. U. (1998). *Cultures of antimilitarism: National security in Germany and Japan.* Baltimore: Johns Hopkins Press.

Beste R., Bornhöft, P., Reuter, W., Schumann, H., & Steingart, G. (2003, autumn). Neue Aufgaben, neuer Kurs. *Der Spiegel* 42/2003, 22–26.

Billig, M. (1995). *Banal nationalism.* London: Sage.

Bothe, M. (2003, March 19). Interview: Vorsitzender der Deutschen Gesellschaft für Völkerrecht. *Berliner Zeitung*, 5.

Bundesministerium der Verteidigung. (1999). *Einsätze der Bundeswehr im Ausland.* Bonn: BMVg.

bw-musix. (n.d.). Retrieved February 3, 2004, from www.bw-musix.de/content/

CDU und CSU uneins über den Irak-Krieg. (2003, March 25). *Frankfurter Allgemeine Zeitung*, 2.

Emnid. 2003. Retrieved May 5, 2004 from www.tns-emnid.com/presse/ntv/ntv-2003_01_17.html

Friedeburg, L. von. (1968). Rearmament and social change. In J. van Doorn (Ed.), *Armed forces and society* (pp. 171–184). The Hague: Mouton.

Geis, M. (2003, April 3). Berlin im Krieg. *Die Zeit*, 9.

Geyer, M. (1986). Krieg als Gesellschaftspolitik: Anmerkungen zu neueren Arbeiten über das Dritte Reich im Zweiten Weltkrieg. *Archiv für Sozialgeschichte* 26, 557–601.

Green, S., & Bavelier, D. (2003). Action video game modifies visual selective attention. *Nature* 423, 534–537.

Henke, A. (2003). 2500 Besucher pro Tag. *Bw aktuell* 12/2003, 12.

Herz, T., & Schwab-Trapp, M. (1997). *Umkämpfte Vergangenheit: Diskurse über den Nationalsozialismus seit 1945* [Disputed History: Discourses about National Socialism after 1945]. Opladen, Germany: Westdeutscher Verlag.

Holbrooke, R. (2003, June 16). Interview. *Frankfurter Allgemeine Zeitung*, 6.

Inacker, M. (2003, June 16). Ein neues Band über den Atlantik. *Frankfurter Allgemeine Zeitung*, 10.

Jakobsen, H.-A. (1975). Zur Rolle der öffentlichen Meinung bei der Debatte um die Wiederbewaffnung 1950–1955. In Militärgeschichtliches Forschungsamt (Ed.), *Aspekte der deutschen Wiederbewaffnung bis 1955* (pp. 117–156). Bonn: Boppard.

Kielinger, T. (2003, March 27). Oberstleutnant Tim Collins und das Ethos des Kriegers. *Die Welt*, 9.

Kohler, B. (2003a, May 16). Ein ungeklärtes Verhältnis. *Frankfurter Allgemeine Zeitung*, 1.

———. (2003b, March 25). Mit Amerika. *Frankfurter Allgemeine Zeitung*, 1.

Kühne, T. (2000). (Ed.). *Von der Kriegskultur zur Friedenskultur?* [From war culture to peace culture?]. Münster, Germany: LIT 2000.

Kühnhardt, L. (2003, April 27). Deutschland: Partner oder Moralist? *Frankfurter Allgemeine Sonntagszeitung*, 4.

Levine, T. (2003, March 19). Nur die Union unterstützt "Ultimatum und Folgen." *Berliner Zeitung*, 5.

Lilienthal, V. (2000, May 24). "Richtig sexy": Militär als Masche: ausgerechnet in den Kulturfenstern. *epd medien*, 3–5.

Luckham, Robin. (1984). Of arms and culture. *Current Research on Peace and Violence* 1, 1–64.

Müller, R. (2003, March 20). Teilnahme an einem Angriffskrieg? *Frankfurter Allgemeine Zeitung*, 12.

Nonnenmacher, G. (2003, March 27). Ernstfall für Europa. *Frankfurter Allgemeine Zeitung*, 1.

Renz, G. (2003, March 11). Ärger mit dem Alphamännchen. *Frankfurter Rundschau*, 3.

Reschke, Jörk-Eckart. (1999). Sicherheitspolitik in neuen Dimensionen. *Der Mittler-Brief* 1, 1–8.

Schmitt, Uwe. (2003. March 20). "Geh und macht die Welt sicher für die Demokratie": Tommy Franks. *Die Welt*, 9.

Schröder, D. (2003, May 17–18). Bye-bye Bismarck. *Berliner Zeitung*, 5.

Stürmer, M. (2003, April 29). Halb Farce und halb Tragödie. *Die Welt*, 8.

Transatlantic Trends. (2003). Retrieved July 18, 2004 from www.transatlantictrends.org.

VH1.com: Shows: Military Diaries. (2003). Retrieved July 18, 2004, from www.vh1.com/shows/dyn/military_diaries/series.jhtml

www.bf42.de. (n.d.). Retrieved February 1, 2004, from www.bf42.de/content/.

3

National Security Strategy and the Ideology of Preventive War

Elisia L. Cohen

In September 2002, the increasing possibility that chemical, nuclear, and biological weapons could fall into the hands of stateless terrorists, coupled with the recent al Qaeda attack in the United States, signaled the breakdown of the deterrence strategy that served the United States throughout the Cold War. Political uncertainty erupted over how U.S. institutions should respond to the situation when containment and deterrence strategies failed to deter multiple threats from subnational sources. In response, the Bush administration detailed the importance of homeland security in a global security environment, specified what it perceived to be significant global threats to the United States, and articulated its new security strategy. The new strategy marked a shift from a deterrence and containment posture to that of a policy embracing preemptive offensive actions to counter the ambitions of rogue states and terrorists.

This chapter traces the shift in security strategy doctrine articulated by the Bush administration after September 11, 2001. At the time, the Bush administration faced the predicament of how to sustain and reposition their arguments for a new security strategy in a global media environment. The administration encountered the difficult need to create a foreign policy rhetoric that simultaneously addressed the dispositions of its international and national audiences. Thus, the chapter will illustrate how the "rhetoric of equivocation" used by the Bush administration cloaked the ideology of its preventive war doctrine. The chapter will argue that the crafted equivocation between preventive and preemptive war became a successful mystification of national security policy. By evaluating the shift in security strategy on its own rhetorical terms, the chapter considers its consequences in the context of the administration's broader goals for the war on terrorism. The chapter will conclude by outlining the significant "blowback" (Johnson 2000) effects for American diplomacy and argue that such equivocation between preventive and preemptive war actions undermined United Nations legal doctrine and diplomatic means of communicating security concerns. Thus, this chapter takes a critical approach toward the Bush administration's arguments justifying the need for a change in security strategy, and illustrates the ways in which these arguments may serve to haunt the United States well into the future.

THE DOCTRINAL SHIFT FROM DETERRENCE TO PREEMPTION

The Bush administration's arguments for change in the United States' global security strategy relied on the shared premise that the September 11 attacks created a new security environment. The 2002 *National Security Strategy of the United States of America* document prominently features rhetoric that works to reinforce the risk posed by terrorism. The document describes the War on Terror and the nature of the enemy, and details how "the United States of America is fighting a war against terrorists of a global reach. . . . The enemy is terrorism—premeditated, politically motivated violence perpetrated against innocents" (*National Security Strategy* 2002, 5). Consistent with President Bush's post–September 11 public rhetoric articulating the "new war" that the United States fights, the *National Security Strategy* dramatizes a global security struggle different from previous national security struggles. This shift in security strategy from a Cold War doctrine of deterrence and containment to a preemptive strike doctrine was alluded to in Bush's speeches prior to the September 2002 release of the *National Security Strategy*.

The revised *National Security Strategy* clearly identifies how in the post–September 11 order, the United States will champion aspirations for human dignity and "oppose those who resist it" (2002, 4). In the twentieth century, nations struggled over divergent ideas—"destructive totalitarian visions versus freedom and equality"—but the Bush doctrine states that today, "That great struggle is over" (*National Security Strategy* 2002, 1).

The Bush doctrine identifies the ascendancy of democratically secured liberties in an era of globalization, and asserts that a clear moral vision will guide American foreign policy. This public discussion of the need to secure liberties is important, because it points to the Bush administration's intention to "also wage a war of ideas to win the battle against international terrorism" (*National Security Strategy* 2002, 6). Although the strategy document maintains that terrorism is not "a single political regime or person or religion or ideology" (6), the battle against terrorist motivations signals a willingness by the United States to engage in a battle over ideological differences.

Additionally, the new strategy document acknowledges the ways in which the threat of the enemy has changed. It states:

> America is now threatened less by conquering states than we are by failing ones. We are menaced less by fleets and armies than by catastrophic technologies in the hands of the embittered few. We must defeat these threats to our Nation, allies, and friends. (*National Security Strategy* 2002, 1)

Thus, the new policy justifies a preemptive military posture to counter the ambitions of rogue states and terrorists. The strategy report maintains:

> Given the goals of rogue states and terrorists, the United States can no longer solely rely on a reactive posture as we have in the past. . . . Traditional concepts of deterrence will not work against a terrorist enemy whose avowed tactics are wanton destructions and the targeting of innocents; whose so-called soldiers seek martyrdom in death and whose most potent protection is statelessness. The overlap between states that sponsor terror and those that pursue WMD compels U.S. to action. (*National Security Strategy* 2002, 15)

At root, the doctrinal shift to preemptive action was grounded in a fortiori argumentation. Aristotle identified "a fortiori" as a rhetorical commonplace practiced when the arguer proves that the opponent acted cruelly in the past by showing at another level that there remains possibility for future cruel actions (Lanham 1991, 167). In the Iraq context, the arguments were designed to forecast the possibilities of future hazards to justify current resolve.

Inherent to Bush's new security strategy doctrine was a redefinition of the United States' position defining its legitimate use of violence. Although after the dissolution of the Soviet threat the United States struggled to reconfigure its foreign policy, it did so within the framework of Cold War analytic structures (e.g., Dauber 1993). Explanations for failures in U.S. foreign policy during the prior Bush administration were often grounded in assessments of the strategic miscalculations that the United States made in its international relations. For example, despite changes in political and military circumstances, Dauber (1993, 159) argues that deterrence theory remained prominent in dictating the "terms of the debate" over post–Cold War defense needs and arms control policy negotiated during the Bush Sr. administration.

In the post–Cold War era, the challenge for the nation is to confront the specter of multiple security threats, including subnational terrorism, coupled with heterogeneous ideologies sparking competition and conflict. After September 11, the Bush administration faced the predicament of how to respond to these threats while simultaneously repositioning their arguments for a new security strategy in a global media environment.

Put simply, President George W. Bush faced a rhetorical situation where processes of globalization have increased the worldwide interconnections between cultural, institutional, and individual networks (e.g., Castells 1996; Giddens 1990). Events such as the Gulf War, the fall of the Berlin Wall, and the massacre in Tiananmen Square, Beijing, among others, have drawn the attention of communication scholars not only by their situatedness as sites of controversial media events, but also as mediated interpretive sites of struggle where distance audiences "remote-sense" them. In the aftermath of the September 11, 2001, tragedies, world leaders, journalists, and audiences were once again confronted with the struggle to encode and decode political meanings (Zelizer & Allen 2002) within this so-called fragmented media environment that communication scholars have acknowledged (Papacharissi 2002).

The fragmented media environment challenged the Bush administration's national public address in two ways. First, although the genre of State of the Union speeches and other national addresses has historically been situated as addressed to national audiences, the global media environment creates an international audience for the address. As Hill and Hughes (1998) contemplate, a global media environment allows for additional transparency of previously "local" (or national) communications. Second, the administration's rhetoric after September 11 became fragmented but re-presented and contested throughout the media system.

THE RHETORIC OF EQUIVOCATION: DEFINING PREEMPTIVE VERSUS PREVENTIVE WAR

As the specter of multiple global security threats to the United States came into focus after September 11, the Bush administration worked to refashion its security doctrine to create a broad public frame of acceptance of its military strategy. The failure of the nation's security umbrella to prevent the September 11 tragedies heightened expectations that the Bush administration must develop a "new" security strategy appropriate to pursue the new War on Terror.

An equivocating rhetoric of preemptive war became prominently featured in presidential address as the administration drew attention to a changed security environment. The arguments for U.S. action to prevent future acts of destruction were pronounced in Bush's early speeches articulating security strategy after September 11. In Bush's June 1, 2002, "Address to the Cadets at West Point," he argued:

Deterrence—the promise of massive retaliation against nations—means nothing against shadowy terrorist networks with no nations or citizens to defend. Containment is not possible when unbalanced dictators with weapons of mass destruction can deliver those weapons on missiles or secretly provided them to terrorist allies. . . . If we wait for threats to fully materialize, we will have waited too long. . . . The only path to safety is the path to action. (2002a, par. 17)

The linkage between the War on Terror at home and abroad also was evident. The threat of weapons of mass destruction created a new security environment where "the battlefield has now shifted to America" (Bush 2002b).

One year and one day after the September 11 terrorist attacks, President Bush was scheduled to appear before the UN to discuss security issues. Although many UN members had anticipated a frenzied discussion about international terrorism in the opening session of the UN Assembly, Bush administration officials signaled in early August that the president would use his opportunity to speak to address the threat Saddam Hussein posed to the world community. President Bush's September 12, 2002, speech to the United Nations detailed the history of international attempts to curtail the spread of weapons of mass destruction by containing Iraq. Bush listed Iraq's history of noncompliance with UN resolutions and showed the possibility of future actions that the regime could unleash to undermine global security at an international level. He then argued:

The first time we may be completely certain that a terrorist state has nuclear weapons is when, God forbid, they use one. And we owe it to our citizens to do everything in our power to prevent that day from coming. (Bush 2002c, par. 27)

When he addressed the nation on September 14, Bush repeated his identification of Saddam Hussein's regime as "a grave and gathering danger" to the global community, and stated, "To suggest otherwise is to hope against the evidence. To assume this regime's good faith is to bet the lives of millions and the peace of the world in a reckless gamble" (Bush 2002d, par. 7).

The speech signaled the shift from a security strategy embracing deterrence and containment to the Bush doctrine emphasizing preemptive action. It also ignited a mediated global political controversy. Concerns were raised about the United States' strategic motivations for a shift in strategy. An Oxford Analytica annual conference reflected the concern that the United States will use preemptive military action "whenever and wherever it perceives a threat—actual or potential—to its national security" (Rowley 2002). The *Irish Times* (O'Clery 2002, 1) reacted to the new policy and described it as "the most radical departure from the past since Harry Truman outlined the

Truman Doctrine in 1947, which guided U.S. foreign policy for more than four decades." London's *Guardian* also sounded its alarm, reporting:

> The world is now undergoing a crash course of political education in the new realities of global power. In case anyone was still in any doubt about what they might mean, the Bush doctrine (set out last Friday in the U.S. National Security Strategy) laid bare the ground rules of the new imperium. The U.S. will in future brook no rival in power or military prowess, will spread still further its network of garrison bases in every continent, and will use its armed might to promote a "single sustainable model for national success" (its own), through unilateral pre-emptive attacks if necessary. (Milne 2002, 20)

U.S. national newspapers also expressed these ideological concerns. The *Washington Post* (DeYoung & Allen 2002, A01) stated that the report, which was

> the first Bush has issued under a 1986 law requiring the president to present Congress with an annual strategic statement . . . gives the United States a nearly messianic role in making the world "not just safer but better."

Globally, senior state diplomats expressed concern that the administration was forgoing diplomatic avenues of threat reduction. German Foreign Minister Joschka Fischer announced that Bush's speech presented a "'very severe, and clear' challenge to the Security Council to contain Iraq" ("Germany 'very concerned'" 2002). A new UN draft resolution proposed by the United States to disarm Iraq initially faced opposition from Russia, France, and China. These nations demanded that the United Nations give full consideration to the ways in which any precedent authorizing the use of force in the Iraqi context would legitimate conflict in future scenarios. Members of the UN Security Council also expressed concern that the United States was prepared to act against a regime that did not evidence preparations to fight the United States. Finally, the legitimacy of the Bush administration itself was challenged as it espoused policy goals first, and then sought United Nations (as well as congressional) approval to pursue its policy objectives.

PREEMPTING THE BUSH DOCTRINE IN THE CONTEXT OF INTERNATIONAL LAW

Part of the international legitimation crisis that the administration faced in justifying the change in American foreign policy was its inconsistency with previous instantiations of American military doctrine. For decades, U.S. war doctrine was justified based on international law, agreements, and norms. In 1960, Robert Tucker embarked on a study of contemporary American doctrine. His book, *The Just War*, examined questions concerning the proper limits of defensive war, the grounds on which a preemptive war has been condemned, as well as the hazards incurred in maintaining a Cold War nuclear deterrence strategy. In depicting the "just war," he clarified the overarching legal and moral limitations on military engagement, arguing:

> The American doctrine is distinguished by the assumption that the use of force is clearly governed by universally valid moral and legal standards; it is distinguished further by the insistence with which these standards are interpreted as making the justice or injustice of war primarily dependent upon the circumstances immediately attending the initiation of force. In substance, the just war is the war fought either in self-defense or in collective defense against an armed attack. Conversely, the unjust—and, of course, the unlawful—war is the war initiated in circumstances other than those of self or collective defense against armed aggression. (Tucker 1960, 11)

The United States has a long history of insisting that "whatever its grievances a state cannot justify initiating war, that whatever its interests a state should not resort to war to preserve or protect those interests" (Tucker 1960, 12). The United States' adherence to the Charter of the United Nations, as well as the various security arrangements it entered after World War II, were used by Tucker (1960) as confirmatory evidence of the orthogonal nature of the United States' moral standards to those of international law. For decades after World War II, the U.S. military engaged in preemptive action to address presumed imminent threats to the nation's interests (e.g., Guatemala, Santo Domingo, Cuba, and Nicaragua). With the exception of the Kosovo campaign, the Clinton administration acted in concert with the United Nations when engaging in military conflict. As Harries notes:

> There were clear U.N. resolutions to use force to expel Iraq from Kuwait; to preserve the no-fly zones in Bosnia; for the United States to act under Article 51, the right of self defense, in Afghanistan; to intervene in Sierra Leone and, more ambiguously, in Kosovo. (2002, 25)

Although the legitimacy of the Kosovo campaign was contested, the United States acted with a commitment to internationalist purposes in concert with a "coalition of willing nations" to stifle ethnic conflict in the Balkans. In contrast to these Clinton administration conflicts, as well as former President George H. W. Bush's campaign against Iraq's incursions into Kuwait, Iraq's military threat posed no immediate danger to another nation. Thus, the United States' justification for confronting Iraq's failure to disarm was perceived by other nations to be steeped with U.S. national interest. Although the United States requested an international commitment to justify its intervention efforts, the rationale for military intervention presented a prima facie case contravening international law against preemptive war.

To justify the Iraq intervention within a security strategy framework that would allow "preemptive" action to be taken in the absence of imminent threat, the Bush administration redefined national security strategy to embrace preemptive actions taken to prevent rogue states and terrorists from exacting mass civilian casualties. In so doing, the administration attempted to create a moral equivalence between historical actions taken by the United States to preempt an enemy attack, and the current ambiguous security actions needed to "prevent" terrorist acts. In effect, Bush argued before the UN that the threshold burden of proof for exacting a preemptive strike should be lowered to account for the "nontraditional" objectives of terrorist nations and networks, and he questioned the adequacy of international law to govern the post–September 11 security environment. As a result, the new security strategy created an ambiguous new meaning for justified preemptive action such that the new meaning would cover understandings of traditional war fighting conducted as "preventive" war:

> For centuries, international law recognized that nations need not suffer an attack before they can lawfully take action to defend themselves against forces that present an imminent danger of attack. Legal scholars and international jurists often conditioned the legitimacy of preemption on existence of an imminent threat—most often a visible mobilization of armies, navies, and air forces preparing to attack. We must adapt the concept of imminent threat to the capabilities and objectives of today's adversaries. Rogue states and terrorists do not seek to attack U.S. using traditional means. . . . Instead, they rely on acts of terror and, potentially, the use of weapons of mass destruction—weapons that can be easily concealed, delivered covertly, and used without warning. . . . As was demonstrated by the losses on September 11, 2001, mass civilian casualties is the specific objective of terrorists and these losses would be exponentially more severe if terrorists acquired and used weapons of mass destruction. (*National Security Strategy* 2002, 15)

The resulting equivocation between preventive and preemptive war is a rhetorical mystification of political ideology that is not without cost to public argument. A legitimate preemptive strike under international law requires that nations show that there is a capability and intention of doing imminent harm by an aggressive state. In contrast, preventive war is without such requirements, but rather engenders mutual fear of a surprise attack. The result may increase global instabilities because motives for arming can be misinterpreted. As Nina Crawford opined:

> Some states may defensively arm because they fear the "pre-emptive/preventive" state; others may arm offensively because they resent the preventive-war aggres-

sor who may have killed many innocents in a quest for total security. A pre-emptive doctrine which has—because of great fear and a desire to control the international environment—become a preventive-war doctrine is likely to create more fearful states and more aggressor states. (2003, A26)

Such an equivocation between preventive and preemptive war actions undermined United Nations legal doctrine and diplomatic means of communicating security concerns. Although Article 51 of the UN charter specifies that acts in self-defense are only legitimate in the face of attack, the doctrine of preventive war rejects the substance and spirit of the article, deeming it irrelevant. As a strategy, preventive war ratchets up political tensions by demanding that nations trust one another to control future dangers. Crawford maintains that if all nations sought to control future dangers with the aim "to crush potential rivals before they gain strength," tensions would escalate internationally across issues that divided nations (2003, A26).

The Bush administration's new security doctrine, then, also may result in blowback for American diplomacy. Chalmers Johnson (2000) argues that "blowback" is the unintended consequences of policies that often serve to haunt the United States well after a change to foreign policy doctrine is complete. He argues that despite processes of globalization and change in military doctrine, global politics in the twenty-first century will be driven by unintended blowback from the Cold War era. Thus, recent foreign policy blowback can be seen in the context of viewing the difficulties that the United States faces in reconstructing Afghanistan after the fall of the Taliban, for it was U.S. Afghanistan policy during the Cold War that supported the covert operations that funded Afghan "freedom fighters," including Osama bin Laden.

Since the introduction of the Bush doctrine, some allied nations have turned the tables to focus political discussion on the rise and power of the United States, and its weapons of mass destruction program, as an international threat. Russia, France, and Germany have pointed to the lack of evidence establishing that Iraq has a nuclear weapons program; in contrast, these nations presented a competitive counternarrative to an international audience, in which U.S. ambitions and military power may be viewed as a threatening problem for the future of global security.

EPILOGUE: THE PREDICAMENTS FOR U.S. FOREIGN POLICY AND RHETORIC

The decision to withdraw from United Nations diplomatic efforts to contain Iraq and to choose invasion instead was not without great political risk for the

Bush administration and U.S. diplomacy. For many members of the international community, how the Bush administration waged war to topple Saddam Hussein confirmed their worst fears about the Bush doctrine. Specifically, the Bush administration's use of its post–September 11 moral claim to aggressively defend itself, coupled with its "go-it-alone" approach to foreign affairs, consistently plays to a broader narrative of U.S. arrogance.

As the Bush doctrine becomes extended in the face of a litany of possible threats, the question remains as to whether or not the policy is sustainable: how can the Bush administration argue for preemptive warfare when even the administration concedes that even a limited engagement might inflict combat fatalities (on a mass scale if WMD actually did become involved) and could result in an escalation of terrorist episodes of greater scope and intensity?

The Bush administration continues to defend its evaluation and justification of the new security doctrine on the basis of three arguments. The first is an argument a fortiori. Throughout its rhetoric justifying intervention in Iraq, the Bush administration claimed that given the strong historical pattern of Iraqi intransigence and the great threat posed by WMD procurement, the best course of action is to act "to prevent" Iraq from threatening the United States or others from a stronger vantage point.

The second line of argument constituted an assessment about the inevitability that the United States must assume a risk of terrorism. The Bush doctrine espouses the belief that terrorists are beyond the reach of our rationality, that they cannot be contained, and that they cannot be deterred. Because this is the case, the doctrine argues that the United States must take preemptive action to deny terrorist groups and rogue nations the ability to commit harm. Bush's January 2003 State of the Union Address cryptically identified the lethal actions his perceived enemies may take, and defined his administration's change of security strategy:

> Before September the 11th, many in the world believed that Saddam Hussein could be contained. But chemical agents, lethal viruses and shadowy terrorist networks are not easily contained. Imagine those 19 hijackers with other weapons and other plans—this time armed by Saddam Hussein. It would take one vial, one canister, one crate slipped into this country to bring a day of horror like none we have ever known. We will do everything in our power to make sure that that day never comes. (2003)

Once the rhetorical stage was set for the possibility of a terrorism incident, possibly on a massive scale, Bush established the grounds for the nation to shift its attention to eradicating these identified terrorist networks and their supporters (since completely avoiding the risk of terrorism is not considered to be plausible).

A third line of argument reflected the zeal afforded to terrorist motivations and the commensurate zeal expressed by the Bush administration in its support of War on Terror objectives. The Bush administration's strategy is premised on the assumption that if individuals are suicidal and will fight to the end, then the United States must also fight to win as well. Fighting with all available technical means—maximizing monitoring, surveillance, detection, and eradication techniques—is crucial to operational success. A preemptive doctrine was the way to assure that the United States would be ready to strike before struck.

The implications of the Bush administration's post–September 11 rhetorical maneuvers are important for scholars of public argument-based security studies to consider. The Bush doctrine marks a sharp turn in U.S. security strategy, and presents a preemptive war doctrine as the appropriate choice to answer the post–September 11 threat environment. However, a preemptive war doctrine was not an inevitable choice; rather, it was the result of a series of arguments made by members of the Bush administration to provide a problem-definition of the security threat and a commensurate solution to the problem. Examining the rhetorical foundation for these institutional arguments in support of the security problem-definition and solution may cast significant doubts on the administration's calculus and the sustainability of the Bush administration's aggressive U.S. security posture.

First, the question remains if the president's declared war on terror and the Bush doctrine will be sustainable in practice. There are many undemocratic nations in which the United States could intervene in civil wars in order to fight terrorism. The prospect of the United States taking aggressive unilateral action in nations that neglect to do so seems unlikely given the possible scenarios for intervention in friendly nations such as Yemen or the Philippines (Eland 2002). While rhetorically bold, the Bush doctrine may ring hollow in policing many sites of potential terrorist threats—and, as all laws, be selectively enforced (e.g., North Korea, Pakistan, and Israel).

Second, critics argue that preemption (à la prevention) sets a dangerous military precedent, inspiring nonnuclear nations to pursue nuclear weapons or inspiring nuclear nations to apply their own version of the Bush doctrine. Either scenario could lead to a preemptive strike, destabilizing global security. However, the argument strategy of the Bush doctrine also bolsters the rationale for a missile defense shield while signaling that this shield may also be included as part of a first-strike agenda.

Although the members of the Bush administration have not announced a "sequel" to the Iraq intervention, Defense Secretary Donald Rumsfeld advised Syria of the serious consequences it would face if it provided safe haven to the former Iraqi regime. A *New York Times* editorial stated, "There have been warnings to other malefactors contemplating weapons of mass destruction to 'draw the appropriate lesson' from the war" ("Aftermath" 2003). However, this message may ratchet up international threat levels. On April 17, 2003, the North Korean government released a statement maintaining "that a 'powerful deterrent' was needed to protect the country in the wake of the American war in Iraq" (French 2003, par. 15). It appears that the Bush doctrine has succeeded in creating a tit-for-tat game of preemptive strike rhetoric, leaving room for miscalculation and misinterpretation of international expectations. Without credible international norms or institutions in place to diffuse such threats—norms and institutions that the Bush doctrine strips of authority—the world may face global instability in the years ahead.

In his first speech after September 11, President Bush declared that he would not differentiate between terrorists and the governments who harbor them. The question remains how the Bush administration will apply its "preemptive" war doctrine to Syrian support for terrorist activities (such as Hezbollah), Iranian efforts to support Shiite Muslim leaders in Iraq, and the nuclear crisis on the Korean peninsula? Clearly, Iran, Syria, and North Korea were three nations singled out by the Bush administration for their foreign policy belligerence to U.S. interests. However, there are other nations acting in pursuit of nuclear materials that the Bush administration is not prepared to threaten, such as Pakistan, India, and Israel, to name a few. The question remains, will the United States' resolve be tested by other nations who seek nuclear capabilities? Furthermore, will the U.S. policy of "anticipatory self-defense" be replicated by other nations, such as in the India-Pakistan conflict over Kashmir, thereby heightening global security threats? These doctrinal issues may challenge the Bush administration as well as future administrations who inherit the Bush doctrine in the years ahead.

Third, there is the issue of the Bush doctrine's effectiveness as a counter-terrorism policy. The Bush doctrine may not succeed in decreasing the risk to the United States posed by global terrorist networks. If the competitive narrative articulated in the international arena (i.e., that the United States acts not in pursuit of justice—in the name of promoting liberty—but actually aspires to achieve global cultural dominance) prevails, then the strategy of preemptive war may embolden the nation's enemies. There are a number of nations with WMDs (e.g., China, India, Israel, North Korea, Pakistan, and Russia) and terrorist groups that do not target the United States (for example, Hezbollah). If the United States' most imminent threat is al Qaeda, a globally networked subnational terrorist organization, then to continue efforts to undermine hostile governmental regimes (or other unlinked subnational groups) seems to divert focus and attention away from the nation's most imminent threat. Moreover, attacking groups and nations that do not pose an imminent threat could activate additional people to join al Qaeda, or other U.S. enemies, thereby increasing the risk of global terrorism to U.S. elite interests and citizen safety.

Finally, a doctrine of preemptive military intervention may threaten democracy if the executive uses the doctrine to usurp power from Congress's constitutional basis for declaring war. The Bush administration's doctrinal values favoring preemptive military action may displace deliberations about prudent foreign policy making, thereby short-circuiting routes of international diplomacy in pursuit of the War on Terror.

REFERENCES

Aftermath: The Bush doctrine. (2003, April 13). *New York Times*. Retrieved April 13, 2003, from www.nytimes.com/2003/2004/2013/opinion/2013SUN2001.html

Bush, G. W. (2002a, June 1). Address to the cadets at West Point. Retrieved June 14, 2002, from www.whitehouse.gov/news/releases/2002/06/20020601-3.html

———. (2002b, September 10). President Bush's remarks at the Embassy of Afghanistan September 10. Retrieved September 12, 2003, from http://usembassy.state.gov/tokyo/wwwhso0242.html

———. (2002c, September 12). President Bush's remarks at the United Nations General Assembly. Retrieved September 12, 2003, from www.whitehouse.gov/news/releases/2002/09/20020912-1.html

———. (2002d, September 14). President discusses growing danger posed by Saddam Hussein's regime: Radio address by the president to the nation. Retrieved September 30, 2002, from www.whitehouse.gov/news/releases/2002/09/20020914.html

———. (2003, January 28). President delivers State of the Union Address. White House (Producer). Retrieved September 10, 2003, from www.whitehouse.gov/news/releases/2003/01/20030128-19.html

Castells, M. (1996). *The information age: Economy, society, and culture*. Volume 1: *The rise of the network society*. Oxford: Blackwell.

Crawford, N. C. (2003, March 16). Wrong war, any time. *Newsday*, A26.

Dauber, C. (1993). *Cold War analytical structures and the post post–Cold War world: A critique of deterrence theory*. Westport, CT: Praeger.

DeYoung, K., & Allen, M. (2002, September 21). Bush shifts strategy from deterrence to dominance. *Washington Post*, A01.

Eland, I. (2002, February 8). War against terrorism expands excessively. Cato Institute (Producer). Retrieved March 15, 2003, from www.cato.org/dailys/02-08-02.html

French, H. W. (2003, April 19). North Korea's atomic bravado incites a host of skeptics. *New York Times*, A2. Retrieved July 19, 2004, from http://www.nytimes.com/2003/04/19/international/asia/19KORE.html

Germany "very concerned" after Bush's Iraq speech. (2002, September 13). *Deutsche Presse-Agentur*, n.p.

Giddens, A. (1990). *The consequences of modernity.* Cambridge: Polity Press.

Harries, R. (2002, August 4). This war would not be a just war: The U.S. must persist with the option for U.N. weapons inspectors to return to Iraq. Argues Richard Harries, Bishop of Oxford: The use of force to remove Saddam Hussein is not a moral option. *Observer,* 25.

Hill, K. A., & Hughes, J. E. (1998). *Cyberpolitics: Citizen activism in the age of the Internet.* Lanham, MD: Rowman & Littlefield.

Johnson, C. (2000). *Blowback: The costs and consequences of American empire.* New York: Henry Holt.

Lanham, R. A. (1991). *A handlist of rhetorical terms,* 2nd ed. Berkeley: University of California Press.

Milne, S. (2002, September 27). We are sleepwalking into a reckless war of aggression. *Guardian* (London), 27.

The National Security Strategy of the United States of America. (2002, September). Washington, DC: White House.

O'Clery, C. (2002, September 21). Bush sets out aggressive national security strategy. *Irish Times,* 1.

Papacharissi, Z. (2002). The virtual sphere: the Internet as a public sphere. *New Media & Society* 4, no. 1, 9–27.

Rowley, A. (2002, September 25). More to Iraq war than just Saddam? U.S. has wider strategic aims, says an international conference. *Business Times Singapore,* n.p.

Tucker, R. W. (1960). *The just war: A study in contemporary American doctrine.* Baltimore: Johns Hopkins University Press.

Zelizer, B., & Allen, S. (Eds.). (2002). *Journalism after September 11.* London: Routledge.

4

Foreign Policy, Public Diplomacy, and Public Relations: Selling America to the World

Sue Curry Jansen

Benedict Anderson (1981) conceives of nation-states as "imagined communities." They are, in a sense, fictions, which are naturalized and reified into reality through legitimating narratives: origin stories, histories, constitutions, laws, maps, border markers, anthems, patriotism, propaganda, and news. Many nations establish formal bureaucratic structures to ensure the resonance of their narratives, for example ministries of culture and state-controlled media systems.

The First Amendment to the U.S. Constitution was intended to provide formative and formidable barriers against this kind of centralized information control. In practice, of course, the U.S. government dedicates considerable resources to cultivating positive perceptions of its policies and practices, both at home and abroad. In 2003, for example, the U.S. government spent $600 million on public diplomacy programs intended to enhance its image abroad; it spent an additional $100 million directly targeting the Middle East through the Middle East Partnership Initiative; and it spent $540 million on international broadcasting, Voice of America, Radio and TV Marti, Radio Free Europe/ Radio Liberty, Radio Free Asia, Worldnet, Radio Farda, and Radio Sawa (Advisory Group on Public Diplomacy for the Arab and Muslim World 2003, 25). These figures do not include funding for U.S. military and intelligence networks' resources dedicated to information warfare including psychological operations and "counterinsurgency" campaigns.

The U.S. Department of State formally distinguishes between public diplomacy and public affairs. Public diplomacy refers to "government-sponsored programs intended to inform or influence public opinion in other countries; its chief instruments are publications, motion pictures, cultural exchanges, radio and television" (U.S. Department of State 1987, 85). Public affairs encompass "the provision of information to the public, press and other institutions concerning the goals, policies and activities of the U.S. Government" to "foster understanding of these goals through dialogue with individual citizens and other groups and institutions, and domestic and international media" (Planning Group for Integration of USIA 1997, 2). The distinction is more than semantic because the Smith-Mundt Bill (1948) prohibits the government from propagandizing the American public.

Public diplomacy programs have seldom been popular in the United States. Many critics across a range of political perspectives regard public diplomacy as a thinly disguised euphemism for propaganda (USIA Alumni Association 2002). Critics on the left tend to see public diplomacy initiatives as part and parcel of U.S. global hegemony (Chomsky 1991; Snow 2002). To critics on the right, public diplomacy has historically been viewed as a wasteful undertaking, which provides employment and subsidies to bureaucrats, artists, performers, scholars, and intellectuals with unreliable, internationalist political loyalties; however, in the wake of the September 11, 2001, terrorist attacks, influential conservative forces have reversed themselves and now endorse reinvigorating and expanding public diplomacy efforts (Heritage Foundation 2004).

Explicitly designed to change the minds of citizens of other sovereign nations—to "move the needle" of public opinion (Advisory Group on Public Diplomacy 2003, 66)—public diplomacy cuts against the grain of American pluralistic ideals, which valorize authority structures that are "legible" and "visible" and dialogic models of free expression (Sennett 1980, 189–190; Dewey 1927; Habermas 1971; Ackerman 1980). Legibility and visibility, public accountability, and dialogic and participatory models of democratic discourse have, of course, always been more richly articulated in theory than practice (Peters 1999; Jansen 1988, 2002).

In wartime and other national emergencies, all nations, whether democracies or dictatorships, tighten their chains of command, practice censorship, and deploy propaganda. Until the mid-twentieth century, however, the United States only invoked systemic government control of information as a temporary measure, to be repealed when the crisis passed, for example, the Committee for Public Information during World War I and the Office of War Information during World War II.

The seismic shifts that realigned global power relations in the immediate aftermath of World War II dramatically changed the U.S. approach to information resources and policies. The United States ended World War II with sizeable overseas assets and information resources: a global radio network and local offices of the U.S. Information Services (USIS) in more than twenty countries. Moreover, the U.S. military had gained control over global information networks, which it was intent on preserving, especially in parts of the world where the weakened British and French colonial nations were losing influence (Dizard 2001). The Cold War, which would lock the United States and the Soviet Union into a global struggle for world dominance for the next forty years, provided both strategic and ideological rationales for maintaining and expanding U.S. control over international information resources.

Founded upon an Orwellian metaphor, the Cold War blurred the distinction between war and peace. The fragile "peace" was to be secured by developing a permanent war economy. Both the United States and the Soviet Union would maintain large standing armies, create vast intelligence networks, engage in intense ideological warfare, and launch periodic hot, subnuclear wars in disputed territories. When the Soviets developed an atomic bomb in 1949, the Cold War "logic" of mutually assured destruction solidified, launching an arms race that would prove enormously costly to both nations and ultimately bankrupt the Soviet Union. This logic was premised upon the assumption that since each nation had nuclear arsenals large enough to destroy the other several times over, neither side would dare to launch a first strike. Nuclear preparedness plus nuclear fear would, it was argued, produce a rational response on both sides: nuclear deterrence cum "peace." The national security apparatus that provided the infrastructure for the stalemate rendered concepts like legibility and visibility largely irrelevant.

In 1953, President Eisenhower created the U.S. Information Agency (USIA) as a Cold War propaganda initiative. Respected journalist Edward R. Murrow was later appointed director of the USIA, and was charged with informing, educating, and promoting international understanding as a means of countering Soviet disinformation and supporting U.S. national interests abroad. The agency continued to operate until 1999 when, in response to legislation sponsored by archconservative Senator Jesse Helms, it was dismantled; its remaining operations were folded into the State Department. At its end, the USIA had 190 posts in 141 countries. Throughout the Cold War era, traditional diplomacy—that is, state-to-state diplomacy—continued to play a dominant role in world affairs; USIA public diplomacy programs functioned in an ancillary role, supporting traditional diplomacy. It should also be noted that the CIA and the U.S. military undertook their own ambitious information initiatives and covert operations, which involved psychological operations and disinformation campaigns. In some instances, the USIA, with its global network of outposts, became fronts for these initiatives.

PAST AS PROLOGUE AND PARABLE

U.S. government attempts to directly influence public opinion in the Middle East began at least as early as 1945, when President Roosevelt called for an expanded U.S. cultural presence in the region. Eleanor Roosevelt suggested using American-produced motion pictures as means of reaching the still largely illiterate populations of the Middle East (Murray 1945).

Major propaganda initiatives were subsequently launched by the Truman and Eisenhower administrations to reaffirm Western dominance in the region by filling the void left by the diminished powers of British and French colonialism after World War II. These initiatives were also charged with countering the growing hostility to the United States, which was generated by the creation of Israel (Battles 2002). This anti-Americanism would be significantly exacerbated by successive U.S. administrations, which would greatly escalate U.S. financial and political support for Israel. The early Cold War efforts were intended to preserve Western access to Middle Eastern oil resources, and to ensure that the region was incorporated in Western alliance in the struggles against the Soviet Union (Battles 2002).

Most of the propaganda efforts were under the auspices of intelligence agencies, including the then newly created CIA; however, the State Department also played a role in developing "psychological" campaigns. These initiatives, which we now know drew upon the expertise of early communication researchers and other social scientists (Simpson 1994), targeted two distinct audiences: the mass audience, which was poor and predominately rural and illiterate; and political and economic elites, professors, teachers, professionals, and mullahs—what Katz and Lazarsfeld's (1955) "two-step flow" model of communication refers to as "opinion leaders."

Documents recently released under the Freedom of Information Act and available through the National Security Archive (2002) offers a rare look inside the normally closed world of information management in the Middle East (see www.gwu.edu/~nsarchiv/ and the excellent accompanying interpretive essay by Battles [2002]). Review of these documents indicates that in the past fifty years little has changed in the way that those responsible for U.S. public diplomacy approach the Middle East, despite the fact that the entire global media and information structure has been radically transformed. As Eleanor Roosevelt had suggested, the early propaganda efforts did use Hollywood and informational films, albeit with mixed results; they also used pamphlets, posters, news manipulation, magazines, radio broadcasts, books, libraries, music, cartoons, educational activities, person-to-person exchanges, religion, and foreign aid to finance programs with "psychological" objectives (Battles 2002). For example, Secretary of State Dean Acheson maintained in 1950 that U.S. propaganda efforts should assert control over news agendas in the region by diverting Arab news organizations away from the Palestine conflict and refocusing their attention on internal social and political problems; by labeling opposition to the United States as "fanaticism"; and by placing "corrective" articles in newspapers and magazines in response to critical news (Acheson 1950, 1).

State Department documents indicate that the United States was very active in Iraq during this period. Although Iraq became an independent nation in 1932, the British retained a strong and troubled neocolonial presence in Iraqi culture and politics well into the 1950s when, for example, in 1955, Iraq, Pakistan, and Turkey signed the Baghdad Pact, which provided these countries with a British-supported mutual defense. This fateful alliance triggered a strong negative reaction among Iraqi factions opposed to the Baghdad Pact and other Iraqi ties to the West; it galvanized anti-Western sentiment and launched the Pan-Arab movement. In 1958 a coup led by army officers overthrew the monarchy, killing King Faisal and Prince Abdul Ilah and declaring Iraq a republic.

It is within this complex and conflict-ridden context that the U.S. and Iraqi governments collaborated in creating and disseminating propaganda during the 1950s. Despite their divergent political and economic interests, the Iraqi government allowed the USIS to target the population at large with anti-Soviet propaganda. The United States provided Iraq with anticommunist materials for dissemination, and the two nations cooperated in creating and distributing newsreels and musical broadcasts directed at the Kurdish minority (Crocker 1950). The United States also asserted its influence by directly subsidizing newspapers, by producing programming for Radio Baghdad, by supporting anticommunist editors, and by using the Fulbright program to introduce pro-American values into the educational system (Berry 1954a, 1954b).

The United States considered Islam an asset to Middle Eastern propaganda efforts during the early Cold War period. As President Eisenhower put it, "The religious approach offers . . . a direct path to Arab interest" (Eisenhower 1958, 1). The three monotheistic world religions were seen as deeply unified in their fight against "godless communism" and its officially sanctioned atheism. Persecutions of Muslims in Soviet satellite states further reinforced Islamic anticommunism.

In reality, however, there were serious tensions in this ecumenical union. From the Iraqi perspective, one of the most effective ways of combating communist influence among its population was to link Zionism and communism—a link that appears to have been sanctioned in some instances by the United States despite its alliance with Israel. Evidence also suggests that the USIS underestimated the differences between Islamic and Western values. USIS propaganda programs assumed that audiences in the Middle East would be impressed by U.S. popular culture and displays of American material success. But Middle Eastern audiences actually responded much more positively to films and other media that were connected to their own lives and cultures. Rural populations in particular tended to be frightened by foreign propaganda and to dislike films that depicted life in foreign cultures, whether American, British, or Russian (Wells 1953). Even the responses of more cosmopolitan audiences in Baghdad often confounded American expectations. Sometimes USIS propaganda efforts backfired as Iraqi audiences interpreted the rampant materialism, godlessness, and perceived immorality of American popular culture to be insults to Islamic values (Lacy 1952).

The Hollywood film *Ninotchka* exemplified the backfire effect. It was frequently cited by members of the American embassy in Baghdad as a cautionary tale for Cold Warriors (Battles, 2002). The Iraqi government had tried to use *Ninotchka* as part of its anticommunist efforts. In the beginning of the film, the character played by Greta Garbo is a stern Soviet. As the plot developed, however, she is transformed into a glamorous figure by her adventures in Paris. Iraqi audiences found the austere Soviet life of Ninotchka far more admirable than her carefree and, from their perspective, immoral life in Paris. After several showings, the Iraqi government withdrew the film (Ireland 1952). It is, however, not clear whether U.S. public diplomacy planners have ever fully internalized this important cautionary tale.

Battles (2002, 16) identifies three dominant themes in U.S. propaganda during the early Cold War era: "The image [of the United States] to be projected was of a society that valued and supported freedom, that was economically and militarily strong, and that supported peace and a role for international institutions in governing intra-state affairs." American propaganda efforts were, however, undermined by the fact that the U.S. government and U.S. economic interests were frequently aligned with the most repressive regimes in the regions; by U.S. support of Israel; and by America's close ties with England and France, the colonial powers that had dominated the region. Anti-American sentiment periodically flared, and, as early as 1952, anti-regime protesters attacked the USIS office in Baghdad.

As the Cold War progressed and the world became even more clearly polarized, some leaders in the Middle East became adept at playing the nuclear chess game by using the competition between the United States and the Soviet Union to their advantage. For example, during the climax of the Iran hostage crisis in 1976, young Islamic revolutionaries exploited the new global power of American television to cultivate support for Islamic fundamentalism among Muslims throughout the world and to humiliate the Carter administration. More routinely, however, Middle Eastern nations were pawns in Cold War struggles; in the Palestinian-Israeli conflict; in Turkey, Lebanon, and Syria; and perhaps most lethally in the eight-year Iran-Iraq war, which may have claimed a million or more lives.

PRIVATIZATION OF PUBLIC POLICY AND
PUBLIC DIPLOMACY: VICTORY CULTURE

Under Western liberalism, democracy and capitalism have always coexisted in creative tension. The privatizing revolutions of the Thatcher and Reagan eras resolved this tension by conflating laissez-faire "free market" economics and democracy, equating economic freedom with political freedom. By definition, this neo- or postliberal resolution favors the wealthiest nations, corporations, and social strata; and it halts, and in many cases reverses, the long, slow, but steady global trend toward greater social equality that began in the eighteenth century. It consolidates the shift from the primacy of public (state) power to private (corporate) power that began early in the twentieth century.

This new configuration of power was in ascent when the Cold War came to an end, so much so that one prominent neoliberal theorist claimed that the West had realized the telos of historical evolution, thereby bringing an "end" to history (Fukuyama 1989). It was from within the euphoria of this "victory culture" that America launched its post–Cold War policy of globalization. Patrick Smith (1999) describes the dangerous narcissism of this triumphalism:

> A widespread complacency—both in and out of government—threatens the institutions of democracy by encouraging Americans to assume their common heritage is eternal, requires no vigilance, and can withstand any abuse. In turn, this has produced a dedication to globalism that borders on religious belief. We may define globalism as the spread of neoliberal economic principles around the world: deregulation, the wholesale privatization of public institutions, and an unshakeable faith in the primacy of unfettered markets. But let us understand the term as it is actually meant. As even its most convinced advocates acknowledge, globalization amounts to Americanization. . . . We have attached a certain finality to this proposition: history has ended; the Hegelian process has run its course, and its end result is the U.S. model. . . . Americans today suffer a kind of narcissism, a failure of vision. As we did after WW II, we have chosen not to see others as they are, or to see ourselves as we are—or finally to see ourselves among others. This is the true meaning of U.S. triumphalism; wherever we look, we see only reflections of ourselves. (42–43)

American triumphalism played a role in the demise of U.S. public diplomacy programs, including the USIA. Indeed, even USIA functionaries whose professional futures were at stake acknowledged that the increased global power and penetration of private media conglomerates, advanced communication technologies, digital convergence, and the Internet, and the emergence of the twenty-four-hour news cycle after the 1991 Persian Gulf War, rendered their own efforts largely obsolete (USIA Alumni Association 1997). CNN and MTV had, in effect, become America's de facto public diplomats. The ersatz public diplomacy efforts of the George W. Bush administration do not, however, appear to have assimilated this crucial insight of USIA experts.

The brief 1991 Gulf War had another significant information outcome. Information and information technologies assumed new significance within warfare theory (Arquilla & Ronfeldt 1997). While resources devoted to both traditional and public diplomacy were declining, assets devoted to information warfare, including psychological warfare, were significantly expanding. Moreover, military personnel were increasingly functioning in roles that had traditionally been played by diplomats (Priest 2003). The net effect was that the face America was presenting to the world was the face that President Eisenhower had warned against in his farewell address in 1959: the aggressive face of the military-industrial complex, with private media and telecommunication companies serving as its nerve center.

NARCISSISTIC FAILURE OF VISION

This was the infrastructure that was in place on September 11, 2001, when the terrorist attacks on New York and Washington, D.C., shattered America's complacency. Ordinary Americans, long insulated against world opinion by a commercial news culture that had grown rich harvesting the easy profits of scandal, celebrity, and infotainment, were genuinely shocked to discover that America had enemies. "Why do they hate us?" people asked in plaintive tones that seemed to express sincere bewilderment during the period of national mourning that followed the attacks.

The Bush administration's response to this question was, predictably, to look to the private sector to repair America's image abroad (Holtzman 2003). It reinvented public diplomacy within the template of neoliberalism. Reasoning that U.S. consumer and popular culture had been contributing factors in the demise of the Soviet Union, the administration believed that its job was to "sell" America to the world, especially to the Middle East with its youthful demographics. Still viewing the world through the distorted lens of the victory culture, it looked to Madison Avenue to transform America's image abroad. Appointing Charlotte Beers, who had served as chief executive of the J. Walter Thompson advertising agency, to the newly created post of undersecretary of state for public diplomacy, the Bush administration conceived of America as a commodity, a brand, to be marketed just as Beers had so successfully marketed Uncle Ben's Rice. In announcing her appointment, Colin Powell said, "I wanted one of the world's greatest advertising experts, because what are we doing? We're selling. We're selling a product" (Leonard 2002, 1). While Powell's description of U.S. national identity as a commodity may be jarring to critics, it is wholly consistent with the assumptions of the territorial branding movement that is now well established within international advertising and marketing.

Beers's approach to selling "Brand America" was to attempt to engage Middle Eastern audiences emotionally rather than discursively. One of Beers's first initiatives was to rename the Voice of America's Arabic service, Radio Sawa (which means Radio Together in Arabic), and to reprogram the service to target a youthful audience, with fast-paced musical offerings featuring Britney Spears, the Backstreet Boys, and popular Arab-language performers, interspersed with U.S. news bulletins that were designed to counter hostile local news reports. Beers also did some of the early groundwork for the creation of the U.S. satellite television network (Middle East Television Network), which was launched in February 2004 to try to compete with Al-Jazeera and Al-Arabiyya.

Beers's other major projects include the production of "Shared Values" people-to-people video profiles for airing in the region, which featured the lives of Muslim Americans, for example teachers, firemen, and basketball players; and *Hi* magazine, a glossy lifestyle magazine aimed at young people. Both of these initiatives appear to have misfired. The intent of the profiles was to send the message that America is an open society that practices religious tolerance, but "Shared Values" lacked credibility in light of the Guantanamo detentions, FBI interrogations of Arab Americans, U.S. deportations, and new visa restrictions. The content of *Hi* was pitched too low for its target audience. It assumed a level of ignorance of America and American values that does not exist among young people in most of the region; consequently, many young Arabs found it boring or overtly propagandistic.

A precipitous decline in favorable attitudes toward America's image worldwide occurred during Beers's short-lived tenure as undersecretary (Pew Research Center 2002); she resigned in March 2003. Beers's detractors claim she failed miserably, while her defenders argue that she was not given adequate resources or time to do the job. Even the Bush administration acknowledged that its public diplomacy efforts in the Middle East had failed; and, in response to congressional pressure, it appointed a blue-ribbon commission, chaired by Edward P. Djerejian, former ambassador to Syria and Israel, to conduct an inquiry (Advisory Group on Public Diplomacy 2003).

The commission's report, *Changing Minds, Winning Peace*, concluded, "At this critical time in our nation's history, the apparatus of public diplomacy has proven inadequate, especially in the Arab and Muslim world" (Advisory Group on Public Diplomacy 2003, 8). The advisory group called for a dramatic transformation in the way the United States communicates its values and policies to the world, and for "an immediate end to the absurd and dangerous under funding of public diplomacy in a time of peril" (2003, 8). The advisory group's report has received a "lackluster" and "disappointing" reception by the administration, according to Republican U.S. Congressman Frank Wolf of Virginia, chair of the House Appropriations subcommittee, which oversees funding for public diplomacy (Regan 2004, 1).

Beers's successor as undersecretary for public diplomacy was Margaret Tutwiler, who brought a background in government public relations to the job. Upon taking office, Tutwiler acknowledged that U.S. standing abroad had deteriorated to such an extent that "it will take us many years of hard, focused work" to restore it. Tutwiler maintained that the "problem does not lend itself to a quick fix or a single solution or a simple plan" (Regan 2004, 1). However, Tutwiler held the position for just three months (December 16, 2003, to March 16, 2004); she resigned to take a position with the New York Stock Exchange just as the first images of the Abu Ghraib prisoner abuses were becoming public. As of this writing (July 2004), the position remains vacant.

The Bush administration has expressed high hopes for the Middle East Television Network, Al Hurra (The Free One). President Bush says that Al Hurra will counter the "hateful propaganda that fills the airways in the Muslim world" and tell "the truth about the values and policies of the United States" (Regan 2004, 2). Costing $62 million for its first year of operation with projected annual operating expenses of $47 million thereafter, Al Hurra, which broadcasts via satellite from Springfield, Virginia, has predictably received a hostile reception by Arab media. The London-based Palestinian expatriate newspaper *Al-Quds al-Arabi* has compared Al Hurra's "guided news" to Saddam's old Ba'ath Party media; it described the approach as forty to fifty years out of date, and used the opportunity to chastise the U.S.-created Iraqi Governing Council for pressuring and censuring local Arab media (*Al-Quds al-Arabi* 2004). Al Hurra also received a "frosty" reception in Cairo and elsewhere in the Middle East (Atia 2004; Craft 2004). Predictably, Al-Jazeera responded with hostility, quoting academic experts who argue that American policies, not Arab ignorance, make America unpopular in the region; these experts point to the ample presence of Western broadcasting in the region, which is readily available through a myriad of satellite offerings, including CNN, BBC, and others (Amayreh 2004). The Bush administration has tried to correct some of its earlier public diplomacy mistakes by staffing Al Hurra with personnel from the region; however, it has clearly gotten off to a bumpy start. Al Hurra's singular accomplishment to date has been to heat up the air wars in the Middle East.

Significantly, Bush's Advisory Group on Public Diplomacy expressed skepticism about the new satellite operation, which was still in the planning stage when their report went to press. They challenged the wisdom of this costly investment in light of the heavy pressures it will put on already scarce public diplomacy dollars. The Advisory Group anticipated Al-Jazeera's verdict: that Al Hurra is unlikely to be able to compete with the well-established presence in the region of Al-Jazeera, Al-Arabiyya, BBC, CNN, MTV, VH1, the Paramount Channel, Orbit news, Sky News, and European programming (Advisory Group on Public Diplomacy 2003; Amayreh 2004). Indeed, the Advisory Group raised serious questions about the overall effectiveness of all of the international broadcasting operations under the authority of the Broadcasting Board of Governors (BBG), the independent, autonomous entity established in 1999 by the Foreign Affairs Reform and Restructuring Act (Public Law 105-277), which oversees all U.S. government sponsored non-military, international broadcasting. Citing a study by the General Accounting Office, the Advisory Group indicated that most public affairs officers found the BBG operations to be of marginal to limited value in their local geographical regions. The Advisory Group contended that in launching the Middle Eastern Television Network (Al Hurra), the BBG was attempting to use twentieth-century technologies to deal with twenty-first-century challenges.

Arab opinion leaders, for example media commentators and intellectuals, with some exceptions, argue that the current U.S. approach is naïve. It assumes, as American propagandists in the early Cold War period assumed, that Arab hostility to the United States is based on ignorance of America. Like the screeners of Garbo's *Ninotchka*, the new public diplomats seem to believe that to know Americans and American popular culture is to love them. Exposure to American culture, it is reasoned, will cultivate a desire for American consumer goods and the American way of life as it did in the former Soviet Union. The Middle East is, however, very different from the Soviet Union. The West has had a powerful and largely exploitive presence in the Middle East for centuries. People in the region know much more about Americans than Americans know about them. The longstanding presence of U.S. corporations (like Bechtel and Halliburton), with their dual-wage standards for Western and regional employees, has provided its own brand of "person-to-person" counterdiplomacy (Chatterjee 2004).

Above all, however, U.S. policy in the region has generated legitimate hostility. And that hostility has escalated dramatically since the 2001 terrorist attacks on the United States as a result of U.S. counterterrorism measures including domestic profiling, interrogation, and detention of Muslims; the detentions at Guantanamo; the continuing chaos in Afghanistan; the invasion and occupation of Iraq; the prison abuse scandals in Iraq, Afghanistan, and

Guantanamo; and what is perceived in the region and in much of the world as U.S. support for Israel's oppression of the Palestinians. To dismiss critics of U.S. policies as "fanatics" or proterrorist elements further inflames that hostility. The long history of inconsistent but politically and economically expedient policies in the Middle East has come back to haunt the United States. The arming and support of Israel in its conflicts with the Palestinians as well as its Arab neighbors, the U.S.-engineered coup in Iran in 1953, the support for Saddam in the brutal war with Iran, the betrayal of the Kurds in the 1991 Gulf War, the sanctions imposed after the 1991 war, the long pattern of support for anti-democratic regimes in the region, and the U.S. invasion and occupation of Iraq cannot be papered over by emotional appeals, the glamour of pop stars, or public relations campaigns. These tactics are likely to further solidify cynicism and antagonism toward the United States among Muslims. Young people in the Middle East rioting against U.S. imperialism while wearing Levis and Nikes may reflect the contradictions of postmodern aesthetics, but the contradictions these young Arabs are seeking to resolve are far more substantive, complex, and intractable than anything a quick fix of commodity fetishism can repair.

Even some former government insiders now regard U.S. unilateralism in the Middle East and the world as the action, if not the intention, of a "rogue state," which places itself above international agreements while insisting (by force if necessary) that other nations honor them (Prestowitz 2003; see also Diplomats and Military Commanders for Change n.d.). From the beginning, the detentions at Guantanamo have provoked outrage in the world press. However, the revelation of the prisoner abuses at Abu Ghraib, at Guantanamo, and in Afghanistan have, as Mark Bowden puts it,

> handed our enemies a propaganda coup that trumps their best efforts. The photos from Abu Ghraib prison portray Americans as exactly the sexually obsessed, crude, arrogant, godless occupiers that our enemies say we are. They have even succeeded in uniting those on both sides of the war issue at home. Everyone is outraged and disgraced. (Bowden 2004, 37)

These photos have confirmed Eleanor Roosevelt's belief in the persuasive power of images in the Middle East. And they have also effectively erased any small pockets of credibility that sixty years of U.S. public diplomacy in the region may have produced.

REFERENCES

Acheson, D. (1950, May 1). Department of State airgram from Dean Acheson. Anti-Americanism in the Arab world. Document 3. Documentation of early cold war

U.S. propaganda activities in the Middle East. *National Security Archive*. Retrieved February 23, 2004, from www.gwu.edu/~nsarchiv/NSAEBB/NSAEBB78/docs.htm

Ackerman, B. A. (1980). *Social justice in the liberal state.* New Haven, CT: Yale University Press.

Advisory Group on Public Diplomacy for the Arab and Muslim World. (2003, October 1). *Changing minds, winning peace: A new strategic directive for public diplomacy in the Arab and Muslim world.* Report released to the U.S. Congress, Washington, DC. Retrieved February 25, 2004, from www.state.gov/documents/organization/24882.pdf

Al-Quds al-Arabi. (2004, February 17). Unsigned editorial. Retrieved February 21, 2004, from *World Press Review*, www.worldpress.org/Mideast/1808.cfm

Amayreh, K. (2004). U.S. TV channel raises Palestinian ire. Retrieved February 15, 2004, from http://english.aljazeera.net/NR/exeres/79A16E4E-4159-8FF0-EAB2F329EE03.htm

Anderson, B. (1981). *Imagined communities: Reflections on the origins and spread of nationalism.* London: Verso, 1981.

Arquilla, J., & Ronfeldt, D. (Eds.). (1997). *In Athena's camp: Preparing for conflict in the information age.* Rand Corporation. Retrieved February 10, 2004, from www.rand.org/publications/MR/MR880/

Atia, T. (2004). Horsing around: When will the Arabs find their own voice? *Al Ahram Weekly.* Retrieved February 21, 2004, from http://weekly.ahram.org.eg/print/2004/678/fr2.htm

Battles, J. (Ed.) (2002). U.S. propaganda in the Middle East: The early cold war version. *National security archive electronic briefing book no. 78.* Retrieved February 12, 2004, from www.gwu.edu/~nsarchv/NSAEBB/NSAEBB78/essay2.htm

Berry, B. (1954a, January 13). United States embassy, Iraq dispatch from Burton Berry to the Department of State. Anti-communist campaign of Iraq Government. Document 118. Documentation of early cold war U.S. propaganda activities in the Middle East. *National Security Archive*. Retrieved February 23, 2004, from www.gwu.edu/~nsarchiv/NSAEBB/NSAEBB78/docs.htm

———. (1954b, January 19). United States embassy, Iraq cable from Burton Berry to the Department of State. Attacking Iraq Neutralism. Document 119. Documentation of early cold war U.S. propaganda activities in the Middle East. *National Security Archive*. Retrieved February 23, 2004, from www.gwu.edu/~nsarchiv/NSAEBB/NSAEBB78/docs.htm

Bowden, M. (2004, July/August). Lessons of Abu Ghraib. *Atlantic*, 37, 40.

Chatterjee, P. (2004, February 23). Operation sweatshop Iraq. *Corporate Watch*. Retrieved February 23, 2004, from www.corporatewatch.org/issues/PRT.jsp?articleid=9508

Chomsky, N. (1991). *Media control: The spectacular achievements of propaganda.* New York: Seven Stories Press.

Craft, M. (2004, February 16). U.S. Arabic channel a turn-off. *Guardian Unlimited*. Retrieved February 21, 2004, from http://media.guardian.co.uk/broadcast/story/0,7493,1149373,00.html

Crocker, E. S. (1950, April 10). United States embassy, Iraq cable from Edward S. Crocker II to the Department of State. Recent developments in connection with the Kurdish-language news bulletin. Document 2. Documentation of early cold war U.S. propaganda activities in the Middle East. *National Security Archive*. Retrieved February 23, 2004, from www.gwu.edu/~nsarchiv/NSAEBB/NSAEBB78/docs.htm

Dewey, J. (1927). *The public and its problems*. New York: Holt.

Diplomats and Military Commanders for Change. Retrieved July 18, 2004, from www.diplomatsforchange.com

Dizard, W. (2001). *Digital diplomacy: U.S. foreign policy in the information age*. New York: Free Press.

Eisenhower, D. D. (1958, July 31). White House letter from Dwight D. Eisenhower to Edward L. R. Elson. Response to letter on the Middle East. Document 133. Documentation of early cold war U.S. propaganda activities in the Middle East. *National Security Archive*. Retrieved February 23, 2004, from www.gwu.edu/~nsarchiv/NSAEBB/NSAEBB78/docs.htm

Fukuyama, F. (1989, summer). The end of history? *National Interest*, 3–18.

Habermas, J. (1971). *Knowledge and human interests*. Boston: Beacon.

Heritage Foundation. (2004, January 13). *Regaining America's voice overseas: A conference on U.S. diplomacy—Proceedings*. Retrieved April 20, 2004, from www.heritage.Org/Research/GovernmentReform/hl817.cfm

Holtzman, M. (2003). Privatize public diplomacy. Retrieved February 9, 2003, from www.allied-media.com/Arab-American /pub-diplomacy.htm

Ireland, P. W. (1952, July 8). Iraq dispatch from Philip W. Ireland to the Department of State. When the communists came. Document 64. Documentation of early cold war U.S. propaganda activities in the Middle East. *National Security Archive*. Retrieved February 23, 2004, from www.gwu.edu/~nsarchiv/NSAEBB/NSAEBB78/docs.htm

Jansen, S. C. (1988). *Censorship: The knot that binds power and knowledge*. New York: Oxford University Press.

———. (2002). *Critical Communication Theory*. Lanham, MD: Rowman & Littlefield.

Katz, E., & Lazarsfeld, P. F. (Eds.). (1955). *Personal influence*. Glencoe, IL: Free Press.

Lacy, D. (1952, October 27). Service letter from Dan Lacy to Datus C. Smith, Jr., guidance for Franklin publications. Document 78. Documentation of early cold war U.S. propaganda activities in the Middle East. *National Security Archive*. Retrieved February 23, 2004, from www.gwu.edu/~nsarchiv/NSAEBB/NSAEBB78/docs.htm

Leonard, M. (2002, June 16). Velvet fist in the iron glove. *Observer Worldview Extra, Guardian Unlimited*. Retrieved January 23, 2004, from http://observer.guardian.co.uk/worldview/story/0,11581,738540,00.html

Murray, W. (1945). Memorandum from Wallace Murray to Archibald MacLeish, letter from Harold B. Hoskins on American movie propaganda. Document 1. Documentation of early cold war U.S. propaganda activities in the Middle East. *National Security Archive*. Retrieved February 23, 2004, from www.gwu.edu/~nsarchiv/NSAEBB/NSAEBB78/docs.htm

National Security Archive, George Washington University. (2002). Documentation of early cold war U.S. propaganda activities in the Middle East. Retrieved February 12, 2004, from www.gwu.edu/~nsarchiv/

Peters, J. D. (1999). *Speaking into the air: A history of the idea of communication.* Chicago: University of Chicago Press.

Pew Research Center. (2002, December 4). *Introduction and summary: What the world thinks in 2002: How global publics view: Their lives, their countries, the world, America.* Retrieved February 4, 2004, from http://people-press.org/reports/display.php3?ReportID=165

Planning Group for Integration of USIA into the Department of State. (1997, June 20). U.S. Department of State. *What is public diplomacy.* Retrieved February 12, 2004, from www.publicdiplomacy.org/1.htm

Prestowitz, C. (2003) *Rogue nation: American unilateralism and the failure of good intentions.* New York: Basic Books.

Priest, D. (2003). *The mission: Waging war and keeping peace with America's military.* New York: W. W. Norton.

Regan, T. (2004, February 9). U.S. image abroad will "take years" to repair. *Christian Science Monitor.* Retrieved February 12, 2004, from www.csmonitor.com/2004/0209/dailyUpdate.html?=entt

Sennett, R. (1980). *Authority.* New York: Knopf.

Simpson, C. (1994). *Science of coercion: Communication research and psychological warfare, 1945–1960.* New York: Oxford University Press.

Smith, P. (1999, September/October). Dark victory. *Index on Censorship* 28 (5), 42–43.

Smith-Mundt Act. (1948). *U.S. code collection, legal information institute.* Retrieved December 12, 2003, from www4.law.cornell.edu/uscode/22/1461.html

Snow, N. (2002). *Propaganda, inc.: Selling American culture to the world.* New York: Seven Stories Press.

U.S. Department of State. (1987). *Dictionary of international relations terms,* 3rd ed. Washington, DC: Department of State Library.

U.S. Information Agency Alumni Association. (Producer). (1997). *Public diplomacy part I: Telling America's story, part II: The road ahead* [Videocassette]. Washington, DC: USIA Alumni Association.

U.S. Information Agency Alumni Association. (2002). *Public diplomacy and propaganda.* Retrieved April 20, 2004, from www.publicdiplomacy.org/1.htm#propaganda

5

The Problem with Patriotism:
Steps toward the Redemption of
American Journalism and Democracy

Robert Jensen

Though it was unintentional, since September 11, 2001, Dan Rather has single-handedly provided enough evidence to destroy one of American journalists' central claims about their special place in a democratic society, while at the same time helping us see why patriotism is morally unacceptable.

Rather's struggles with the conflicts between his role as a journalist and his desire to be patriotic demonstrated why contemporary U.S. journalism falls well short of its claim to be politically neutral. For this service, journalists should be grateful to Rather, for if we can bury that peculiar ideology of contemporary commercial journalism it might be possible to rebuild a media system that better serves a democratic society and its citizens.

At the same time, Rather's declarations about citizenship during wartime have demonstrated why the problem with patriotism is not how to define it properly, but how to eliminate it. For this service, citizens should be grateful, for if we can leave behind that morally and intellectually bankrupt ideology it might be possible to dismantle the American empire to make way for a meaningful American democracy.

WHY DAN RATHER?

Rather, anchor of the *CBS Evening News* and the dean of American television journalism, spoke more openly after 9/11 than any other mainstream commercial journalist, appearing on numerous talk shows to discuss his reaction to the tragedy and media coverage. The flash point was his appearance less than a week after 9/11 on David Letterman's talk show, for which he was both criticized and lauded for his declaration of loyalty to the president.

67

But much more important than that initial reaction have been comments that Rather has continued to make since 9/11 as he has tried—and failed—to reconcile the contradictions in his conception of what it means to be a journalist and a U.S. citizen. In that failure—which is not his alone but the whole profession's—we can see how intellectually incoherent and politically debilitating are the current ideologies of journalism and patriotism.

The basic claim that journalists make about their role in society is simple: In a democracy predicated on the notion that the people—not leaders—are sovereign, the people need information independent of the centers of power, especially the government. The larger and more complex the society, the more difficult it is for individuals to gather for themselves that information. Enter the journalists, who offer themselves as independent watchdogs on power who don't take sides in partisan struggles. In the contemporary United States, journalists claim to be neutral sources of information.

Since 9/11, it has been painfully clear that the mainstream commercial news media have not been, on the whole, that much-needed critical, independent voice and are far from neutral politically. Just as important, the current posture of journalism shows that such simplistic claims to political neutrality tend to undermine the ability to be critical and independent; nowhere is that more evident than in discussions of patriotism.

Dan Rather helps make this plain as day.

Some have written him off as an aging crank who not only can sound goofy on the air (his sometimes strained colloquialisms have been dubbed "Rather Blather") but also, more importantly, doesn't represent the views of most journalists. I see it just the opposite: Rather is a fairly typical journalist, just unusually blunt and honest in public. That's precisely why he so often embarrasses the profession; he isn't good at self-censorship.

Using Rather's comments as a starting point, I will lay out a case against the typical journalistic claim to the importance of political neutrality and the typical American claim to the nobility of patriotism, arguing that both are incoherent and destructive to democracy.

PATRIOTIC JOURNALISM

This argument rests on the simple assertion that patriotism is not politically neutral, which is both obvious and steadfastly ignored. In fact, in the United States invocations of patriotism are routinely coupled with declarations of bipartisanship, evidence that one has gotten "beyond politics." Yet patriotism is inherently political, not only in the way it is used by politicians—often cynically—to justify particular policies regarding war but also in the fundamental way it defines citizenship in relation to a nation-state. More on that later, after an examination of Rather's post-9/11 performance.

Rather's first foray into the issue came on the *Letterman* show on September 17, 2001, when he said, "George Bush is the president. He makes the decisions, and, you know, it's just one American, wherever he wants me to line up, just tell me where, and he'll make the call" (Bozell 2001, A18).

Such a direct declaration of subordination to the authority of a political leader made many—especially many journalists—nervous, and though Rather never retracted the remark he tried to refine his ideas in subsequent discussions. As he consistently reasserted his patriotism without apology, he struggled to articulate it in a fashion consistent with a conception of journalists-as-neutral-observers. For example, Rather—the same man who offered to line up wherever the president ordered—would not wear a flag pin on the air, as some other journalists did. In a September 22, 2001, interview on *CNN Tonight* with Howard Kurtz (the *Washington Post* media critic who also appears on the cable news channel), Rather explained, "It doesn't feel right to me. I have the flag burned in my heart, and I have ever since infancy. And I just don't feel the need to do it. It just doesn't feel right to me" (all quotes from television broadcasts are, unless otherwise indicated, taken from transcripts retrieved from the Dow Jones Interactive database).

Shortly after 9/11, the American flag became a symbol of "America standing tough," which quickly became fused with "America going to war." So Rather was correct in recognizing that journalistic neutrality, as it is conventionally understood, would be compromised by wearing a flag. But in that same interview, Rather was asked by Kurtz if he thought that journalists, out of a fear of a public backlash, might be reluctant to criticize the administration. Rather's answer exhibited his inability to move past a sense of patriotism as subordination to authority:

> I want to fulfill my role as a decent human member of the community and a decent and patriotic American. And therefore, I am willing to give the government, the president and the military the benefit of any doubt here in the beginning. I'm going to fulfill my role as a journalist, and that is ask the questions, when necessary ask the tough questions. But I have no excuse for, particularly when there is a national crisis such as this, as saying—you know, the president says do your job, whatever you are and whomever you are, Mr. and Mrs. America. I'm going to do my job as a journalist, but at the same time I will give them the benefit of the doubt, whenever possible in this kind of crisis, emergency situation. Not because I am concerned about any backlash. I'm not. But because I want to be a patriotic American without apology.

Rather's contradictions are striking. He won't wear a flag pin, but he'll claim to be patriotic without apology. He will ask tough questions, but if those tough questions elicit responses from officials that seem questionable, he will give officials the benefit of the doubt. Rather's answer to Kurtz came just eleven days after the terrorist attacks, when one could plausibly believe that the shock of the event led people to speak in ways they might otherwise not. But Rather offered the same assessment on June 4, 2002, on the *Larry King Live* show on CNN, when King asked if there was "a thin line between patriot and reporter." Rather replied:

> No. I don't think it's a thin line at all. I've never had any difficulty with that line. What's sometimes a thin line, and where I do have some difficulty, is what's appropriate and what's the appropriate time? That's what I've just tried to outline in the wake of September 11. And then when the war first started, early in October, you know, when there's doubt to be given, we should give the military those doubts.

On October 9, 2001, Rather managed to contradict himself in the same interview, with former NBC and CBS reporter Marvin Kalb. After declaring, "I don't think you can be too patriotic; when in doubt, I would much prefer to err on the side of too much patriotism as opposed to too little," Rather went on to define a patriotic journalist as a "skeptical and independent journalist, not cynical." For Rather, that means "the measure of a journalist's patriotism is does he have the wisdom, does he have the savvy and does he or she have the guts to ask the tough questions, even though it might be deemed to be quote unpatriotic." Later in that interview he stated, "As a journalist, I never want to place a single American fighting man or woman's life in danger. And I'm fully prepared to give the government military spokesman the benefit of every reasonable doubt on that score" ("Conversation with Dan Rather" 2001). Kalb either didn't see Rather's contradictions or didn't think they warranted comment.

It is not clear on what principle Rather would refuse to interrogate political leaders early in a crisis or war. On the surface, it would seem just the opposite rule should apply; in the wake of an attack like 9/11, it's likely that politicians would move quickly to take advantage of public shock and grief, making journalistic intervention and tough questioning all the more important early, when people are most emotional and most vulnerable to manipulation. Likewise, given the history of military officials shielding themselves from scrutiny and covering up mistakes with claims that releasing information would endanger men and women in the field, Rather would have to explain how one can ask "the tough questions" while giving military officials the benefit of the doubt.

While many journalists were nervous about Rather's pronouncements, the performance of the commercial mainstream news media after 9/11 suggests he was merely articulating what others believed and were doing; journalistic scrutiny of administration claims for months after 9/11 was timid at best, and claims by American officials that were intensely scrutinized in the foreign press and alternative media were accepted at face value in the U.S. commercial mainstream news media.

Curiously, shortly before his appearance on the June 2002 *Larry King Live* show, Rather had given an interview to the BBC in which he ruminated on the dangers of excessive patriotism. On *BBC Newsnight* on May 5, 2002, Rather said:

> I worry that patriotism run amok will trample the very values that the country seeks to defend. In a constitutional republic based on the principles of democracy such as ours, you simply cannot sustain warfare without the people at large understanding why we fight, how we fight, and have a sense of accountability to the very top. (Holt 2002)

This "surge of patriotism," Rather said, leads to a journalist saying, "I know the right questions, but you know what, this is not exactly the right time to ask them." But, he continued, "It's unpatriotic not to stand up, look [officials] in the eye, and ask the questions they don't want to hear" (Holt 2002). Though Rather had said in the earlier interview with Kurtz that he didn't fear a backlash from a hyperpatriotic public, to the BBC reporter he compared the problems that American journalists faced regarding patriotism with the practice of "necklacing":

> It is an obscene comparison. You know I am not sure I like it. But you know there was a time in South Africa that people would put flaming tires around peoples' necks if they dissented. And in some ways the fear is that you will be necklaced here, you will have a flaming tire of lack of patriotism put around your neck. Now it is that fear that keeps journalists from asking the toughest of the tough questions. . . . And again, I am humbled to say, I do not except myself from this criticism. (Holt 2002)

Rather's flip-flopping—between (1) declarations that he would defer to authority, followed by (2) promises that he would ask the tough questions, except (3) when it wasn't the right time to ask tough questions, followed by (4) an acknowledgment that he and his colleagues weren't asking the tough questions even when they should—was not an aberration from, but an honest account of, the position of most American journalists.

Whatever his confusion about the role of journalists, Rather seems clear about the role of citizens in wartime: the majority will either support administration policy or, when war does come, quickly get in line. On November 2, 2001, on CNN's *Larry King Weekend*, Rather said,

> The whole country is right in saying, look, whatever arguments one may or may not have had with George Bush the younger before September 11, he is our

commander-in-chief, he's the man now. And we need unity, we need steadiness. I'm not preaching about it. We all know this.

Do we all agree with this call for unity? The existence of an antiwar movement that began organizing immediately after 9/11 suggests otherwise. And, why in a democracy should we value such unity? Unity toward what goal? Given that in a democracy people are supposed to determine the goals, and that invariably there will be many differences of opinion about the proper goals, what can unity mean other than the obedience and acceptance of authority? On *Larry King Live* on November 4, 2002, Rather made that explicit:

And, you know, I'm of the belief that you can have only one commander-in-chief at a time, only one president at a time. President Bush is our president. Whatever he decides vis-à-vis war or peace in Iraq is what we will do as a country. And I for one will swing in behind him as a citizen . . . and support whatever his decision is.

In that interview, Rather's conception of the role of the news media in governance came into sharper focus. When arguing that the U.S. military can be too restrictive in the information it releases and the access it provides journalists, Rather's rationale for greater openness was that in a "constitutional republic based on the principles of democracies such as our own that there must be— it is imperative there be a higher degree of communicable trust between the leadership and the led."

This is, in a nutshell, Dan Rather's political theory: As a citizen, he will swing in behind a president's decision to go to war; as a journalist, he will provide the information to create trust between politicians and citizens. The obvious problem is that this inverts the relationship of citizen to elected officials in a democracy. Citizens in a democracy are not supposed to be "the led." In a meaningful democratic system, citizens should not be limited to a role only in the selection of leaders (an incredibly thin conception of democracy) or in the selection of policies from a set of limited choices presented to them by leaders (still a very thin conception). In a democratic system with a rich sense of participation, citizens would have an active, meaningful role in the determination of which issues are most important at any moment and in the formation of policy options to address those issues. And journalists would be their ally in that task.

THE PROBLEM WITH PATRIOTISM

Whatever the differences of opinion—about how much journalists should talk in public about patriotism, or whether they should wear flag pins on their lapels, or how aggressive their questioning of officials should be—I know of no mainstream commercial journalist in the United States who publicly renounced patriotism after 9/11. Despite the flak he took for various comments, Dan Rather was probably accurate when he told the Texas Daily Newspaper Association in March 2002: "There's a lot of talk today about being patriotic. And we all want to be patriotic" (Tolson 2002, 19). The only potential disagreements have been about what constitutes patriotic behavior for journalists.

Bill Kovach, chairman of the Committee of Concerned Journalists, was one of the strongest spokespersons for tough, critical journalism after 9/11. He did not trumpet patriotism, but implicitly endorsed the concept in his defense of journalists:

> A journalist is never more true to democracy—is never more engaged as a citizen, is never more patriotic—than when aggressively doing the job of independently verifying the news of the day; questioning the actions of those in authority; disclosing information the public needs but others wish secret for self-interested purposes. (Kovach 2002)

An editor at one of the top U.S. journalism reviews also implicitly endorsed patriotism in arguing that journalists serve their country best when asking "tough, even unpopular questions when our government wages war." He distinguished "patriotism, love of one's country" from "nationalism—the exalting of one's nation and its culture and interests above all others. If patriotism is a kind of affection, nationalism is its dark side" (Baker 2002, 78–79).

There is only one problem with all these formulations: patriotism cannot be distinguished from nationalism; patriotism in general is morally indefensible; and patriotism in today's empire, the United States, is particularly dangerous to the continued health of the planet. I argue that everyone—citizens and journalists alike—should abandon patriotism and strive to become more fully developed human beings with allegiances not to a nation but to humanity. At first glance, in a country where patriotism is almost universally taken to be an unquestioned virtue, this may seem outrageous. But there is a simple path to what I consider to be this logical, moral conclusion.

If we use the common definition of patriotism—love of, and loyalty to, one's country—the first question that arises is, What is meant by country? Nation-states, after all, are not naturally occurring objects. In discussions with various community groups and classes since 9/11, I have asked people to explain which aspects of a nation-state—specifically in the context of patriotism in the United States—they believe should spark patriotic feelings. Toward whom or what should one feel love and loyalty? The answers offered include the land itself, the people of a nation, its culture, the leadership, national policies, the nation's institutions, and the democratic ideals of

the nation. To varying degrees, all seem like plausible answers, yet all fail
to provide an acceptable answer to that basic question.

Land: Many people associate patriotism with a love of the land on which
they were born, were raised, or currently live. Certainly people's sense
of place and connection to a landscape is easy to understand; most of us
have felt that. I was born and raised on the prairie, and I feel most comfortable, most at home, on the prairie. But what has that to do with love
or loyalty to a nation-state? Does affection for a certain landscape map
onto political boundaries? If I love the desert, should I have a greater affection for the desert on the U.S. side of the border, and a lesser affection when I cross into Mexico? Should I love the prairie in my home
state of North Dakota, but abandon that affection when I hit the Canadian border? In discussing connections to the land we can sensibly talk
about watersheds and local ecosystems, but not national boundaries. And
ties to a specific piece of land (i.e., the farm one grew up on) have nothing to do with a nation-state.

People: It's also common to talk about patriotism in terms of love and affection for one's countrymen and women. This can proceed on two levels: either as an assertion of differential value of people's lives or as an
expression of affection for people. The former—claiming that the lives
of people within one's nation-state are more valuable than lives of people outside it—is immoral by the standards of virtually all major moral
philosophies and religions, which typically are based on the belief that
all human life is equally valuable. It may be true that especially in
times of war, people act as if they value the lives of fellow citizens
more, but for most people that cannot be a principle on which patriotism can rest.

Certainly everyone has special affection for specific people in their
lives, and it's likely that—by virtue of proximity—for most of us the majority of people for whom we have that affection are citizens of the same
nation. But does that mean our sense of connection to them stems from
living in the same nation-state? Given the individual variation in humans, why assume that someone living in our nation-state should automatically spark a feeling of connection greater than someone elsewhere?
I was born in the United States near the Canadian border, and I have
more in common with Canadians from the prairie provinces than I do
with, for example, the people of Texas, where I now live. Am I supposed
to, by virtue of my U.S. citizenship, naturally feel something stronger for
Texans than Manitobans? If so, why?

Culture: The same arguments about land and people apply to cultures. Culture—that complex mix of customs, art, stories, faith, and traditions—does not map exactly onto the often-artificial boundaries of nation-states. More importantly, if one rejects the dominant culture of the nation-state in which one lives, why should one have affection for it or loyalty to it?

Leaders: In a democracy, it is clear that patriotism can't be defined as loyalty to existing political leaders. Such patriotism would be the antithesis of democracy; to be a citizen is to retain the right to make judgments about leaders, not simply accept their authority. Even if one accepts the right of leaders to make decisions within a legal structure and agrees to follow the resulting laws, that does not mean that one is loyal to that leadership.

Policies: The same argument about leaders applies to specific policies adopted by leaders. In a democracy, one may agree to follow legally binding rules, but that does not mean one supports them. Of course, no one claims that it is unpatriotic to object to existing policy about taxes or transportation planning. War tends to be the only policy over which people make demands that everyone support—or at least mute dissent about—a national policy. But why should war be different? When so much human life is at stake, is it not even more important for all opinions to be fully aired?

Governmental structures: If patriotism is not loyalty to particular leader or policies, many contend, at least it can mean loyalty to our governmental structures. But that is no less an abandonment of democracy, for inherent in a real democracy is the idea that no single set of institutions can be assumed to be, for all times and places, the ultimate expression of democracy. In a nation founded on the principle that the people are sovereign and retain the right to reject institutions that do not serve their interests, patriotism defined as loyalty to the existing structures is hard to defend.

Democratic ideals: When challenged on these other questionable definitions of patriotism, most people eventually land on the seemingly safe assertion that patriotism in the United States is an expression of commitment to a set of basic democratic ideals, which typically include liberty, justice, and equality. But problems arise here as well. First, what makes these values distinctly American? Are not various people around the world committed to these values and working to make them real in a variety of ways? Given that these values were not invented in the United States and are not distinct to the United States today, how can one claim them as the basis for patriotism? If these values predate the formation of the United States and are present around the world, are they not human ideals rather than American?

The next move many make is to claim that while these values are not the sole property of Americans, it is in the United States that they have been realized to their fullest extent. This is merely the hubris of the powerful. On some criteria, such as legal protection for freedom of speech, the United States certainly ranks at or near the top. But the commercial media system, which dominates in the United States, also systematically shuts out radical views and narrows the political spectrum, impoverishing real democratic dialogue. It is folly to think that any nation could claim to be the primary repository of any single democratic value, let alone the ideal of democracy.

Claims that the United States is the ultimate fulfillment of the values of justice also must come to terms with history and the American record of brutality, both at home and abroad. One might want to ask indigenous people and black Americans, victims of the America holocausts of genocide and slavery, about the commitment to freedom and justice for all, in the past and today. We also would have some explaining to do to the people of Guatemala and Iran, Nicaragua and South Vietnam, East Timor and Laos, Iraq and Panama. We would have to explain to the victims of U.S. aggression—direct and indirect— why it is that our political culture, the highest expression of the ideals of freedom and democracy, has routinely gone around the world overthrowing democratically elected governments, supporting brutal dictators, funding and training proxy terrorist armies, and unleashing brutal attacks on civilians when we go to war. If we want to make the claim that we are the fulfillment of history and the ultimate expression of the principles of freedom and justice, our first stop might be Hiroshima.

After working through this argument in class, one student, in exasperation, told me that I was missing the point by trying to reduce patriotism to an easily articulated idea or ideas. "It's about all these things together," she said. But it's not clear how individual explanations that fall short can collectively make a reasonable argument. If each attempt to articulate patriotism fails on empirical, logical, or moral grounds, how do they add up to a virtue?

Any attempt to articulate an appropriate object of patriotic love and loyalty falls apart quickly. When I make this argument, I am often told that I simply don't understand, that patriotism is as much about feeling as about logic or evidence. Certainly love is a feeling that often defies exact description; when we say we love someone, we aren't expected to produce a treatise on the reasons. My point is not to suggest that the emotion of love should be rendered bloodless but to point out that patriotism is incoherent because there is no object for the love that can be defended, morally or politically. We can love people, places, and ideas, but it makes no sense to declare one's love or loyalty to a nation-state that claims to be democratic.

BEYOND PATRIOTISM

My claim is that there is no way to rescue patriotism or distinguish it from nationalism, which most everyone rejects as crude and jingoistic. Any use of the concept of patriotism is bound to be chauvinistic at some level. At its worst, patriotism can lead easily to support for barbaric policies, especially in war. At its best, it is self-indulgent and arrogant in its assumptions about the uniqueness of U.S. culture and is willfully ignorant about the history and contemporary policy of this country. Emma Goldman was correct, I believe, when she identified the essentials of patriotism as "conceit, arrogance, and egotism," and went on to assert that

> patriotism assumes that our globe is divided into little spots, each one surrounded by an iron gate. Those who have had the fortune of being born on some particular spot, consider themselves better, nobler, grander, more intelligent than the living beings inhabiting any other spot. It is, therefore, the duty of everyone living on that chosen spot to fight, kill, and die in the attempt to impose his superiority upon all the others. (Goldman 1969, 128–129)

This is not a blanket denunciation of the United States, our political institutions, or our culture. People often tell me, "You start with the assumption that everything about the United States is bad." But I do not assume that; it would be as absurd a position as the assumption that everything about the United States is good. No reasonable person would make either statement. Nor do I "blame America first," as some often assert about radical analysis. Instead, I take seriously the moral obligation to be accountable for one's own behavior and, in a democracy, to be responsible collectively for the behavior of the nation in which I am a citizen.

To do that, we must move beyond patriotism. We can retain all our affections for land, people, culture and a sense of place without labeling it as patriotism and artificially attaching it to national boundaries. We can take into account the human need to feel solidarity and connection with others (what Randolph Bourne [1918] described as the ability "to enjoy the companionship of others, to be able to cooperate with them, and to feel a slight malaise at solitude") without attaching those feelings to a nation-state. We can realize that communication and transportation technologies have made possible a new level of mobility around the world, which leaves us with a clear choice: either the world can continue to be based on domination by powerful nation-states (in complex relationships with multinational corporations) and the elites who dictate policy in them, or we can seek a new interdependence and connection with people around the world through popular movements that cross national boundaries based on shared values and a common humanity.

To achieve the latter, people's moral reasoning must be able to constrain the destructive capacity of elite power. As Goldman suggested (1969), patriotism retards our moral development. These are not abstract arguments about rhetoric; the stakes are painfully real and the people in subordinated nation-states have, and will continue, to pay the price of patriotism in the dominant states with their bodies.

As the Bush administration makes good on its post-9/11 promise of an unlimited war against endless enemies, the question of patriotism is particularly important in the United States. The greater the destructive power of a nation, the greater the potential danger of patriotism. Despite many Americans' belief that we are the first benevolent empire, this applies to the United States as clearly as to any country. On this count, we would do well to ponder the observations of one of the top Nazis, Hermann Goering. In G. M. Gilbert's book on his experiences as the Nuremberg prison psychologist, he recounts this conversation with Goering:

> "Why of course the people don't want war," Goering shrugged. "Why would some poor slob on a farm want to risk his life in a war when the best that he can get out of it is to come back to his farm in one piece? Naturally, the common people don't want war; neither in Russia nor in England nor in America, nor for that matter in Germany. That is understood. But, after all, it is the leaders of the country who determine the policy and it is always a simple matter to drag the people along, whether it is a democracy or a fascist dictatorship or a Parliament or a Communist dictatorship."
>
> "There is one difference," I pointed out. "In a democracy the people have some say in the matter through their elected representatives, and in the United States only Congress can declare war."
>
> "Oh, that is all well and good, but, voice or no voice, the people can always be brought to the bidding of the leaders. That is easy. All you have to do is tell them that they are being attacked and denounce the pacifists for lack of patriotism and exposing the country to danger. It works the same way in any country." (Gilbert 1947, 278–279)

IF NOT PATRIOTISM?

If our political lives should not be organized around patriotism and nation-states, then what? The simple answer is both the local and the global; politics must, over time, be devolved down to levels where ordinary people can have a meaningful role in governing their own lives, while at the same time maintain a sense of connection to the entire human family and understand that the scope of high technology and the legacy of imperialism leave us bound to each other across the globe in new ways. This is a call for an internationalism that understands that we live mostly at the local level but can do that ethically only when we take into account how local actions affect others outside our view.

My goal here is not a detailed sketch of how such a system would work; any such attempt would be unrealistic. The first step is to envision something beyond what exists, a point from which people could go forward with experiments in new forms of social, political, and economic organization. Successes and failures in those experiments would guide subsequent steps, and any attempt to provide a comprehensive plan at this stage cannot be taken seriously. It also is important to realize that the work of articulating alternative political visions and engaging in political action to advance them has been going on for centuries. There is no reason today to think that national identification is the only force that could hold together societies; for example, political radicals of the nineteenth and early twentieth centuries argued for recognizing other common interests. As Goldman put it:

> Thinking men and women the world over are beginning to realize that patriotism is too narrow and limited a conception to meet the necessities of our time. The centralization of power has brought into being an international feeling of solidarity among the oppressed nations of the world; a solidarity which represents a greater harmony of interests between the workingman of America and his brothers abroad than between the American miner and his exploiting compatriot; a solidarity which fears not foreign invasion, because it is bringing all the workers to the point when they will say to their masters, "Go and do your own killing. We have done it long enough for you." This solidarity is awakening the consciousness of even the soldiers, they, too, being flesh of the flesh of the great human family. (Goldman 1969, 142–143)

We can, of course, go even further back in human history to find articulations of alternatives. As Leo Tolstoy reminded us in his critique of patriotism published in 1900, a rejection of loyalty to governments is part of the animating spirit of Christianity: "Some 2,000 years ago . . . the person of the highest wisdom, began to recognize the higher idea of a brotherhood of man." Tolstoy argued that this "higher idea, the brotherly union of the peoples, which has long since come to life, and from all sides is calling you to itself" could lead people to "understand that they are not the sons of some fatherland or other, nor of Governments, but are sons of God" (Tolstoy 1900).

In a more secular form, this sentiment is summed up in an often-quoted statement of the great American labor leader and socialist Eugene Debs, who said in 1915: "I have no country to fight for; my country is the earth, and I am a citizen of the world" (Debs 1915).

CAN JOURNALISTS BE NEUTRAL?

Whatever one's assessment of the intellectual and moral status of patriotism, one thing should be readily evident: a declaration of patriotism is a declaration of a partisan political position. For the purposes of this portion of my argument, it matters not how any particular journalist conceptualizes patriotism or what might be the best way for journalists to make good on their patriotism. Just as rejecting patriotism as a framework is political, so is accepting it. How, then, can journalists both openly proclaim a political position and continue to make the claim they are politically neutral?

Of course, individual journalists hold political positions on many subjects; no journalist claims to be politically inert. The conventional argument is not that journalists are devoid of opinions, but that professional practices of fairness, balance, and objectivity help ensure that the news is gathered and presented in a way that is not inordinately influenced by those opinions. As part of that, journalists typically avoid making public pronouncements about their political beliefs and affiliations. This is where patriotism is different; journalists typically agree that patriotism is a good thing and struggle in public with what it means for their work. On this matter, they are openly political yet see no conflict between this and an obviously contradictory claim to neutrality.

The most plausible explanation is that these journalists take patriotism to be the kind of political judgment that is so universally accepted that to publicly accept it is uncontroversial. For example, it's likely true that all American journalists believe slavery is wrong, and if asked in public no journalist would hesitate to state that belief. The statement would be a moral and political judgment about the rights and obligations of people, but no one would see it as compromising an accompanying claim to neutrality because to argue for slavery would place one well outside current social norms. It would be seen as an indication of pathology, personal and political.

But unless the argument against patriotism is evidence of such pathology—making me, Debs, Goldman, Tolstoy, and many others, both today and in the past, pathological—patriotism can't be in that category of a moral or political truism. The only way to pretend that declarations of patriotism are not political and open to critique is to erase the many arguments against patriotism. Indeed, a review of contemporary American mainstream commercial journalism would suggest that is exactly what happens.

Does any of this matter? Does it affect the news that U.S. readers and viewers get, especially on matters of war and peace? Yes, for this patriotism systematically clouds the vision of American reporters, and not just since 9/11. The most thorough account of this is contained in *Manufacturing Consent*, in which Edward S. Herman and Noam Chomsky (2002, xv) extensively review the systematic slanting of the news of foreign affairs toward the official view-point of the dominant culture's political elites. But, if one doesn't trust such radical sources, let's return to Dan Rather.

In 1996 Rather gave a talk on journalism ethics at the University of Texas, where I teach. More interesting than the lecture was his response to one question. A student asked Rather about the failures of the news media in covering the 1991 Gulf War—boosterish coverage of the military, failure to examine the Bush administration's claims (many of which turned out to be lies), and a gee-whiz approach to the high-tech weapons. The student laid out a clear and compelling case for journalistic malfeasance, and Rather acknowledged that he couldn't argue with most of what the young man said.

But, Rather shrugged, in time of war, "journalism tends to follow the flag" (Rather 1996).

Rather was right, and I suppose we can admire him for being honest. But he seemed to miss the point of the question: yes, journalists do tend to follow the flag, but should they? Rather's acceptance of the student's analysis indicated that he understood how a democratic system suffers when journalists too readily accept the pronouncements of the powerful during a war, how people can't really make intelligent decisions about policy options without independent information. But his reaction also indicated that he believed the "follow the flag" instinct was inevitable, perhaps a law of journalistic nature.

Of course, there are no laws of nature for journalists. Instead, there are institutional realities, professional routines, and ideologies that shape behavior, as Herman and Chomsky (2002) lay out in their propaganda model. The importance of these influences on the news is obscured by the professional ideology of political neutrality, which keeps both journalists and citizens from understanding the relationship between power and the news media. Any claim to such neutrality is illusory; there is no neutral ground on which to stand anywhere in the world. One need not be overtly partisan or propagandistic to be political. The politics of journalists' choices about which stories to cover, from which angle, and using which sources cannot be eliminated by a claim to have established neutral professional practices. The question is not whether one is neutral, but whether one is independent in a meaningful way from powerful forces.

Mainstream commercial journalists are quick to answer, "Yes, of course we are independent." In fact, government officials rarely attempt to impose legal restraints on journalists, and editors and reporters work relatively free of direct governmental control. (Of course, journalists are not independent of the corporations that employ them, but the focus here is on independence from government.) All governments routinely attempt to control the information that journalists receive from officials, especially during wartime, but the U.S.

government does relatively little, in terms of direct repression, to impede journalists from their work. (One exception to that is in the war theater itself, which is a complex issue I won't take up here.)

What do journalists do with that freedom from most legal control? For the most part during war, not much. The slavish dependence on official sources and the ideology of patriotism keep the vast majority of American journalists trapped in a fantasy world in which U.S. war aims are always just and anything bad that happens is the product of either an honest mistake or the rogue action of a "bad apple" in an otherwise decent system. The result is painful to come to terms with: times of war—when a democracy most desperately needs a critical, independent journalism working outside the ideological constraints of the culture—are precisely when the U.S. commercial mainstream news media fails most profoundly. A final anecdote to illustrate:

> During the question period following a 1999 speech at the National Press Club, Dan Rather discussed the decision of U.S. military planners in the attack on Yugoslavia to target that nation's power grid. Of course, there is an apparent contradiction between Rather's use of the pronoun "we" in describing U.S. military action while claiming to be a neutral journalist. Rather acknowledged it was a difficult issue, but he made no bones about where he came down on the question: "I'm an American, and I'm an American reporter. And yes, when there's combat involving Americans—criticize me if you must, damn me if you must, but—I'm always pulling for us to win." (Rather 1999)

Unstated in Rather's response, of course, is the assumption that Americans in combat fight on the right side. But what if U.S. leaders sent Americans into battle for a cause that was not just? What if leaders pursued a war that was, in fact, decidedly unjust? What if the United States fought a war not for freedom and justice but instead to extend and deepen its own control over crucial strategic regions of the world? Let's say, just for the sake of argument, this war took place in a region of the world that held the majority of the easily accessible oil reserves, in an era in which the world's industrial economy ran on oil, and therefore control over the flow of oil and oil profits meant real power. What if American troops were sent into combat for the objective of such control? What if, because of the way U.S. military planners fight wars, one could be reasonably certain that large numbers of civilians would die? Just for the sake of argument, if that were to happen, would it be acceptable for anyone— journalist or ordinary citizen—to be "pulling for us to win"? Should journalists be open to the possibility that the leadership of their country might be capable of such a war plan? And if journalists were not open to such a possibility, would we call them neutral? Would we trust them to provide us with the information we need to make decisions as citizens in a democracy?

As I have argued throughout this essay, Dan Rather's public comments are important not for the way in which they occasionally are idiosyncratic, but for the way in which they are completely conventional. When Rather talked about "pulling for us to win," the most disheartening moment was not the comment itself, which was hardly surprising given Rather's history and public comments. More troubling was that at the National Press Club—in a room full of some of the most experienced and influential working journalists in the nation's capital—the audience broke out in applause.

REFERENCES

Baker, R. (2002, May). Want to be a patriot? Do your job. *Columbia Journalism Review*, 78–79.

Bourne, D. (1918). War is the health of the state. Retrieved October 23, 2003, from http://struggle.ws/hist_texts/warhealthstate1918.html

Bozell, L. B. (2001, September 25). Media coverage at its best. *Washington Times*, A18.

A conversation with Dan Rather. (2001, October 9). *The Kalb report: Journalism at the crossroads* [CD-ROM]. Also retrieved April 2, 2004, from www.gwu.edu/~kalb/

Debs, E. V. (1915). Speech. Retrieved October 23, 2003, from http://bari.iww.org/iu120/local/Scribner12.html

Gilbert, G. M. (1947). *Nuremburg diary*. New York: Farrar, Straus.

Goldman, E. (1969). *Anarchism and other essays*. New York: Dover.

Herman, E. S., & Chomsky, N. (2002). *Manufacturing Consent*, rev. ed. New York: Pantheon.

Holt, M. (2002, May 16). Is truth a victim? [Electronic version]. *BBC News*. Retrieved May 5, 2004, from http://news.bbc.co.uk/1/hi/audiovideo/programmes/newsnight/1991885.stm

Kovach, B. (2002, April 30). Journalism and patriotism. Lecture to annual meeting of Organization of News Ombudsmen. Retrieved October 23, 2003, from www.newsombudsmen.org/kovatch.html

Rather, D. (1996, November 26). Ethics in journalism. Lecture. College of Communication, University of Texas, Austin.

———. (1999, June 25). Speech. National Press Club, Washington, DC. Retrieved October 23, 2003, from www.fair.org/activism/husseini-rather.html

Tolson, M. (2002, March 19). Remain objective despite war, Rather tells Texas journalists. *Houston Chronicle*, 19.

Tolstoy, L. (1900). Patriotism and government. Retrieved April 24, 2004, from http://dwardmac.pitzer.edu/Anarchist_Archives/bright/tolstoy/patriotismandgovt.html

6

Culture as Persuasion: Metaphor as Weapon

William B. Hart II and Fran Hassencahl

> In the beginning we create the enemy. Before the weapon comes the image.
> We think others to death and then invent the battle-axe or the ballistic mis-
> siles with which to actually kill them. Propaganda precedes technology.
>
> Keen (1991, 10)

The first purpose of this study is to further integrate and update the literature on the dehumanization of enemies by use of metaphor (Hart & Hassencahl 2002). The second and main purpose of this study is to understand
how specifically U.S. editorial cartoonists used visual metaphor when drawing Saddam Hussein and the Iraqi military during the buildup to the U.S.-
Iraq war and how the use of metaphor in presidential rhetoric relates to this
process.

In a speech in Cincinnati on October 7, 2002, to America's heartland,
President Bush utilized a variety of metaphors, one of which was Hussein as
"a student of Stalin" (Bush 2002). This metaphor was then repeated in an editorial in the *Washington Post* (Hogland 2002), on *MSNBC Countdown*
(MSNBC 2002), on the *Oprah Winfrey Show* (Hudson 2002), and by syndicated columnist Cal Thomas (Thomas 2002). Cartoonists' visual metaphors
when coupled with President Bush's verbal metaphors and widely disseminated by the press make a case for the invasion of Iraq by the United States.
By conducting a content analysis of editorial cartoons related to the U.S.-
Iraq war, we empirically test claims about the use of visual metaphor during
times of war.

METAPHOR AND WAR

Metaphors are evident in the way we talk about war. We can talk, for example, of war as a game. Edelman (1988) pointed out in his chapter, "The Construction and Uses of Political Enemies," that the game metaphor explains the transformation of an antagonist into an adversary. The task then becomes "finding and pursuing winning tactics . . . whether the stakes are small or vast" (67). President Bush, for example, used the war-as-game metaphor in his call for a preemptive strike on Iraq (Bush 2003b, 2003c, 2003d, 2003e). On February 6, 2003 (Bush 2003b), in reference to Hussein's continued denial of possession of biological, chemical, and nuclear weapons, Bush predicted, "No doubt he will play a last-minute game of deception." Bush bluntly told the world, "The game is over."

Edelman (1971) described metaphors as devices that simplify and give meaning "to complex and bewildering sets of observations that evoke concern" (65). In times of uncertainty, like war, when we need to reduce dissonance between conflicting value premises about the world and to formulate appropriate political action, metaphors "create and filter out value premises" (70). Edelman (1971) further explained this reduction of dissonance with the example of how a value premise core value can be erased by a political metaphor when "strike capacity" is translated as "power to kill people" (70–71). When Bush called the invasion of Iraq a "preemptive strike" rather than an invasion or war, the task appeared to be quick and surgical rather than a long trek through enemy fire from Basra to Baghdad. A quick preemptive strike is acceptable to a public who is uncertain about going to war, since it suggests fewer losses of life and that U.S. soldiers will not stay in Iraq for a long period of time.

Edelman (1971) further observed that leaders use metaphors as a means to build mass support for political violence. Definitions of the enemy as a stranger, an alien, or a subhuman are repeated themes, which "will most potently create and mobilize allies" (114). The causes and remedies for wars are complex, but metaphors "permit [people] to live in a world in which the causes are simple and neat and the remedies are apparent" (Edelman 1971, 83). Metaphors are a "powerful legitimizer" of governmental policy and can even be used to dampen dissent against certain policy (Edelman 1971, 72).

Metaphors are common in international relations discourse and are often used to justify foreign policies and actions (Lakoff 1991; Chilton & Lakoff 1995). Lakoff (1991) examined the metaphors used by the George Bush Sr. administration during the Gulf War. He argued that the metaphors used by the Bush administration helped justify the military actions that the U.S. and coalition forces took during the war. The "Nation As a Person" metaphor, for example, frames "War is a fight between two people." Such a mindset or metaphor, according to Lakoff, frames Hussein as Iraq and ignores Iraqi civilians and the potential casualties of those civilians. Lakoff (2001) applied his form of metaphorical analysis to the U.S. war in Afghanistan against al Qaeda and the Taliban. Within the rhetoric of the George W. Bush Jr. administration, Lakoff identified such metaphors of bin Laden as animals (such as rodents and snakes) and as an evildoer. More recently, Lakoff (2003) reported that the "Nation As a Person" metaphor used to justify the war against Iraq in 1991 has returned for the Iraq-U.S. war:

> What the metaphor hides, of course, is that the 3000 bombs to be dropped in the first two days will not be dropped on that one person. They will kill many thousands of the people hidden by the metaphor, people that according to the metaphor we are not going to war against. (Lakoff 2003)

Like verbal metaphors in wartime rhetoric, visual metaphors also are used to justify war and the killing of the enemy. The visual metaphors initially found by Keen (1984) were enemy-as-barbarian, enemy-as-rapist, enemy-as-animal, enemy-as-enemy-of-God, and enemy-as-death. While Dower (1986) did not use the term "metaphor" in his detailed description of enemy images used by the United States and Japan during World War II, he nonetheless found the enemy being framed as animals, primitives, children, madmen [sic], and demons. Dower saw these enemy images as evidence of strong racism during war. While Dower studied the images that the United States and Japan had of each other during World War II, Keen's 1986 book, *Faces of the Enemy*, is an historical analysis of the visual metaphors used by artists during many different wars. In the book's more than 300 propaganda posters, editorial cartoons, and other artwork, the artists, according to Keen, draw upon "archetypes of a horrible imagination" to dehumanize the enemy. Keen's analysis showed that in times of war, the enemy is dehumanized through visual metaphor and, moreover, this process is universal. Each side dehumanizes the other. Keen found twelve types of dehumanizing visual metaphors (e.g., enemy-as-barbarian or enemy-as-animal; for list, see below). Keen argued that dehumanization of the enemy justifies the killing of the enemy. If the enemy is not a civilized human like us, then, according to Keen, the guilt associated with killing then enemy is greatly lessened. If the enemy is thought of as an animal, (e.g., a rat or snake), then killing the enemy becomes easier.

EDITORIAL CARTOONS, RHETORIC, AND WAR

Rhetorical criticism tends to focus on the verbal (spoken or written) rather than upon the visual. However, through the analysis of political cartoons, the critic is forced "to grapple with nonverbal or visual elements of the text" (Benoit, Kluykovski, McHale, & Airne 2001, 372). In their study of over 2,000 cartoons on the Clinton-Lewinsky-Starr affair, Benoit et al. (2001) refer to the cartoons as "Rhetorical Texts." While rhetorical critics begin to see cartoons as rhetorical texts, cartoonists are seeing themselves as rhetors who create the visual counterpart of the commentary on the editorial page of newspapers. Daryl Cagle, cartoonist and creator of the Professional Cartoonist Index website at Slate.com (Cagle 2004), observed that America has a rich tradition of wartime cartoons.

> Cartoons aren't necessarily funny, they're also poignant. They can bring a tear to the eye and make you think. So I wouldn't think of cartoons as jokes. Cartoonists are really graphic commentators. We're like columnists but we use pictures instead of words and pictures communicate better than words when feelings are visceral at [a] time like this. (Cagle, quoted in Hays, Morris, & Willis 2003)

Rhetorical critics not only examine texts, but also attempt to determine what effect these texts have on audiences. Cartoonists can read their e-mail and get some sense of audience response. Cagle observed that people tear out cartoons and put them on their refrigerators, but they do not tear out the news story or the editorial and put it on their refrigerators. Cartoonist David Horsey, winner of a Pulitzer Prize in 2003, says that readers like editorial cartoons, and when they hate them, "They like hating them!" He argues that the worth of cartoons is that they are "a point of entry into newspapers and they give people something to argue about" (Astor 2003). Central to the act of calling another person's attention to the cartoon is the creation of a shared perspective. By virtue of appearing in a daily newspaper and being archived on the Web, these cartoons have the potential to focus attention on political events and to foster a collective consciousness about events.

By what process do cartoonists, as rhetors, use visual metaphor to influence a reader's viewpoint toward an enemy? Three studies (DeSousa 1984; Conner 1998; Hart & Hassencahl 2002) specifically used metaphorical analysis to study depictions of enemies in editorial cartoons. All three studies are examples of quantitative rhetorical criticism, which attempts to analyze the use of language and images to persuade audience's views of during war. DeSousa (1984), in his study of 186 cartoons depicting Ayatollah Khomeini during the 1979–1980 U.S.-Iran hostage crisis, draws upon "commonplace images within American culture to explain what was happening to our citizens held in a foreign land" (217). The metaphors used for Khomeini were Khomeini-as-madman, Khomeini-as-religious-fraud, and Khomeini-as-manipulator. DeSousa suggested that the metaphorical images in the cartoons gave the American public a venue for venting their hostilities in a situation where little else could be done.

Artz and Pollock (1995) studied approximately eighty political cartoons of Saddam Hussein during the buildup to the 1991 Gulf War. The cartoons appeared in four major newspapers and *Newsweek*. Artz and Pollock found that cartoons of Hussein can be grouped into two main categories: (1) Hussein as dangerous, and (2) Hussein as uncivilized, irrational, and barbaric. From their analysis of media images of Hussein, Artz and Pollock concluded that

> the laughter, sarcasm, and anger directed at Hussein through political cartoons helped mobilize an American public to tolerate the killing of over 100,000 people in Iraq. Joined with the media's "video game" portrayal of the war, the images helped dehumanize the enemy. (132)

Conners's (1998) study of cartoonists' portrayal of Saddam Hussein during the 1991 Gulf War specifically used Keen's categories of enemy images. Conners surveyed 965 cartoons in three large circulation newspapers and *Newsweek* over a period of seven months (August 1990–March 1991). Of the 397 cartoons that dealt with the Gulf War, 170 of the cartoons (43 percent) dehumanized Hussein (i.e., used one of Keen's dehumanizing visual metaphors). Hussein was most frequently portrayed as an aggressor (48 percent of 170) and criminal (24 percent of 170). Conners concluded that the cartoons "reflected Bush administration rhetoric labeling Hussein as a threat that the United States needed to control" (110).

Hart and Hassencahl (2002) used Keen's categories to analyze the images of bin Laden, al Qaeda, and the Taliban between September 11, 2001, and October 8, 2001 (shortly before the U.S. invasion of Afghanistan). Of the U.S. editorial cartoons containing the enemy, 91 percent dehumanized the enemy with Keen's metaphors. The most prominent metaphors used to portray the enemy were enemy-as-animal (e.g., rat, snake, germ; 29 percent) and enemy-as-aggressor (21 percent). Hart and Hassencahl argued, "In order to better and more completely understand the motives and future actions of Osama bin Laden and the al Qaeda, we may find value in not accepting too quickly oversimplifying metaphor" (151).

CARTOONS AND DEHUMANIZATION

Within the context of the U.S.-Iraq war and based on the work covered above, we propose the following research questions: (1) To what extent is the enemy (i.e., Hussein and the Iraqi military) shown in the editorial cartoons during the buildup to the U.S. Iraq War? (2) To what extent is the enemy dehumanized in the editorial cartoons? (3) Which types of dehumanization (Keen's visual metaphors) were most prominent? How often is each of the dehumanization types used? Do any new types emerge? (4) How do the results of the present study compare to the dehumanization of the enemy in previous wars? What are the similarities and differences?

The American Association of Editorial Cartoonists has approximately 150 members categorized as full-time editorial cartoonists who are employed as cartoonists for newspapers and other periodicals (American Association of Editorial Cartoonists, personal communication, March 4, 2002). Typically, past studies of cartoons relied on small samples of cartoonists found in a few major newspapers and newsmagazines. More recent editorial cartoon studies (Benoit et al. 2001; Hart & Hassencahl 2002) have used the large amount of cartoons available in Internet archives (which allows for a much wider, near-census sample).

The present study analyzed 2,446 cartoons drawn by eighty-eight cartoonists available in an online database of editorial cartoonists, Daryl Cagle's Professional Cartoonist Index (Cagle 2004). The sample of 2,446 cartoons was gathered between January 28, 2003, and March 27, 2003 (between the 2003 State of the Union Address until a week into the U.S.-Iraq war). The eighty-eight cartoonists had 1,300 war-related cartoons in the database during the time period under study (53 percent of the 2,246 total). This study focused only on the 1,300 war-related editorial cartoons. The authors independently coded each of the war-related cartoons using Keen's dehumanizing types, and then met and reached consensus on how each cartoon was to be coded. Since cartoonists could include more than one metaphor into any single cartoon, some cartoons were coded into more than one of Keen's types.

For the purposes of this study, Keen's dehumanizing types were operationally defined as follows:

> *Enemy-as-Animal*: Cartoon with repulsive animals (e.g. rat, reptile, insect, or germ), including plants such as weeds; showing the enemy doing animal-like actions (e.g., hiding or living under a rock); a character doing actions toward the enemy that are typically done to repulsive animals
>
> *Enemy-as-Desecrator-of-Civilians*: Cartoon with Iraqi civilians (women, children, and/or men) who have been (or are being) harmed (physically or psychologically) through physical contact, intimidation, repression, and so on
>
> *Enemy-as-Torturer-of-Prisoners*: Cartoon containing Iraqi political prisoners being tortured by the enemy (e.g., hanging by thumbs or being beaten)

Enemy-as-Barbarian: Cartoon with an image of the enemy as primitive/uncivilized/not modern (e.g., wearing clothing associated with prehistoric cave people), as small person, or as a "brute/monster" (e.g., with exaggerated features like elongated teeth or claws)

Enemy-as-Criminal: Cartoon with an image of the enemy as criminals, as deceitful (e.g., shown on a wanted poster or in a criminal lineup)

Enemy-as-Greedy: Cartoon containing an image of the enemy taking (from others) land, money, or other resources

Enemy-as-Enemy-of-God: Cartoon with an image of the enemy as a desecrator or opponent of Christian religious symbols (e.g., the Bible) or Christianity (e.g., being the Devil or associated with the Devil)

Enemy-as-Death: Cartoon containing an image of the enemy as a skeleton (or skull) or as the Grim Reaper

Enemy-as-Faceless: Cartoon with an image of the enemy who has only one or no facial features (e.g., only eyes); images of more than one enemy, who all look alike or identical

Enemy-as-Aggressor: Cartoon containing images of the enemy carrying weapons (e.g., gun or knife). Cartoon showing the enemy dressed in a military uniform, with a fist in the air, and so on

Enemy-as-Abstraction: Cartoon with an image of the enemy as a nonliving object (e.g., robot, target, or smoke)

Enemy-as-Human: Cartoons containing the enemy but not falling into any of the above categories (i.e., enemy that is not dehumanized)

In addition to the images within the cartoons, cartoons also were coded into the above categories based on words used within the cartoon (e.g., within captions).

PORTRAYAL AND DEHUMANIZATION OF THE ENEMY IN EDITORIAL CARTOONS

The enemy (Saddam Hussein and the Iraqi military) was represented in 434 (33 percent) of the 1,300 war-related editorial cartoons studied. The remaining 67 percent of war-related cartoons, which did not portray the enemy, focused on President Bush or others in the Bush administration. Some enemy cartoons had as many as four different Keen metaphors in one cartoon. Of the 434 enemy cartoons, 414 cartoons contained 715 dehumanization metaphors. Twenty cartoons were coded as humanized with no dehumanizing metaphors used by cartoonists. Stated another way, 96.4 percent of the cartoons, which portrayed Hussein or the Iraqi military, dehumanized the enemy in some way.

TYPES OF DEHUMANIZATION USED

When the enemy was dehumanized, certain of Keen's types were more prominent than others (χ^2 = 1345.8, 11df, p < .001). As shown in table 6.1, the prominent metaphors used in the cartoons were enemy-as-aggressor (used 293 times) and enemy-as-death metaphors (used 118 times), while enemy-as-torturer metaphor appeared only six times and the enemy-as-greedy metaphor appeared only four times. The percentages in the parentheses below are the percentages of enemy metaphors fitting the category under discussion divided by the total number of enemy metaphors used (N = 715). See table 6.1 for percentages based on the total number of cartoons. This pattern continues for the other metaphor types.

Enemy-as-Aggressor (47.0 percent). The most prominent metaphor portrayed the enemy as an aggressor. While guns and knives were present, the majority of the weapons shown were weapons of mass destruction. Some forty-three cartoons either showed or verbalized about such weapons, and only fifteen showed conventional weapons. Since military uniforms were part of the coding, cartoons showing the Iraqi army and Saddam Hussein in uniform were included in the 142 of the total 231 instances.

Table 6.1.   A Comparison of Visual Metaphors Used by Wartime Editorial Cartoonists

Enemy Metaphor	Hussein (2003) Frequency	%	Bin Laden (2001) Frequency	%	Hussein (1991) Frequency	%
Animal	43	10	76	31	10	6
Desecrator	27	6	11	5	0	0
Torturer	6	1	1	0	8	5
Barbarian	29	7	20	8	6	4
Criminal	94	22	11	5	42	26
Greedy	4	1	0	0	12	7
Enemy of God	20	5	16	7	1	1
Death	118	27	6	2	2	1
Faceless	21	5	12	5	0	0
Aggressor	293	68	54	22	82	50
Abstraction	40	9	31	13	0	0
Human*	20	5	22	9		
Total Cartoons	434		242		163	
Total Metaphors Used	715		260		163	

* Conners (1998) did not provide data on the number of "humanized" cartoons.

Enemy-as-Death (18.9 percent). The most prevalent image of death was the presence of skulls. A separate subcategory was created that was labeled "death beret," because thirty cartoonists transformed the military insignia on Hussein's military beret into a skull or into a skull and crossbones. Seventy-two percent of the cartoons in this category showed skulls on his beret and uniform.

Enemy-as-Criminal (13.5 percent). Three common themes occurred within the enemy-as-criminal category. Several cartoons showed Hussein on wanted posters, or in a "High Noon" shootout with President Bush appearing as the sheriff. Hussein appears in seven instances as an exiled criminal. He is shown working at Wal-Mart and as a participant in a *Survivor* television program while in exile from Iraq. This is likely in reference to the forty-eight hours given by Bush as an ultimatum for Hussein to leave Iraq. The other major theme was that of the trickster.

Enemy-as-Animal (6.9 percent). The enemy-as-animal metaphors consisted of such subcategories as enemy-as-rat, enemy-as-reptile, and enemy-as-insect. Within this category, the enemy was most frequently depicted as a rat and reptile (e.g., snake). The enemy was also portrayed as a cockroach, a germ, a gorilla, and a dog. Six cartoonists within the context of February 2, celebrated in the United States as Groundhog Day, depicted Saddam rising from the ground to see the shadow of war over his head.

Enemy-as-Abstraction (6.4 percent). The major metaphors used here were smoke replacing Saddam's head and Hussein disappearing into sand. Iraq was also depicted as a smoking gun, and Hussein was shown in the center of a target.

Enemy-as-Barbarian (4.7 percent). Within this category, the enemy was portrayed almost equally as a brute, a miniature person, a child, and lacking in intelligence. With his thumbs in his ears and tongue extended, Saddam was depicted as a tiny person mocking the United States. Saddam was also shown as a toddler, sucking his thumb and clutching a United Nations blanket. He is shown twice as a child sitting on the floor and playing with parts of a missile.

Enemy-as-Desecrator-of-Women-and-Children (4.3 percent). Only one cartoon contained depictions of the enemy desecrating American or coalition women, and this was an American woman who was one of those who volunteered to be human shields in Iraq. Cartoons did depict the enemy as a desecrator of Iraqi women and children, and showed an innocent population being used as shields or left above ground to face the bombs while Hussein was hidden under ground.

Enemy-as-Faceless (3.4 percent). Enemy-as-faceless takes two forms:
(1) all members of the enemy group look the same, and (2) an enemy
missing facial features. Several show the enemy all looking alike.

Enemy-as-Enemy-of-God (3.2 percent). Enemy-of-God cartoons most frequently portray the enemy as being in hell with the Devil. Saddam was
depicted as the Devil in disguise, because under his angel wings and
robe were cloven hoofs and a long forked tail.

CONTEXTS OF METAPHOR

The previous work of Edelman (1971, 1988), Ivie (1980, 1984, 1996, 2003),
Lakoff (1991, 2001, 2003), Dower (1986), Keen (1984, 1986, 1991, 2001),
DeSousa (1984), Artz and Pollock (1995), Conners (1998), Hart and Hassencahl (2002), and Hassencahl (2004) suggest that metaphors play an important role in wartime rhetoric, and the present study shows that this phenomenon of dehumanizing the enemy continues. In the present study,
dehumanizing metaphors of the enemy were used by cartoonists in 32 percent
(414) of the 1,300 war-related cartoons. Past studies had this percentage at approximately 20 percent (see Hart & Hassencahl 2002). Further comparisons
of the results of this study to the past studies of Hart and Hassencahl (2002)
and Conners (1998) are provided in table 6.1. Comparisons of special note are
as follows: (1) bin Laden was depicted as an animal in 31 percent of the enemy cartoons, while Hussein was shown as an animal in only 6 percent of the
cartoons for the Gulf War and 10 percent for the U.S.-Iraq war; (2) Hussein
was shown as a criminal for the Gulf War in 26 percent of the enemy cartoons
and 22 percent of the enemy cartoons for the U.S.-Iraq war, while bin Laden
was shown as criminal in only 5 percent; (3) for both the Gulf War and the
U.S.-Iraq war, Hussein was shown as an aggressor for a high percentage of
the cases (50 percent and 68 percent, respectively); on the other hand, bin
Laden was depicted as an aggressor in only 22 percent of the enemy cartoons;
and (4) Hussein was depicted as death in 27 percent of the enemy cartoons
for the U.S.-Iraq war, but only 1 percent of those for the Gulf War, while bin
Laden had a low percentage of only 2 percent.

These differences may be explained to some degree by the different contexts in which the enemy was portrayed. The reason why bin Laden was dehumanized more as an animal may be explained by a stronger hate or anger
toward bin Laden for the thousands of U.S. lives taken during the terrorists'
attacks. The reason why Hussein was depicted as a criminal at a relatively
high percentage and bin Laden was not depicted as a criminal as strongly may
be connected to the attempts in presidential rhetoric to argue that Hussein is

a breaker of UN law and a deceiver who possesses weapons of mass destruction. The difference between Hussein and bin Laden for enemy-as-aggressor may also be explained by presidential rhetoric. The argument was that Hussein had weapons of mass destruction and would use them.

In 27 percent (118) of the enemy cartoons, Hussein was depicted as death. Of these 118 cartoons, eighty-five cartoons showed Hussein wearing a military beret on which a skull or skull and crossbones insignia was placed by the cartoonists. An inspection of actual photos shows that Hussein's military beret does not have a skull insignia. Why, then, would thirty different cartoonists (approximately one-third of the total number of cartoonists) over the time of this study all use this motif, which we labeled the "death beret"? A study of past military uniforms shows that the Nazi SS during World War II wore skull and crossbones (or *totenkopf*, death head) insignias on their military hats. Cartoonists may be consciously or unconsciously drawing on imagery of Nazi SS from newsreels, films about World War II, or other media.

Two other recurring subcategories of major categories are worthy of comment. First, under the broader category of enemy-as-barbarian, cartoonists portrayed Hussein seven times as a small child who needed to be controlled. Lakoff (2003) notes this enemy-as-child metaphor when he speaks of the pervasive metaphor of "Nation as a Person" and notes that "in the International Community, peopled by Nation-Persons, there are Nation-adults and Nation-children." Nation-adults are rational and industrialized, but Nation-children are the "developing" nations who need guidance and must be disciplined when they misbehave. Iraq is a Nation-child and, although it was "the cradle of civilization, is seen via this metaphor as a kind of defiant armed teenage hoodlum who refuses to abide by the rules and must be 'taught a lesson'" (Lakoff 2003). In one cartoon Bush, the Nation-adult, is portrayed as administering a spanking to the bare behind of the Nation-child Saddam.

Under the broader category of enemy-as-criminal, we found the enemy-as-trickster metaphor worthy of note, especially given the concern over hidden weapons of mass destruction. Cartoonists portrayed the enemy-as-trickster in seventy-two of the ninety-four enemy-as-criminal cartoons. Instances of such behavior showed Hussein masquerading as a "fat lady" opera singer and as Anna Nicole Smith with huge pointy bombs enhancing his bosom. Hussein is shown several times in denial of having weapons, and the next frames show him smiling with missiles substituting for teeth. Hussein is a master of disguises and is often disguised as Groucho Marx or interacting with his body doubles. He is shown fooling the arms inspectors when he brings them to a mannequin factory and tells them that this is his "arms" factory.

This study also found a metaphor not addressed in Keen's group of enemy metaphors. In fourteen cartoons, Iraqi soldiers are depicted as surrendering or running away—enemy-as-cowards. Two cartoonists showed the Iraqi soldiers raising the new Iraqi flag, a white flag of surrender.

What are the sources for the cartoonists' dehumanizing metaphors? Where do they get their imagery? In addition to popular culture and its images (Keen 1986) that provide stock representations, a more immediate, significant source is that of presidential rhetoric. News is largely defined by what government leaders say and do (Miller 2003). When a leader utilizes metaphors that depict an enemy as evil, an animal, a rapist, a criminal, and an aggressor, then these dramatizations are likely to be covered in the media. In his State of the Union Address in January 2002, Bush included Iraq in the "axis of evil, arming to threaten the peace of the world," and stated that the United States is "called to a unique role in human events" (Bush 2002b). In his State of the Union Address before the invasion of Iraq in March 2003, President Bush continues to use the metaphor of Hussein as the desecrator-of-the-innocent when he refers to the gassing of the Kurds in the Iran-Iraq war and suggests that Hussein will use chemical weapons again (Bush 2003a).

The dictator who is assembling the world's most dangerous weapons has already used them on whole villages—leaving thousands of his own citizens dead, blind, or disfigured. Iraqi refugees tell us how forced confessions are obtained—by torturing children while their parents are made to watch. International human rights groups have categorized other methods used in the torture chambers of Iraq: electric shock, burning with hot irons, dripping acid on the skin, mutilation with electric drills, cutting out tongues, and rape. If this is not evil, then evil has no meaning (Bush 2003a).

Clearly these acts are, to use the metaphor of enemy-as-criminal, evidence of an "outlaw regime." Bush presented in his speech of January 2003 an extensive list of the weapons of mass destruction held by Iraq and characterized Hussein as a master of deception, who led the United Nations weapons inspectors on a "scavenger hunt" (Bush 2003a).

The cartoonists in this study reflect the metaphors used by President Bush to frame Hussein as a criminal, as a desecrator of women and children, and as an outlaw regime. More importantly, the American public has heeded these metaphors that are spoken by President Bush and repeated in cartoons, news, and news-talk shows that dehumanize Hussein as the enemy. Hussein is seen as a dangerous, armed man with weapons of mass destruction. A poll released in October 2002 by the Pew Research Center for the People and the Press showed that 79 percent believed that Hussein either possessed or was close to possessing nuclear weapons, and 60 percent of those polled said that getting rid of weapons of mass destruction and preventing future terrorism were reasons to go to war with Iraq (Rampton & Stauber 2003). The president's phrase "axis of evil" frames the enemy and becomes a composite of Iraq,

Iran, and al Qaeda. They are all evil and working together. According to the Pew poll, 66 percent of Americans believed that Saddam Hussein was involved in the 9/11 attacks on the United States (Rampton & Stauber 2003).

"This gap between reality and public opinion was not an accident" (Rampton & Stauber 2003, 79). In their book, *Weapons of Mass Deception: The Uses of Propaganda in Bush's War on Iraq*, Sheldon Rampton and John Stauber (2003) from the Center for Media and Democracy discuss and document the information and disinformation campaign conducted by the White House after 9/11. They suggest that the public had a limited understanding of the facts and accepted erroneous information about Iraq similar to the way that they believed the story that Iraqi soldiers dumped Kuwaiti babies from hospital incubators during the first Gulf War. The American public listened to "a steady drumbeat of allegations and insinuations from the Bush administration, pro-war think tanks and commentators" that were often "false and misleading and whose purpose was to create the impression that Iraq posed an imminent threat" (80).

In this study, we have shown that dehumanizing metaphors continue to be used in wartime, and we have argued that there are some important dangers to using metaphor in foreign policy discourse. Metaphors oversimplify a complex situation and may hide important facts. Edelman cautions that a metaphorical view becomes the organizing conception, a filter that is then used by the public and its leaders to select and to interpret new information. Metaphors are self-perpetuating and "help all kinds of groups to believe that their political beliefs and loyalties are rational and to maintain them" (72). On the eve of the U.S.-Iraq war, Lakoff (2003) cautions that Americans have been led "by the administration, the press, and the lack of an effective Democratic opposition" to accept the metaphors of "the nation-as-person" and Hussein the tyrant who must be stopped, and to believe that the war in Iraq is a "just war." These metaphors also hide the fact that the thousands of bombs dropped will not fall upon the tyrant. Lakoff concludes that these bombs will kill or maim large numbers of innocent Iraqi civilians who are "hidden by the metaphor, people that according to the metaphor we are not going to war against" (Lakoff 2003). Metaphors oversimplify complex situations. Metaphors can hide important facts. Metaphors can be dangerous. "The lesson to be learned is what every good general knows, it is dangerous to believe your own propaganda" (Keen n.d.).

REFERENCES

Artz, L., & Pollock, M. (1995). Limiting the options: Anti-Arab images in U.S. media coverage of the Persian Gulf crisis. In Y. R. Kamalipour (Ed.), *The U.S. media and the Middle East: Image and perception* (pp. 119–135). Westport, CT: Greenwood Press.

Astor, D. (2003, April 14). Pulitzer Prize—Editorial cartooning: Seattle Post-Intelligencer (David Horsey wins). *Editor & Publisher*. Retrieved from Lexis/Nexis database.

Benoit, W. L., Kluykovski, A. A., McHale, J. P., & Airne, D. (2001). A fantasy theme analysis of political cartoons on the Clinton-Lewinsky-Starr affair. *Critical Studies in Mass Communication* 18 (4), 377–394.

Bush, G. W. (2001a, September 16). Remarks by the president upon arrival. Retrieved January 8, 2002, from www.whitehouse.gov/news/releases/2001/09/20010916-2.html

———. (2001b, October 7). Presidential address to the nation. Retrieved January 14, 2000, from www.whitehouse.gov/news/releases/2001/10/20011007-8.html

———. (2002a, October 7). President Bush outlines Iraqi threat. Retrieved January 17, 2004, from www.whitehouse.gov/news/releases/2002/10/20021007-8.html

———. (2002b, January 29). Bush State of the Union address. Retrieved January 30, 2002, from cnn.allpolitics.print . . . 396811692199674&partnerID=2001.

———. (2003a, January 28). President delivers "State of the Union." Retrieved February 10, 2004, from www.whitehouse.gov/news/releases/2003/01/20030128-19.html

———. (2003b, February 6). President Bush: "World can rise to this moment." Retrieved February 10, 2004, from www.whitehouse.gov/news/releases/2003/02/20030206-17.html

———. (2003c, March 6). President George Bush discusses Iraq in national press conference. Retrieved February 10, 2004, from www.whitehouse.gov/news/releases/2003/03/20030306-8.html

———. (2003d, March 16). President Bush: Monday "moment of truth" for world on Iraq. Retrieved February 10, 2004, from www.whitehouse.gov/news/releases/2003/03/20030316-3.html

———. (2003e, March 23). President discusses military operation. Retrieved February 10, 2004, from www.whitehouse.gov/news/releases/2003/03/20030323-1.html

Cagle, D. (2004, February). Daryl Cagle's professional cartoonist index. Retrieved December 11, 2003, from http://cagle.slate.msn.com

Chilton, P., & Lakoff, G. (1995). Foreign policy by metaphor. In C. Schaffner & A. L. Wenden (Eds.), *Language and peace* (pp. 37–59). Amsterdam, the Netherlands: Harwood Academic.

Conners, J. L. (1998). Hussein as enemy: The Persian Gulf War in political cartoons. *Harvard International Journal of Press/Politics* 3 (3), 96–114.

DeSousa, M. A. (1984). Symbolic action and pretended insight: The Ayatollah Khomeini in U.S. editorial cartoons. In M. J. Medhurst & T. W. Benson (Eds.), *Rhetorical dimensions in media: A critical casebook* (pp. 204–230). Dubuque, IA: Kendall/Hunt.

Dower, J. W. (1986). *War without mercy: Race and power in the Pacific War*. New York: Pantheon Books.

Edelman, M. (1971). *Politics as symbolic action: Mass arousal and quiescence.* Chicago: Markham.

———. (1988). *Conducting the political spectacle.* Chicago: University of Chicago Press.

Hart, W. B., & Hassencahl, F. (2002). Dehumanizing the enemy in editorial cartoons. In B. S. Greenberg (Ed.), *Communication and terrorism: Public and media responses to 9/11* (pp. 137–151). Cresskill, NJ: Hampton Press.

Hassencahl, F. (2004, May). American and European political cartoonists pen/pin Saddam Hussein: An analysis of U.S.-Iraq war editorial cartoons. Paper presented at 2nd International Conference on Communication and Mass Media, Athens, Greece.

Hays, K., Morris, V., & Willis, G. (2003, March 19). Editorial cartoonists draw on a fine line during times of war. *Flipside.* Retrieved from Lexis/Nexis database.

Hogland, J. (2002, October 10). [Editorial]. Absorbing Iraq's "unique" evil. *Washington Post,* A33. Retrieved from Lexis/Nexis database.

Hudson, D. A. (Executive Producer). (2002, October 9). *Oprah Winfrey Show* [Television broadcast]. Chicago: Harpo. Transcript retrieved from Lexis/Nexis database.

Ivie, R. L. (1980). Images of savagery in American justification for war. *Communication Monographs* 47, 279–291.

———. (1984). Speaking "common sense" about the Soviet threat: Reagan's rhetorical stance. *Western Journal of Speech Communication* 48, 39–50.

———. (1996). Tragic fear and the rhetorical presidency: Combating evil in the Persian Gulf. In M. J. Medhurst (Ed.), *Beyond the rhetorical presidency* (pp. 153–178). College Station: Texas A&M University Press.

———. (2003). Democracy and the rhetoric of evil. Retrieved March 1, 2004, from www.indiana.edu/~ivieweb/rhetevil.htm

———. (forthcoming). *Democracy and America's war on terror.* Tuscaloosa: University of Alabama Press.

Keen, S. (1984, February). Faces of the enemy. *Esquire,* 67–72.

———. (1986). *Faces of the enemy: Reflections of the hostile imagination.* New York: Harper & Row.

———. (1991). *Faces of the enemy: Reflections of the hostile imagination,* 2nd ed. New York: HarperCollins.

———. (2001). The new face of the enemy. In Beliefnet (Ed.), *From the ashes: A spiritual response to the attack on America* (pp. 122–125). Emmaus, PA: Rodale.

———. (n.d.). Ideas in process: How shall we respond to our enemy? Retrieved April 2, 2002, from www.samkeen.com/fontsize2bwonderingsbfontp/

Lakoff, G. (1991). Metaphor and war: The metaphor system used to justify war in the Gulf. *Peace Research* 23 (2–3), 25–32.

———. (2001, September 16). Metaphor of terror. Retrieved January 7, 2002, from www.press.uchicago.edu/News/911lakoff.html

———. (2003, March 18). Metaphor and war, again. *Alternet.* Retrieved December 10, 2003, from www.alternet.org/story.html?StoryID=15414

Medhurst, M. J., & DeSousa, M. A. (1981). Political cartoons as rhetorical form: A taxonomy of graphic discourse. *Communication Monographs* 48, 197–236.

Miller, M. (2003, November/December). A tyranny of symbols. *Columbia Journalism Review* 6. Retrieved November 18, 2003, from www.cjr.org/issues/2003/6/campaign-miller.asp

MSNBC. (2002, October 30). Countdown: Iraq 22:00 [Television broadcast]. Secaucus, NJ: MSNBC Cable L. L. C. Transcript retrieved from Lexis/Nexis database.

Rampton, S., & Stauber J., (2003). *Weapons of mass deception: The uses of propaganda in Bush's war on Iraq*. New York: Tarcher/Penguin.

Thomas, C. (2002, October 9). The president makes his case. *Chattanooga Times Free Press*. Retrieved January 28, 2004, from Lexis/Nexis database.

7

The Invisible Ally: Australia's War in Iraq

Andrew Jakubowicz and Liz Jacka

The Iraq war has revealed much about the Australian state, the media, and their interrelationships in time of crisis. Australia was the invisible ally, unnoticed by other countries, and in many ways untouched by its involvement in the war. However, the war was the first for at least a generation where government and opposition were not in accord, and where a majority of the population was skeptical if not opposed to the whole exercise (Goot 2003). It was also a war about which most Australians believed their government had misled them (Barker 2003; Gaita 2003; Megalogenis 2003; Toohey 2004). The role of the media has proved to be crucial in the dynamics of the relationship between the public and government, for the media have been the source of or conduit for information, and the locus of critique and assessment of events and policies. Outside Australia, the media have already been shown to have played some rather compromised roles in relation to the public sphere (Kellner 2003; Miller 2004; Rampton & Stauber 2003).

The Australian nation occupies a continent settled by Europeans over the past 200 years, its population overwhelmingly Christian, and its government democratic (Australian Bureau of Statistics 1994). Over the past thirty years, it has ostensibly redefined itself as a multicultural nation and opened itself to immigration from societies that are neither European nor Christian (Australian Bureau of Statistics 2003). Over the past decade, it has become increasingly uneasy as globalization has tested its borders, and terrorism has unsettled its sense of security and cohesion.

Australia prides itself on having a vibrant and robust civil society, with an active and challenging public sphere. While print and television media ownership is concentrated, there is a diversity of alternative sources of information from the public or community sector in broadcasting and over the Internet. Citizens in general have access to information about decisions taken by government, and the Westminster system based on the British parliamentary tradition of ministerial responsibility for their own actions and those of their public servants. The national government is led by Liberal Party Prime Minister (PM) John Howard, a thirty-year parliamentary veteran with a political sensitivity finely attuned to the murmurings in the electorate. In Australia, the Liberal Party promotes conservative political philosophies and neoliberal economics.

This chapter examines the relationship between the Australian government, the media, and the public in the lead-up to, pursuit of, and aftermath of the war on Iraq in 2003. Australian troops were committed early, suffered no casualties, and were withdrawn from active engagement on the ground soon after the Coalition of the Willing claimed its victory and instituted the occupation— while Australia accepted a continuing patrol and training role it declined to be part of the official occupation force. Prior to the invasion, Australian public opinion was in general opposed to involvement, with large demonstrations for peace, steady public skepticism of government announcements, and the opposition Labor Party voicing its strong reservations about embarking on war without specific United Nations endorsement.

Within a week of the war commencing, public opinion had moved dramatically in support of the exercise, and the antiwar movement was increasingly marginalized and excluded from the public debate. Soon after the war began, the government, modeling its behavior on the U.S. government's, shifted the motive for the war from WMD detection and eradication to regime change. In that process, it began a sustained attack on the balance of reporting in the media, and in particular on the "antiwar" stance that it claimed had been adopted by the government-owned Australian Broadcasting Corporation (ABC).

The media management adopted by the government was apparently successful in achieving its first goal—the neutralizing of oppositional public opinion. It then moved public opinion around toward support, but was unable to achieve this change across the whole social spectrum—the upmarket broadsheets (other than the *Australian*, owned by Rupert Murdoch) and the national broadcaster did not follow suit, and retained their skepticism about the whole process.

How, then, did the government seek to achieve its strategy for managing public opinion about the war? We argue that it adopted a marketing strategy based on the use of cognitive dissonance theory, a technique that had worked for the conservative coalition of parties in the 2001 federal election, and in which the government and its media managers were becoming extremely proficient. The government had to convince itself, its supporters, the media, and through them the majority of the population that despite no signs of an existing WMD program, and despite the government's acceptance of, if not support for, dictatorial regimes elsewhere, the Iraq adventure was necessary for Australia's national interest because there was an active and immediately threatening WMD program in place in Iraq, and it was appropriate if the opportunity presented itself to overthrow Saddam Hussein and replace him with another, undefined regime. Why would the Australian government, ruling a nation of some 20 million and positioned just to the south of the Green Crescent Islamic nations, decide that its national interests lay 16,000 kilometers away, halfway across the world?

DEPUTY SHERIFF: THE AMERICAN–AUSTRALIAN ALLIANCE

Australia has cherished the American alliance since at least 1942, when the defeat of the British east of Suez by the Japanese prompted Australia to look elsewhere for its strategic protectors (Harries & Australian Broadcasting Corporation 2004; Watson 2001). While the Labor Party has tended to be more interested in a multilateral defense umbrella, the conservative parties have been more attracted to a close one-on-one relationship with the United States. This closeness has taken on an almost symbiotic melding, with Australia increasingly adopting a strategy that places U.S. interests at the forefront, on the grounds that only a morally indebted United States can be depended on to come to Australia's aid in a crisis.

In a series of imperial adventures since 1945, Australia has either prompted or followed the United States (and the United Kingdom) into land wars in Asia—Korea, Malaya, Indonesia, and Vietnam. Most recently, Australia has been involved in the expulsion of Indonesia from East Timor, a multilateral incursion under Australian command to ensure the fair election of an independent government in the territory. In this process, U.S. President George W. Bush commended Australia as America's "deputy sheriff," implying that there were some smaller conflicts that the United States would like Australia to manage for it. The United States also has a number of secret intelligence installations located in Australia, protected by treaties that place them effectively under sovereign control by Washington. Even a powerful insider to government policy, Professor Paul Dibb, has noted that "now, the question is being asked whether Australia has become an overly compliant ally of the U.S. and whether Australia's commitment of forces to military action in Iraq will damage our diplomatic relations in Asia" (Dibb 2003).

The current Australian defense strategy proposes a capacity to operate overseas in distant places (assumedly at the behest of the U.S. government), as attacks from near neighbors are deemed unlikely. Thus, the strategic thinking of government indicates that it accepts American definitions of Australia's priorities, in order to ensure the overall security of Australia under the U.S. umbrella. All action flows from this precept.

THE MEDIA ENVIRONMENT IN THE WAKE OF BALI

Australian public confidence in the security of the nation was badly shaken by a rapid sequence of events beginning in 2000. The refugee crisis began to expand, with onshore detainees rioting for the prime-time television cameras, raids by refugee supporters on desert prisons to "liberate" the inmates, and an apparently endless armada of leaky fishing boats overburdened with asylum seekers sailing into Australian waters from Indonesia. Then the September 11, 2001, attacks in the United States brought home a sense of the vulnerability of Western nations to well-planned and calculating terrorist attacks.

In the 2001 federal election, the PM used the presence of refugee boats off Western Australia to imply that refugees were illegitimate, manipulative, and untrustworthy (Mares 2001). The material on which he based the calumny was drawn from unverified statements alleging that asylum-seeking parents had thrown their children overboard in order to intimidate Australian officials into allowing them to stay. This social anxiety had been the background to the so-called Tampa affair, when a Norwegian container ship of that name had rescued distressed refugees; they were then forcibly expelled from Australian waters and held under armed guard in Nauru, a small island nation northeast of Australia (Mares 2002). The media in general reported the government uncritically about the "children overboard" claims. Despite its soon-revealed and evident falsity, already identified by critics of the government at the time, the material proved to be very effective through the weeks before the election (Healey 2002), a period that saw the conservatives surge forward, leaving the Labor Party without a position on immigration that could possibly pass any test of clarity (Jayasuriya 2003; Marr & Wilkinson 2003).

In October 2002, over eighty Australians (among people of many other nationalities and a large number of Balinese) were killed and many more injured in a double firebombing of two popular nightclubs in Kuta Beach, Bali, a longtime rendezvous for holiday-making Australians. The Australians were targeted, according to the perpetrators, because of their alliance with the United States, their role in excising East Timor from Indonesia, and their white, Western culture.

The Australian media plunged into the Bali catastrophe, eulogizing its victims, celebrating the role of the Australian police in "solving" the crime with the Indonesians, and warning Australians of the encroaching ring of terror in the region. The War on Terror had become a reality, and there was widespread media agreement that Australia now stood in the front line. In such a climate, the more traditional skepticism of the media toward government pronouncements became submerged in a sense of national unity in this new war. Government publicity intensified such a perspective, as few wanted to argue with the growing jingoism and the reiteration of the call to arms that underlay most ministerial speeches.

AUSTRALIAN MEDIA

There is quite a diversity of news and information sources available in Australia. There are five free-to-air television networks, two of which (ABC and SBS) are public-service broadcasting; there is a forty-five-channel pay TV service with 20 percent penetration that carries CNN, Sky News, Fox News, and BBC World. There are up to twelve public-service and commercial radio stations in each city, as well as a large number of community radio stations, most of which, however, do not have the resources to carry out independent news coverage. There is wide availability of the Internet with 60 percent of the Australian population connected at home or work, and of course no restrictions on access to sites. The newspaper industry is quite concentrated, with virtually only three owners dominating city and regional newspapers.

In Sydney and Melbourne, the two biggest cities, there are three daily newspapers—two broadsheet (a national one owned by the Murdoch empire, the other owned by the more progressive Fairfax organization) and one tabloid (owned by Murdoch). In the other capital cities, there is one daily owned by Murdoch. In our survey of media coverage and in particular of how the war was "spun" by the government, we looked at two contrasting Sydney newspapers, the broadsheet, the *Sydney Morning Herald* (*SMH*), owned by Fairfax; and the tabloid, the *Daily Telegraph* (*DT*), owned by Murdoch. The *SMH* is generally considered to be a high-quality paper that sits toward the left of center of the political spectrum. The *DT* is less liberal, but its reporting is generally accurate, if at times partial. However, like most tabloids, it is capable of some very sensationalist headlines, especially on the front page, where in three or four words the whole tone of what is really a very complex matter is set. However, it is by no means a rabid tabloid like London's *Sun* or New York's *New York Post* (although, of course, they are all part of the international Murdoch stable).

In examining certain events or phases in the war more closely, we have also made reference to some of the more populist media outlets, in particular, the Sydney AM stations, 2UE and 2GB, where talkback kings, John Laws and

Alan Jones respectively, reign supreme. In particular, 2GB's Alan Jones, the most powerful radio broadcaster in Australia, commands about 20 percent of the breakfast audience and, in keeping with the type, runs a highly colorful, right-wing populist line, and is an ardent supporter of the Howard government (he once was Howard's adviser) and a bitter opponent of the "urban liberal elites." If politicians have an urgent message to convey to the electorate, they vie to get on 2GB so that they can convey it in person and at length. Because of the significance of talkback radio in commanding the populist vote, we look at some instances where Howard used this route to try to persuade the electorate of the merits of his position.

PUBLIC OPINION AND COGNITIVE DISSONANCE: ALERT OR ALARMED?

The growing repetition by the government that war might well be impossible to avoid, and that Australia would be part of it, created a sense of inevitability of the violence to come. It was as though that war "over there" would somehow purge the frustrations that terror had generated "over here."

Even though the media and the government were increasing the level of apprehension, an alternative discourse was abroad (appearing mainly in the *SMH* and on the ABC)—one that proposed that only common action by the nations of the world could actually "defeat" terrorism and reassert the global rule of law. Unilateral acts would in fact undermine this possibility, even if they achieved short-term outcomes such as the defeat of the Hussein regime. At least one whistleblower, former Office of National Assessments intelligence officer Andrew Wilkie, provided a focus for the view that there was no clear and present danger from Iraq and the war was a grievous mistake (Barker 2003). He became the media foil for the government's campaign in favor of immediate war.

The alternative discourse fitted comfortably with Australian public culture among the urban liberal middle classes, up until 1996 (and the return of the conservative government)—that Australia was a civilized nation among civilized nations, that it had been an ardent advocate of the United Nations, and that it played a leading role as a rational and peaceful middle-range power. Yet this public culture had been changing, as the conservative government developed a series of alternative value stances. The United Nations was increasingly presented as a "toothless tiger," controlled by authoritarian and corrupt Third World regimes. Australia would have to stand up for itself and take a tougher line on refugees—the Convention Relating to the Status of Refugees, adopted in 1951 and enforced from 1954, was seen as no longer helpful in a world with millions of refugees. The Asian Tigers had been shown up as economic disasters (especially Indonesia), and Australia should reassert itself as a Western rather than Asian nation—history should dominate geography.

Australians are not unlike most other peoples—they prefer consistency to inconsistency in public life, and they seek reinforcement for their values. When they commit to a course of action, they will tend to seek information and evidence that reinforces the correctness of that line. In the germinal work on "cognitive dissonance," Leon Festinger (1957) has pointed to the central importance of arousal in the process of attitude formation and behavioral change. When people experience unpleasant arousal, they will try to reduce their discomfort by modifying their attitudes to support the behavioral change necessary to reassert a state of personal comfort. By early 2003, it would be fair to say that the whole of Australian society was in a state of unpleasant arousal—a sense self-consciously captured in the February/March government antiterrorism campaign slogan of "Be Alert but Not Alarmed" (Minchin *The Age*, March 4, 2003).

There were numerous inconsistencies in the public discourses about the world and Australia's place in it. These inconsistencies were to provide the arena in which the specific government strategy to sell the war would take place. The critical message to communicate would be the necessary link between going to war and both personal self-interest and national security. The starting point was an environment dominated by the statements of UN weapons' inspectors that they could find nothing in the way of weapons of mass destruction (WMDs), while there was also a well-established and healthy export trade for Australia in wheat and meat to Iraq. The national perception was that the real problems of security were close to home—refugee penetration of the national "skin," and Muslim anti-Australian terrorism in an out-of-control Indonesia.

In mobilizing cognitive dissonance, attitude change proponents need to ensure that the issues are salient, the level of unpleasant arousal is high, the cost of changing to the new attitude is low, and the attitude change once committed is regularly reinforced and given social approval.

SELLING THE WAR: WMDS, REGIME CHANGE, AND BEING A "WESTERN NATION"

The process of shifting public opinion to support the war was identified by Howard, when he indicated in his "going to war" speech (www.pm.gov.au/news/speeches/speech79.html) that once Australian troops were on the ground, opposition in Australia would wane. Initially, the government depended on references to expertise—the technical failure of the regime to respond to the demands that it display its WMDs for the UN inspectors, then the demand that it actively cooperate to point out the WMDs, and then the referral to Iraqi defector information about the WMDs (of which more below). The outflow of information from the government increased, so that the public experienced an "overload" of information: too much material, unverified and untestable, arriving very quickly. There was simply no time for the public to assess or reflect on the information provided and the conclusions the government had reached based on this information. Such a situation exemplifies the environment where attitude change can be forced, or, more correctly, where behavioral change can be instigated, which then drags attitude change along in its wake. The behavior that changed was the willingness of the center ground of people to agree with the government's decision to go to war—the self-rationalizations soon followed.

Moreover, once the government announced troops were in battle, public opinion moved into support of the PM, especially as the WMD rationale was soon replaced by the cry of "regime change" (Barker 2003). The support held through the war but began to dissipate soon after. That is, as the salience of the war declined at the announcement of the ostensible end of Australia's role, and thereby the pressures of cognitive dissonance moved back against the government position, support slipped away.

Public opinion polls through this period reveal the dynamics of the process at work—thirteen were undertaken by Newspoll, the News Ltd. market research firm, between August 2002 and April 2003 (www.newspoll .com.au). In August 2002, when the war talk was beginning to grow and before Bali, a Newspoll of 1,200 people commissioned by the multicultural broadcaster SBS reported that 50 percent were opposed to any action to overthrow Hussein, while 39 percent favored it. A month later, a Newspoll survey of 700 people again gave 50 percent opposed, rising to 74 percent if the UN had not sanctioned the action. While up to 54 percent would support Australian involvement if there were strong evidence and a detailed argument from the prime minister, 85 percent agreed that he should provide this evidence prior to going to war, while 80 percent also felt that any alliance with the United States against Hussein would increase terrorist threats to Australia. As Geoffrey Barker (2003) has argued, this requirement for "hard evidence" drove the government's information strategy (unqualified statements of threat), with information delivery accelerating in response to poll results. The Bali bombings, specifically identifying Australians as targets because of the government alliance with the United States on Iraq, occurred in October 2002.

By January 2003, and with the Bali bombings recent traumatic memories, polls showed an increase in opposition to involvement, with 60 percent still refusing to support unilateral action, and support for involvement falling from 39 percent to 30 percent; 57 percent of women and 50 percent of men now believed that Australia would be attacked by terrorists within the year. Increasingly, then, the Bali experience intensified Australians' concerns about an effective defense against terrorism at home, rather than building their commitment to a suspect adventure on behalf of the Americans thousands of miles away.

In early February, the government released its "Let's Look Out for Australia" campaign, geared toward "protecting our way of life from a possible terrorist threat." This campaign was designed to "bounce" the issue in terms of its salience, linking graphically and emotionally (though not rationally and critically) the points of the terrorism/personal safety/Iraq war triangle. Saturation advertising and national mailing, despite widespread skepticism and criticism, raised anxiety levels and made the Saddam Hussein/terrorism link, however illogical and unsupported, more salient for the population. The campaign directly targeted the concerns about local dangers, connecting the international situation with local anxieties. Thus, as the weeks slipped by toward war, the opposition to war began to be eroded, with majority support for the war if the UN supported it (rising from 57 percent to 67 percent). Despite this, in the wake of a weekend of protests, support for the government briefly weakened again.

By March, it was clear that UN support would be critical as a factor in public opinion, though some movement toward the government position of unilateral action in alliance with the United States was evident (from 18 percent to 22 percent). Strong opposition to the war from women led the prime minister into a national statement on the humanitarian justification for war (a new overt rationale) with a major TV speech being directed toward "mumsland," the women viewers of daytime television. With the inevitability of the war and the feeling that "our boys and girls in Iraq cannot be abandoned" came a swing in public opinion. The polls show that with the commitment of troops, there was an even split on whether to go to war. Within a day or so of the first bombs falling, the majority was in favor with only a strong but falling minority opposed.

A cross-national poll taken in Australia, the United States, and the United Kingdom a week into the war showed Australian support more muted than in those countries—52 percent compared to 54 percent in the UK and 74 percent in the United States. By this time, with the war well advanced, much of the debate had become academic. The polls thereafter showed a rapidly rising support for the prime minister and his political coalition.

The war was declared officially over in early April 2003. Like Bush and Blair, Howard trumpeted the success of the mission and declared that "every single major prophesy of doom" had not been realized (*SMH* 2003c) and that the intelligence on which the decision had been based was totally credible (*SMH* 2003d). Polls in mid-April and early May indicated that the war had had a sizable positive affect on Howard and the government's popularity, due in part to the Labor opposition's indecision about its position. In a speech at the UN, Howard declared that the question of the international legitimacy of the invasion of Iraq should be dropped now that the conflict had ended (*SMH* May 7, 2003)

However, the triumphal phase did not last long. On May 29, 2003, Andrew Gilligan's infamous report about "sexed up British intelligence" went to air on BBC radio, and the "weapons of mass destruction" story began to unravel. In Australia, as in the United States and the United Kingdom, the story after that was one of the government trying to argue that the intelligence on which they went to war was accurate. Over the following months, as it became clear that there had been no WMDs, the debate in Australia became whether the prime minister knowingly misled the parliament and the people, or whether he himself was misinformed. The holes in the WMD story led to a slide in support for the war and for the Coalition government. By February 2004, 62 percent of Australians believed they were misled over the WMDs, with as many as 36 percent reporting they were knowingly misled (Newspoll, reported in the *Australian* 2004).

GOING TO WAR

The Howard government began to make a case for Australia to join the United States and the United Kingdom in a possible invasion of Iraq in August 2002. Media support for the government line was mixed, reflecting the confusion in government arguments, the political position taken by proprietors (with Rupert Murdoch's outlets strongly in support of the Bush/Blair/Howard triad, as the Fairfax group was more cautious and skeptical), and the freedom available to individual journalists to reflect on what they were reporting.

In December 2002, Howard—no doubt in "deputy sheriff" mode—mentioned the possibility of preemptive military strikes against terrorists "beyond Australia's borders" (*Channel Nine Sunday*, reported in *SMH*, 2002), at which the governments of the Philippines, Malaysia, and Thailand expressed extreme displeasure. As early as January 12, 2003, Howard announced the advance deployment of 2,000 troops to the Persian Gulf (*SMH*

2003a) and continued to follow the United States and the United Kingdom in their condemnation of the failure of the Iraqi government to allow weapons inspectors. The *Daily Telegraph* (West Jan. 12, 2003) heavily emphasized the imminent threat from North Korea and followed the Howard government's logic (following Bush) of equating a number of otherwise unconnected "rogue states" into an "axis of evil," thus implying that a threat from one was a threat from all.

By the third week of January, Howard was giving farewells to the ground troops about to depart for the Gulf in the HMAS *Kanimbla*. The *Daily Telegraph* gave front-page coverage to Howard's assertion of "Why I had to send them," reporting that Howard

> experienced his career's most tearful farewell to battle units. . . . As the naval band on the Garden Island dock yesterday played Waltzing Matilda, We are One and Advance Australia Fair, parents, children, brothers, sisters, and lovers said their goodbyes aboard the transport ship. On board the Kanimbla, tears flowed freely as loved ones spent their final moments with the troops. (*DT* Jan. 24, 2003, 1)

Howard later told the *Daily Telegraph* that he had spoken to 200 to 300 people, but just one told him deploying troops to the Middle East had been a mistake. The *SMH* ran almost as emotional a report, though concluded rather obliquely, "Probably none [i.e., any overseas military action] has had such little public support as this one" (Stephens, *SMH* Jan. 24, 2003).

Talkback host John Laws (generally considered right wing and a gung ho nationalist) conducted a fairly tough interview with Howard on January 24 (www.pm.gov.au/news/interviews/Interview178.html), pressing him on the issue of the advance commitment of troops and on the question of what secret commitment may have been made to the United States. In contrast, Alan Jones, the most influential talkback host in Australia, conducted a much more sympathetic interview with Howard (*2GB* 2000; see www.pm.gov.au/news/interviews/Interview186.html).

Howard's next move was the release of the antiterrorism pamphlet, and then a formal address to Parliament on the issues at stake. He mentioned all the key themes: "weapons of mass destruction" or variations on it was used throughout; Iraq was called a "rogue state"; the tone used was somber and threatening; the sense of immediate danger to Australians was emphasized; the link with worldwide terrorism was made; and the close parallels between Iraq and the much closer (to Australia) territory of North Korea were invoked. The speech echoed what was being said by Bush and Blair: the weakness and ineffectiveness of the UN sanctions, the link between WMDs and the War on Terror, and Howard explicitly quoted both British and U.S. intelligence as the source and basis for Australia's position.

The prime minister's reaction to antiwar protests was to label protesters as supporters of Saddam Hussein—a line repeated by right-wing commentators (see *SMH* 2003b). The prime minister made a televised address to the nation on the day troops were committed, March 23, 2003 (www.pm.gov.au/news/speeches/Speech79.html), moving from WMDs to generalized terrorism to terrorists on our doorstep to Australia as part of a generalized "West," hated by the "terrorists" for our values. But a new theme began to emerge in the PM's discourse—the brutality of the Saddam Hussein regime—thus laying the groundwork for a possible modification of the rationale for war from defense against WMDs and terrorism, to one of regime change.

By the end of March, a week into the war, the government was actively working the media to press for emotional support for the troops in battle, whatever the position that citizens might hold on the war itself. This was always going to be a major element in the media massage. The *Daily Telegraph* soared in its emotional manipulation of jingoistic imagery, featuring headlines like "PLEASE DON'T HATE OUR DADS"—pictures of toddlers seeing their fathers off to war (*DT* 2003b).

In early April, as coalition forces neared Baghdad and were meeting relatively little resistance, discussion began about the postwar regime, including some fairly unattractive jockeying by U.S., UK, and Australian business interests for a slice of the reconstruction action. Howard foreshadowed the pullout of Australian troops and signaled that Australia would be part of the coalition transitional authority in Iraq, no doubt with a view to the commercial advantage that might be associated. However, criticism of the war had continued throughout the actual engagement and was, if anything, intensified by the details that were emerging about civilian casualties on the ground in Iraq, in part due to coverage by Arabic channels, including Al-Jazeera, whose footage was available via both pay TV and broadcast networks like SBS.

The war was declared officially over on April 16, when George Bush made his *Top Gun*–type landing on the USS *Abraham Lincoln* in front of a sign, "Mission Accomplished." Like Bush and Blair, Howard trumpeted the success of the mission, and declared that "every single major prophesy of doom" had not been realized (*SMH* 2003c) and that the intelligence on which the decision had been based was totally credible (*SMH* 2003d).

Yet the media story was not as single-mindedly supportive as Howard liked to claim. While some Australian journalists were embedded with the U.S. and British forces and carrying whatever they could extract from the military situation, some, like the *SMH*'s Paul McGeogh, were "embedded" in Baghdad, reporting the war from the side of those awaiting the invasion to overrun them. Others found their role as journalists rather more complex, with disastrous consequences.

THE DEATH OF THE CAMERAMAN

In March 2003 Australian journalist/cameraman Paul Moran, on contract to the ABC, had entered northern Iraq to cover fighting between Kurdish forces and Iraqi and al Qaeda–linked forces. He was filming a group of Kurdish fighters near Halabja when a car drew up and exploded next to him. He was killed instantly and an Australian ABC journalist, Eric Campbell, was injured. Moran's death was covered widely in the Australian media, and his heroism celebrated (*ABC News* 2003). Over the following months, however, it became clear that Moran was rather more than just a heroic media worker killed in the line of duty. Moran had been working in Iraq since 1990, and had undertaken a number of contracts for the Iraqi National Council (INC), the exile organization established by the Rendon Group (a Washington, DC, PR firm) on behalf of the CIA. He had also undertaken other contracts for Rendon (Radio National Breakfast 2002), which was employed by the American government in Afghanistan and Iraq. During the first Gulf War in 1990, Rendon had organized the "spontaneous" waving of U.S. flags by Kuwaitis greeting the liberating Americans (Rampton & Stauber 2003).

Moreover, Moran had been the only international television journalist provided with access by the INC in 2001 to the Iraqi defector, Adnan Ihsan Saeed Al Haideri, ostensibly a chemical and biological weapons engineer. It was Al Haideri's unsubstantiated intelligence that was then disseminated globally and formed the nucleus of American, British, and Australian claims about Saddam's weapons of mass destruction program. It is still not clear whether Moran was a conscious conduit for this probable disinformation, or more a naïve and enthusiastic advocate of the Kurdish cause who had been used by Rendon and the CIA for their purposes—an argument made by the Special Broadcasting Service Insight program in July 2003 (Hoskins 2003).

There was almost no reporting in the Australian media of the SBS claims, with the ABC simply asserting that "Paul Moran was a highly professional and brave cameraman/journalist whose editorial integrity the ABC had no reason to doubt" (Australian Story 2003). The ABC did not deny his work for Rendon—though the Australian Story documentary made by his family through the ABC to rebut the SBS story sought to make light of it.

It is still not known whether Moran was murdered for his past associations or as a target of opportunity. (He was memorialized with other journalists killed on duty at the Freedom Forum memorial in Virginia, in May 2004.) The Moran saga indicates that simple distinctions between the media and the state are hard to make—even more so when the media are consciously provided with false information by intelligence agencies, or are employed or suborned by them. One conclusion would seem that the media should always view government-sourced information as initially suspect, to be validated by at least some triangulation from independent sources. Yet this is not just a question of the veracity of reported news. In an analysis of the impact of the Iraq war on journalists, and in particular the case of Paul Moran, Tim Gopsill has argued that the close ties between some journalists and intelligence agencies have increased the dangers for all journalists—they are all now potential activists rather than representatives of the public interest (Gopsill 2003) and thus likely targets from any side of a conflict.

SILENT HEROES

While there were journalists embedded in the British and American forces racing toward Baghdad, Australia's forces were free of any such distractions. There appear to be two reasons for this situation—one tactical, the other political. An early article on Australia's media policy noted that

> the ADF initially agreed to embed Australian reporters and news crews, but quickly withdrew the offer. Of the 56 pages of coverage which the Sydney Morning Herald devoted to the first week of the conflict in Iraq, fewer than four paragraphs concerned what the Australian SAS, the Royal Australian Air Force (RAAF) and Navy were doing. . . . Perhaps the government's rationale for the lack of access to the ADF is to distract the world's attention from the fact that Australia is part of the "coalition of the willing." If so, it is a successful strategy. Iraqi and other Arab leaders, denouncing what they see as the aggressors, invariably mention the US, Britain and Israel. Rarely do they add Australia to the list. (Collins 2003)

In its selected history of the Australian Defence Forces (ADF) in the Middle East (Australian Department of Defence 2004), the Australian Department of Defence indicated it was aware that there had been public interest in the war but that operational security was of paramount concern. While Australian naval personnel patrolled the Gulf, gave supporting fire to British marines near Basra, and cleared mines from booby-trapped harbors, the main Australian strength was contained in Special Air Service and Commando troops engaging in long-distance desert patrols in the west, seeking to interdict potential Iraqi Scud attacks (none were discovered) on Israel and elsewhere. Many of these troops operated behind enemy lines, later lying hidden close to Baghdad, where they directed air sorties against Iraqi command and control targets.

The Australian government was concerned to ensure that only good news stories about the Australians came out of Iraq. There were regular allusions to the highly secret nature of the SAS sorties, while the Defense Public Affairs and Corporate Communication Division (part of the operational command for the war) ran daily briefings for the media in Canberra, and for a short time in Kuwait (until Australian military commanders were rather too open and engaged with Australian journalists—who were then interviewed by the international media, which had been fed almost no information by the U.S. command). The briefing transcripts (Australian Department of Defense Public Affairs and Corporate Communication 2003) demonstrate that the military would tell their story and the media would ask rather unthreatening questions—a comfortable partnership.

Australian military history traditionally views the Middle East as a theater of valorous engagements, from the time of the Great War desert battles in Palestine (the Light Horse charge on the Ottoman troops at Beersheba) to the Rats of Tobruk stopping Rommel's advance in World War II. The Light Horse have provided the paradigmatic image of the Australian male at war, tough bronzed men in a hard dry land using courage, resourcefulness, and wit to outflank and defeat larger and usually Arab or Turkish foes. The SAS and their Commando comrades fit the modern makeover of this image. Where the Americans were nightly displayed as heavily armored and Leviathan-like in their inexorable rumbling toward Baghdad, and the British were seen in a Northern Ireland remake of close fighting in urban centers such as Basra, the Australians (who were rarely seen on television) were wraith-like figures moving at will across desert landscapes, shadows on the moonlit sands. The photographs chosen by the ADF for their report on the war reinforce this sense of distant wonder— lithe men in desert camouflage, Oakley wraparound sunglasses, and Bedouin headdresses abound, riding in cut-down trucks with heavy-caliber machine guns, clearing demolished remote airfields, or guarding captured facilities.

Media coverage of the ADF report demonstrates the ease with which this image could be circulated. In its summary of the report, the broadsheet *Melbourne Age* newspaper followed the military narrative without question:

Australia's crack Special Air Services were engaged in fierce fighting throughout the first week of the Iraq war, a review of Australia's military operations in Iraq revealed today. For the first week of the war, the enemy was actively seeking out the Australian force. . . . The SAS met the Iraqi forces head-on with fire power and tenacity that shocked the enemy. . . . Other SAS patrols were flown deep into the western desert by American helicopters. For several days they were the closest coalition ground forces to Baghdad. They watched key roads and military facilities, undetected by nomadic Bedouin or enemy patrols. (Feb. 23, 2004)

The report makes no mention of any Australian casualties, nor of any significant moment when the Australian forces were anything other than heroic, well behaved, legally informed, and magnanimous in victory. Its final "Lesson Learned" was that "Defense will continue to emphasize operational information security but will seek to balance the need to protect our forces with the need to keep the public informed of the employment and performance of the ADF" (Australian Department of Defence 2004). Rather, it may well have learned that reinforcing heroic myths is critical to selling war, as it did in cooperating with the commercial television program *Sunday* in featuring these same images for a feature on quiet heroes, broadcast on Australia's war memorial Anzac Day (April 26) in 2004.

THE BIG LIE

As discussed earlier, the Howard government did not enjoy its triumphal phase for long. The holes in the WMD story led to a slide in support for the war and for the Coalition government. By February 2004, a year after the ramping up of the war was at its height, 62 percent of people believed they were misled over the WMD, with as many as 36 percent reporting that they were knowingly misled (Newspoll, reported in the *Australian* 2004).

In spite of ample evidence from both the United States and the United Kingdom that the prewar intelligence was faulty, Howard continued to tough it out and insist that the government had acted in the best interests of both the Australian and the Iraqi people, amply assisted by sympathetic headlines such as the *DT*'s "Howard's War: I Have No Regrets" (Farr, Jan. 27, 2004). However, by early February 2004, Howard was admitting that the intelligence might have been wrong (*DT* 2004, 2). A Senate inquiry reporting on these issues cleared the government of actively misleading the population, but recommended a further inquiry (see www.aph.gov.au/house/committee/pjcaad/WMD/report.htm). Meanwhile, the Foreign Minister Alexander Downer admitted that Australia's alliance with the United States would have weakened "very substantially" if the government refused to go to war against Iraq (*SMH* 2004), an admission that further undermined the WMD story.

Even though the whole Iraq adventure was demonstrated to have shaky foundations, the equivalence that government discourse had managed to create between Iraq, generalized terrorism, Islamic fundamentalism, threats to our borders from the north, and so on, continued to create a climate of unease in Australia.

THE MINISTER HAS A PROBLEM . . .

The fallout from the somewhat fraught relationships between some of the media and the government continued as the WMD fiasco unwound, particularly in relation to the Australian Broadcasting Corporation (ABC). The ABC (founded 1932) is the major public broadcaster in Australia (it shares the field with the multicultural Special Broadcasting Service). Although, unlike the British Broadcasting Corporation on which it is modeled, it has never had a commanding position in the ratings (about 20 percent of the radio audience and 16 percent of TV), its reach and influence far outreach its ratings performance. Quality news and current affairs are central to its mission.

The ABC has a long history of abrasive relations with governments of either political persuasion on controversial matters. During the 1991 Gulf War, for instance, the Labor Party prime minister of the day, Bob Hawke, was incensed at the use by the ABC of a commentator on the war who was neutral in his views rather than uncritically supportive of the government. A decade later, the second Gulf War triggered ire from a conservative government for essentially similar alleged transgressions. Then-Minister Alston became angry about "gratuitous barbs" directed toward the American president George W. Bush that suggested his administration was producing propaganda in its war briefings to the media.

This incident represented a larger argument within the elites, between neoconservative and more liberal perceptions of the role of the national broadcaster—over how the parameters of the public sphere would be set, and what power government would seek to use in controlling the discursive terrain of policy debate. While the ABC has not faced the same sort of pressure as the BBC (in the Hutton Inquiry), it has been a major conduit for the arguments of government critics such as ex-ONA intelligence assessor Andrew Wilkie. The ABC had reported his attacks on the government's credibility: "The Government lied every time," Mr. Wilkie said. "It skewed, misrepresented, used selectively, and fabricated the Iraq story. . . . The Government lied every time that it associated Iraq with the war on terror" (see www.abc.net.au/news/newsitems/s930536.htm).

THE STATE, THE MEDIA, AND PUBLIC OPINION

The Australian government was clearly able to mobilize a complex of preexisting fears and rising apprehensions to swing popular support behind its commitment to the Coalition of the Willing, albeit only when Australian troops were committed to war, and then for barely longer than the formal war lasted. Yet in doing this they were far less successful than the U.S. government, facing continuing criticism from the national broadcaster and parts of the Fairfax press. This uncontrollable media element (unlike the constant support from the Murdoch press) undermined government capacity to dominate totally the public agenda and set the terms for debate. Although the Australian government did not face the sustained alternative worldviews offered by newspapers such as the *Guardian* and the *Independent* in the United Kingdom, nor the head-to-head confrontations that marked the relationship between Blair's government and the BBC, it was not unaffected by media criticism.

The high volatility of public opinion could be easily swayed by changing circumstances, as competing discourses found salient resonance with a frightened citizenry (Goot 2003). Yet the importance of public service journalism cannot be overestimated. Public service journalism sought to retain some capacity for independent assessment, endeavoring to avoid too close an integration with government worldviews, despite sustained public and behind-the-scenes pressures to conform with government opinion as the only legitimate version of the national interest. Journalists were able to sustain some continuing interrogation of the government agenda (as with Paul Mc-Geogh, the Fairfax journalist embedded in Baghdad who reported on the effect on civilians of American bombing and stayed to report the endless urban insurgency that followed the declaration of victory).

The Iraq war showed Australians that they could easily be implicated in global adventures over which they had little control, and in the service of the American government, with little real benefit to Australia. Their media could be as confused and "misled" as the prime minister sheepishly accepted he had been in the wake of U.S. and British admissions of mistaken readings of the WMD evidence. The Free Trade Agreement between Australia and the United States signed in February 2004, supposedly a return to Australia for its loyalty to the United States, proved in the end to be more in the United States' favor than Australia's. In March 2004, Australia announced that it would purchase fifty-nine refurbished Abrahams heavy tanks from the United States, their "survivability" proven on the desert sands of Iraq, but of no value at all in the jungles of Australia's locality. This time, the media were willing to reflect on the irony.

REFERENCES

ABC News. (2003, 23 March). Tributes flow for Australian cameraman. *ABC News Online*. Retrieved from www.abc.net.au/news/newsitems/s813802.htm

Australian Bureau of Statistics. (1994). *Australian Social Trends 1994: Population-Population Growth: Birthplace of Australia's settlers.* Retrieved from www.abs .gov.au/ausstats
———. (2003). *2015.0 2001 Census reveals Australia's cultural diversity.* Retrieved June 21, 2002, from www.abs.gov.au/ausstats
Australian Department of Defence. (2004). *The War in Iraq: ADF operations in the Middle East in 2003.* Canberra: Australian Department of Defence. Retrieved from www.defence.gov.au
Australian Department of Defence Public Affairs and Corporate Communication. (2003). Media Briefing Australia's contribution to global operations. Defence Media Release. Retrieved from www.globalsecurity.org/wmd/library/news/iraq/2003/iraq-030416-australia01.htm
Australian Story. (2003, 13 October). First Casualty. Australian Broadcasting Corporation. Retrieved from www.abc.net.au/austory/content/2003/s964135.htm
Barker, G. (2003). *Sexing it up: Iraq, intelligence and Australia.* Sydney: UNSW Press.
Collins, P. (2003, 3 April). War is deeply embedded in hearts of Australians. *Irish Times.* Retrieved March 9, 2004, from www.ireland.com
Dempster, Q. (2000). *Death Struggle: How political malice and boardroom power-plays are killing the ABC.* Crows Nest, Australia: Allen & Unwin.
Dibb, P. (2003). Australia's alliance with America. *Melbourne Asia Policy Papers 1,* no. 1.
Festinger, L. (1957). *A theory of cognitive dissonance.* Stanford, CA: Stanford University Press.
Gaita, R. (Ed.). (2003). *Why the war was wrong.* Melbourne: Text Publishing.
Goot, M. (2003). Public opinion and the democratic deficit. *Australian Humanities Review.* Retrieved from www.lib.latrobe.edu.au/AHR/archive/Issue-May-2003/goot.html
Gopsill, T. (2003). Target the Media. In D. Miller (Ed.), *Tell me lies: Propaganda and media distortion in the attack on Iraq* (pp. 251–261). London: Pluto.
Harries, O., & Australian Broadcasting Corporation. (2004). *Benign or imperial? Reflections on American hegemony.* Sydney: ABC Books for the Australian Broadcasting Corporation.
Healey, J. (2002). *Australia's immigration debate.* Rozelle, Australia: Spinney Press.
Hoskins, J. (2003, July 23). Paul Moran Story. *Dateline.* Retrieved from www.sbs .com.au/dateline/trans.php3?dte=2003-07-23&title=Paul+Moran+Story
Independent Complaints Review Panel (ICRP). (2003). *Review of 68 complaints made by the minister for communications, information technology and the arts, Senator Richard Alston, carried out at the request of the managing director of the ABC.* Retrieved February 23, 2004, from www.abc.net.au/corp/pubs/ICRP.pdf
Jayasuriya, K. (2003, 7 March 2003). *Howard, Tampa, and the politics of reactionary modernisation.* Retrieved June 17, 2003, from www.econ.usyd.edu.au/drawing board/digest/0303/jayasuriya.html
Kellner, D. (2003). *From 9/11 to terror war: The dangers of the Bush legacy.* Lanham, MD: Rowman & Littlefield.

Mares, P. (2001). *Borderline: Australia's treatment of refugees and asylum seekers.* Sydney: UNSW Press.

———. (2002). Refugees: Why were we surprised by the Tampa? *Australian Policy Online, http://www.apo.org.au/webboard/items/00024.shtml.*

Marr, D., & Wilkinson, M. (2003). *Dark victory.* Sydney: Allen & Unwin.

Megalogenis, G. (2003). *Fault lines: Race, work and the politics of changing Australia.* Melbourne: Scribe.

Miller, D. (Ed.). (2004). *Tell me lies: Propaganda and media distortion in the attack on Iraq.* London: Pluto Press.

Radio National Breakfast. (2002, May 21). War on terror PR. Australian Broadcasting Corporation. www.abc.net.au/rn/talks/brkfast/stories/s559930.htm

Rampton, S., & Stauber, J. (2003). *Weapons of mass deception.* Sydney: Hodder Headline.

Toohey, B. (2004, February 2–29). Media and mass deception. *Weekend Australian Financial Review,* 26–27.

Watson, D. (2001). *Rabbit syndrome: Australia and America.* Melbourne, Australia: Black Inc.

8

The Construction of Arabs as Enemies: Post-9/11 Discourse of George W. Bush

Debra Merskin

Make no mistake, we will find the enemy and we will kill the enemy.

The Siege (1998)

Make no mistake, the United States government will hunt down and punish those responsible for these cowardly acts.

George W. Bush (2001)

In the post–September 11 world, the administration of George W. Bush, through media presentations of his speeches, has anthropomorphized courage and bravery. At the same time, his rhetoric also puts a face on terror (and it is Arab) by employing words and expressions such as "them," "they," "evil," "those people," "demons," and "wanted: dead or alive" to characterize people of Arab/Middle Eastern descent. While these descriptions have largely been applied to non-U.S. citizens, they cannot help but include the approximately 3 million Arab individuals living in the United States, many of whom were born in the States as well as others who have adopted America as home—Iraqis, Iranians, Palestinians, Egyptians, Saudis, Yemenis, and others.

Popular culture and mass media in the United States have generated and sustained stereotypes of a monolithic evil Arab; these stereotypes constructed all Muslims as Arab and all Arabs as terrorists. Using representations and language in news, movies, cartoons, and magazine stories, the media and popular culture have participated in the construction of an evil Arab stereotype that encompasses a wide variety of people, ideas, beliefs, religions, and assumptions (Artz & Pollock 1995; Ghareeb 1983; Hamada 2001; Jackson 1996; Shaheen

1998, 2001; Suleiman 1988, 1999; Terry 1985). For example, movies such as *The Siege* (1998), *True Lies* (1994), *Hostage* (1986), and several news-magazines presented dark images of Middle Eastern men, or what Shaheen (1995, 191) calls "America's bogeyman." In recent films, "Barbarism and cru-elty are the most common traits associated with Arabs" (Jackson 1996, 65). These stereotypes, "which tend to lump Arabs, Muslim, Middle East into one highly negative image of violence and danger," are composed largely from collective memory rather than from actual experience (Jackson 1996, 65).

Historically, a combination of (mis)information has worked to construct an enemy image in the popular imagination that has an important function in the maintenance of political power, or hegemony, through ideology. Conse-quently, the "Face of Terror" became not only that of Osama bin Laden and Saddam Hussein, but also all persons of Arab descent, evoking the simu-lacrum of all Middle Eastern–looking males as the face of terror/ism (Gha-reeb 1983; Hamada 2001; Suleiman 1999).

This chapter links stereotypes of Arabs, enemy image construction, and ideology to the rhetoric of President George W. Bush as delivered during four speeches subsequent to the September 11, 2001, attacks. It is my intention to demonstrate how depictions of Arab enemies in popular culture and em-ployed by the media were mobilized by the Bush administration and fed to a receptive public. These carefully cultivated stereotypes, used to justify the in-vasion of Afghanistan and occupation of Iraq, were affirmed during the months following September 11, 2001, and reified by the time troops invaded Iraq in 2003.

Spillman and Spillman's (1997, 50–51) model of enemy image construc-tion is used as a framework for an interpretive textual analysis (Chandler 2002; Hall 1975) that chronologically traces the development of the Arab en-emy image in this rhetoric. This model posits that feelings and reactions to enmity can be described as a syndrome, one that draws on a historically con-structed foundation from which stereotypes are built and enemy images emerge. The resultant extraction of an enemy image reinforces ancient ideo-logical dichotomies of good versus evil and us versus them, rigidifying an agreed-upon stereotype with referential function. Over time, an "enemy image," defined as a "culturally influenced, very negative and stereotyped evaluation of the 'other'" (Fiebig-von Hase 1997, 2), is reinforced and rein-vigorated via the words of political opinion leaders and mass media repre-sentations. The present study reveals that the accumulation of historically, po-litically, and culturally cultivated negative images and words of Arabs resembles the word choices and allusions used in the carefully constructed, post–September 11 speeches of President George W. Bush. A necessary part of this analysis is to "bracket the historical question of guilt and innocence, and focus on the recurring images that have been used . . . to characterize the enemy" (Keen 1986, 13). The analysis demonstrates how presidential verbal rhetoric built upon and was informed by cultural artifacts (movies, television, newspaper stories, and comics) and is consistent with Spillman and Spillman's (1997) model of evil enemy image construction. There is a standard repertoire of propagandistic words and images that serves to dehumanize the "other" as part of the construction of an enemy image in the popular imagination and thus makes a retaliatory backlash against human beings seem logical and natural. The results of this study are important for scholars, governmental decision makers, media creators, and citizens. They add to the limited literature on the construction of enemy images and Arab stereotyping in the media, and extend and exemplify the Spillman and Spillman (1997) model. As evidenced by policies such as those enacted by the newly created Department of Homeland Security, by the Patriot Act, and by the detainment of suspects without due process of the law, these findings have human rights as well as foreign and domestic policy implications (Feehan 2003; Valbrun 2003).

MAKING ENEMIES

Nations "need" enemies. Governments use the idea of a common enemy as a method of social control, of reinforcing values of the dominant system, and of garnering participation in the maintenance of those beliefs (Keen 1986; Spillman & Spillman 1997). As a hegemonic device, a common enemy can serve to distract attention and divert aggression and energy toward a common threat. In addition, a common enemy is important in organizing evolutionary-based survival strategies that rely on perceptual and behavioral patterns that are a fundamental part of human nature.

Differences in age, race, religion, culture, or appearance can be the characteristic(s) that stimulate resentment toward other groups. The unfamiliar and strange evoke strong emotions and reactions such as aggression, fear, hate, aversion, and expulsion. Xenophobic and racist reactions create "an artificial binary opposition that is resolved through the physical annihilation of one side by the other" (Kibbey 2003, 2). The resultant "we-they" dichotomy produces a kind of "groupthink" that supports the separation of particular racial, religious, ethnic, or cultural groups, positioning them as hostile and alien. As Said (1997) points out, "Sensationalism, crude xenophobia, and insensitive belligerence are the order of the day, with results on both sides of the imaginary line between 'us' and 'them' that are extremely unedifying"(xlviii).

Cultural factors also play an important role in forming and regulating human behavior as part of the "phenomenology of the hostile imagination" (Keen 1986, 13). Despite changing times and circumstances, the "hostile imagination has a certain standard repertoire of images it uses to dehumanize the enemy" (Keen 1986, 13). This process includes what Jung refers to as the shadow archetype, which, in this case, becomes the "archetype of the enemy" (Hyde & McGuinness 1994, 86). In the collective sense, according to this theory, shadowy qualities and unsavory characteristics are often projected onto other people, resulting in "paranoia, suspiciousness, and lack of intimacy, all of which afflict individuals, groups, and even entire nations" (Hopcke 1989, 82). Spillman and Spillman (1997) explain the development of the collective unconscious that comes to support viewing others as enemies. They describe enemy image construction as a syndrome of deeply rooted perceptual evaluations that take on the following characteristics:

Negative Anticipation. All acts of the enemy in the past, present, and future become attributed to destructive intentions toward one's own group. Whatever the enemy undertakes is meant to harm us.

Putting Blame on the Enemy. The enemy is thought to be the source of any stress on a group. They are guilty of causing the existing strain and current negative conditions.

Identification with Evil. The values of the enemy represent the negation of one's own value system, and the enemy is intent on destroying the dominant value system as well.

Zero-Sum Thinking. What is good for the enemy is bad for us and vice versa.

Stereotyping and Deindividualization. Anyone who belongs to the enemy group is ipso facto our enemy.

Refusal to Show Empathy. Consideration for anyone in the enemy group is repressed due to perceived threat and feelings of opposition. There is nothing in common and no way to alter that perception. (50–51)

STEREOTYPES AND PROPAGANDA

First the image, then the enemy.

Keen (1986, 10)

Thought of as overgeneralized, reductionist beliefs, stereotypes are collections of traits or characteristics that present members of a group as being all the same. This signifying mental practice provides convenient shorthand in the identification of a particular group of people.

As available methods for organizing the "great blooming, buzzing confusion of the outer world" (Lippmann 1922, 81), stereotypes "get hold of the few simple, vivid, memorable, easily grasped, and widely recognized characteristics about a person, *reduce* everything about the person to those traits, *exaggerate* and *simplify* them, and *fix* them without change or development to eternity" (Hall 1997, 258; emphasis in original).

Certainly, it would be impossible to function in the world without simplifying visual and verbal information to manageable units. As Gandy (1998) suggests, "It seems likely that stereotypes become part of our understanding of our surroundings from the first moments of our efforts to make sense of the world around us" (83). Stereotypes serve as building blocks of the "fortress" of social tradition (Lippmann 1922, 96). They are part of the "maintenance of social and symbolic order" that facilitates the binding of people together as an us and sends those who are not us into "symbolic exile" as *them* (Hall 1997, 258). Once an individual is constructed as an outsider, this person is no longer thought of as having humanity. The intimidating outsider is "surely an animal in human form" (Green 1993, 327). In the absence of direct personal experience, stereotypes serve as a way of filling in the blanks in terms of expectations (or lack thereof) of those different from the individual imagining them. Construction of an enemy image becomes the "mental background for aggression, distrust, guilt, projection, identification with all evil, and stereotyping" (Fiebeg-von Hase 1997, 2).

The people and government of the United States have a long history of selectively demonizing and dehumanizing others, including their own citizenry, in the interest of acquisition and preservation of resources and power (Said 1997; Takaki 1993; Zinn 1995). Further, a joining of politics and religion is useful in propagating hegemonic beliefs. To accomplish this, both theologians and political rhetoricians frequently invoke images of Satan (Pagels 1996). This practice can be traced at least as far back as Luther, when rebelling peasants were declared to be "agents of the devil" (Keen 1986, 27). For purposes of this essay, however, there are ample examples in the recent past that can best be explained under the rubric of two structural factors tied to enmity: (1) "some concrete facts that permit the enemy image to appear as plausible and real," and (2) "the political system itself" (Fiebig-von Hase 1997, 24). Attitudes among European Americans that would permit extermination attempts of indigenous Americans, the enslavement of Africans, and Japanese internment are a few examples of the extremes to which enemy construction has reached. These beliefs are not simply erased over the passage of time. Rather, through the messages of dominant social and cultural institutions, such as the government and the media, selective versions of "reality" are presented in a way that provides justification for past, present, and future action and reaction to constructed enemies.

The political system is the second structural source of social conflict and enmity (Fiebig-von Hase 1997). In American bureaucracy, tension often arises between an individual's beliefs and expectations of government and political control. In the guise of political rhetoric, propaganda, defined in its broadest sense as controlling information to influence "human action by the manipulation of representations," is often used to ameliorate psychological dissonance (Lasswell 1934/1995, 13). Propaganda can be found in "spoken, written, pictorial or musical" forms and has been used as a way of mobilizing sentiment around an idea, image, or product. Moreover, it attains "eminence as the one means of mass mobilizations that is cheaper than violence, bribery, or other possible control techniques" (Lasswell 1934/1995, 17).

Embedded in official doctrine, hate propaganda draws strength and longevity from well-established underlying attitudes and beliefs:

> For mobilization of national hatred the enemy must be represented as a menac-
> ing, murderous aggressor, a satanic violator of the moral and conventional stan-
> dards, an obstacle to the cherished aims and ideals of the nation as a whole and
> of each constituent part. Through the elaboration of war aims, the obstructive
> role of the enemy becomes particularly evident. (Lasswell 1934/1995, 18–19)

Through the use of symbols or symbolic words that not only are popular but also resonate with preexisting points of view, propagandist representations must spontaneously induce acceptance and elicit necessary changes in order to bring about permanent adaptation. Stereotypes, "especially negative ones of Arabs, have been used as a weapon that has proved to be as effective as some of the military, economic, or political weapons" (Suleiman 1988, ix).

THE ARAB STEREOTYPE IN AMERICAN POPULAR CULTURE

Al tikrar biallem il hmar. [By repetition, even the donkey learns.]

Arab proverb

All the information a child or young adult learns becomes assimilated into a particular worldview and is compressed into categories of understanding (stereotypes) that are consistent with widespread social norms (Gandy 1998; Hall 1997; Merskin 2001; Spyrou 2002). From early childhood on, media and popular culture teach both Arabs and non-Arabs about "Arab-ness" by bombarding them "with rigid, repetitive and repulsive depictions that demonize and delegitimize the Arab" (Shaheen 1990, 7) and appear to represent consensus. These distorted representations can be found in music (remember "Ahab the Arab"?) cartoons, advertisements, comic strips, editorials, political rhetoric, and even children's textbooks (Ghareeb 1983; Hamada 2001; Shaheen 1988, 2001; Terry 1985). The movie quotations at the beginning of this article suggest that Hollywood has been a particularly powerful and consistent outlet for vilification of others. According to Jeanine Basinger (Lyman 2001, E1) "We've had the IRA as villains, we've had international drug dealers, we've had Arabs, we've had vague Asians who weren't quite sure what country they were from." In other words, according to Hall (as quoted in Gavrilos 2002, 428) "The media are not simply institutions that reflect consensus but also institutions that produce consensus and 'manufacture consent.'" The system of representation thereby "becomes a stable cultural convention that is taught and learned by members of a society" (Kates & Shaw-Garlock 1999, 34). Markers of the nation-state, these signifiers serve as key components of ideology in a hegemonic system that requires a great number of people to "buy in" to the dominant belief system, the one held to be "right." Stories and beliefs about what is "true" thereby become fertile fodder for the construction and maintenance of Arab stereotypes.

In an exhaustive study of more than 900 films over the last twenty years that portray Arab men, women, and children, Shaheen (2001) found that, in all but a few, Arabs were presented as "Public Enemy #1—brutal, heartless, uncivilized religious fanatics, and money-mad cultural 'others' bent on terrorizing civilized Westerners, especially Christians and Jews." Other examples include stereotypical representations such as "brute murderers, sleazy rapists, religious fanatics, oil-rich dimwits, and abusers of women" (Shaheen 2001, 1–2).

After the dismemberment of the Soviet Union and the end of the Cold War, U.S. policy makers found a new enemy, a global bad guy, "a new foreign devil" (Said 1997, xxviii). Cultural, political, educational, and media environments were well in place to make the threat Arab. The 1991 Gulf War provoked "an ugly wave of anti-Arab racism in the United States with Arab-Americans insulted or beaten or threatened with death. Bumper stickers said, 'I don't brake for Iraqis'" (Zinn 1995, 587), and political cartoons of Arabs reinforced the sentiments (Artz & Pollock 1995). By then, the construction of an enemy "of Middle Eastern descent" was well established, as evidenced by the rush to judgment when an Arab American man (Abraham Ahmad) was falsely arrested only a few hours after the April 19, 1995, Oklahoma City bombing ("False bombing" 1995).

A lack of representation (symbolic annihilation) can also reinforce stereotypes. In an extensive three-year study (1993–1996) of TV content on ABC,

CNN, PBS, and NPR, Lind and Danowski (1998) found very little coverage of Arabs and less of Arab culture. This reinforcement of dominant stereotypes through an overwhelming association with war, violence, and threats resulted in the representation of Arabs who "were identified most strongly in terms of their relations with Israel" (165).

With regard to the conflict with Osama bin Laden, Pilon quoted Attorney General John Ashcroft at a National Press Club luncheon as saying that Americans had "seen the face of evil," that they were dealing with "irrational madmen," and that they were "at war against international terrorism" (Pilon 2001). The "axis of evil" became the presidential mantra of the moment. Fish (2001, A19) points out,

> We have not seen the face of evil; we have seen the face of an enemy who comes at U.S. with a full roster of grievances, goals, and strategies. If we reduce the enemy to "evil," we conjure up a shape-shifting demon, a wild-card moral anarchist beyond our comprehension.

In a *New York Times* article following George W. Bush's September 15, 2001, speech, D. T. Max (2001) wrote,

> He called the terrorists "folks" and referred to the coming battle as a "crusade." He called for "revenge," called Osama bin Laden the "prime suspect," and asked for him "dead or alive." He said "make no mistake" at least eight times in public remarks. It was beginning to look like "bring me the head of Osama bin Laden." (1)

In the following months, evil was seamlessly transferred from bin Laden to Hussein.

RHETORIC IN ACTION

An interpretive textual analysis was used to examine four speeches given by President George W. Bush shortly after September 11, 2001. Specifically, these speeches are the September 11 presidential address to the nation, remarks Bush made upon arrival at the White House from the South Lawn on September 16, a speech before a joint meeting of Congress on September 20, and the State of the Union address on January 29, 2002. These speeches were selected because the discourse provides insight into the enemy-building process that Spillman and Spillman (1997) describe.

The first step of the analysis involved "a long preliminary soak" (Hall 1975, 15) in the text by studying complete speeches. This step was followed by a "close reading" to identify the rhetorical characteristics of enemy image construction and an interpretation of the findings (Feldstein & Acosta-Alzuru 2003, 159). Goffman's (1974, 11) frame analysis is used as a guide for understanding the words and phrases in Bush's rhetoric, the organization of which governs events as well as "our subjective involvement in them."

Representative "strips," defined as a "slice or cut from the stream of ongoing activity, including . . . sequences of happenings, real or fictive, as seen from the perspective of those subjectively involved sustaining interest in them" (Goffman 1974, 10), are used to illustrate characteristics of enemy image construction. The characteristics include, as described above, negative anticipation, putting blame on the enemy, identification with evil, zero-sum thinking, stereotyping and deindividualization, and refusal to show empathy (Spillman & Spillman 1997).

Transcripts were collected from www.whitehouse.gov. Since the Spillman and Spillman (1997) categories are not mutually exclusive, the results are presented and discussed chronologically.

September 11, 2001: Statement by the President in His Address to the Nation

In this brief (593-word) address to the nation, President Bush laid the foundation upon which his future rhetoric would build, solidifying the evil enemy image. The term "evil" was mentioned four times in this first address, God was mentioned once, and Psalm 23, "Even though I walk through the valley of the shadow of death, I fear no evil, for You are with me," was recited. The Spillman and Spillman (1997) characteristics of enemy construction, negative anticipation, blaming the enemy, identification with evil, and stereotyping and deindividualization are pulled together in this rhetoric. For example, in the first few sentences, Bush invoked the concepts of good versus evil and us versus them when he provided an initial reason for the attack: "Our very freedom came under attack. . . . America was targeted for attack because we're the brightest beacon for freedom and opportunity in the world . . . thousands of lives were suddenly ended by evil, despicable acts of terror." This is the first of many uses of the word "evil" that transmogrified into "evil folks" and "evildoers" in later addresses. He noted that "today, our nation saw evil" and that "the search is underway for those who are behind these evil acts." Zero-sum thinking, stereotyping, and deindividualization are evident in the statement, "We will make no distinction between the terrorists who committed these acts and those who harbor them."

September 16, 2001: Remarks by the President
upon Arrival at the White House

George W. Bush's remarks to the nation from the South Lawn of the White House offered less scripted, more spontaneous rhetoric. At this point, terms such as "evildoers," "evil folks," and "barbarism" had entered the vernacular. Arab enemy image construction is evident in the president's persistent references to evil in his speeches and the accompanying pervasive images of Arab suspects in the news media. In his remarks from the South Lawn, Bush said,

> We're a nation that can't be cowed by evildoers. . . . We will rid the world of evildoers. . . . There are evil people in this world. . . . Evil folks still lurk out there, never did anybody's thought process [sic] about how to protect America did we think that the evildoers would fly not one, but four commercial aircraft into precious U.S. targets. That's why I say to the American people we've never seen this kind of evil before. But the evildoers have never seen the American people in action, before, either—and they're about to find out.

The idea of evil in Bush's remarks was accompanied by the idea of goodness, frequently expressed in Christian terms and expressions. In this speech, the word "faith" was used six times, either in references to Sunday, September 16, being "the Lord's day," "this day of faith," or of the American people having "great faith." Bush said he had "faith in our military," "faith in America," and "great faith in the resiliency of the economy."

The animalistic nature of stereotyping and deindividualization is evident as well in his assurance that "my administration is determined to find, to get 'em running, and to haunt [sic] 'em down, those who did this to America."

September 20, 2001: President Bush's Address
before a Joint Meeting of Congress

In this speech, Bush identified four questions he felt Americans were asking: (1) who attacked our country? (2) why do they hate us? (3) how will we fight this war? and (4) what is expected of us? In response to the first question, Bush engaged negative anticipation by pointing out previous attacks and bombings by Arab-affiliated groups. At this time, he not only used terms such as "evildoers" but also began referring to a more precise group identified as the Taliban. Bush described how the Taliban would pay a price for not meeting his demands. He drew upon the stereotypical, deindividualized characteristics of enemy image construction when he described the people as animalistic and brutal in act and ideology: "The terrorists may burrow deeper into caves and other entrenched hiding places. Our military action is also designed to clear the way for . . . relentless operations to drive them out and bring them to justice," since "they hide in your land." The statement to the Taliban that they must act immediately and "hand over the terrorists or they will share in their fate" illustrates zero-sum thinking.

In commenting that the Muslim faith is respected and freely practiced by individuals in America and around the world, Bush's ecumenical effort to be inclusive was subsumed by the statement that followed: "Those who commit evil in the name of Allah blaspheme the name of Allah." According to Hathout (1999, 1), "Islam is probably the most misunderstood American reality," and "studies have shown that Americans' knowledge of the Islamic faith is 'tragically laughable.'" As a result, "Most of the time we're mentioned, it's sensationalized, ugly or weird. And when a group is generalized, it becomes an object of fear" (Hathout 1999, 1).

"Why do they hate us?" was the second question Bush posed. His response: they hate us because "Americans show a deep commitment to one another and an abiding love for country." The implication was that "they" do not share a similar sense of national pride. Bush compared an unknown image to a known stereotype by stating, "Al Qaeda is to terror what the Mafia is to crime." The act of blaming the enemy—and the representation of the enemy as greedy, insatiable, and possessing no limits or boundaries—provide justification for doing whatever is necessary to preserve the American way of life. In this speech, Bush used the abstract concept of freedom as being under attack, not individuals. For example, he said that "enemies of freedom committed an act of war against our country. . . . The terrorists' directive commands them to kill Christians and Jews." Negative anticipation is illustrated in this speech when Bush stated that America and Americans are hated because of

> what they [the terrorists] see right here in this chamber, a democratically elected government. Their leaders are self-appointed. They hate our freedoms, our freedom of religion, our freedom of speech, our freedom to vote and assemble and disagree with each other.

A clear example of zero-sum thinking is found in Bush's ultimatum,

> Every nation in every region now has a decision to make. Either you are with us or you are with the terrorists. From this day forward, any nation that continues to harbor or support terrorism will be regarded by the United States as a hostile regime.

Refusal to show empathy is illustrated when Bush made this declaration about sympathizing nations: "They will hand over the terrorists or they will share in their fate." The American military would either "bring our enemies to justice or bring justice to our enemies." It was alongside this statement that Bush announced the creation of a cabinet-level position that would report directly to him—the Office of Homeland Security.

In this speech, Bush extended the evil paradigm when he drew parallels with Nazism:

> We have seen their kind before. They are the heirs of all the murderous ideologies of the 20th century. By sacrificing human life to serve their radical visions, by abandoning every value except the will to power, they follow the path of fascism, Nazism and totalitarianism.

When he presented the third question, "How will we fight this war?" Bush's response returned to the characterization of the enemy as evil, barbaric, and animalistic when he said the U.S. military would " starve terrorists of funding, turn them one against another, drive them from place to place until there is no refuge or no rest."

Finally, negative anticipation, identification with evil, blaming the enemy for domestic tensions, zero-sum thinking, and stereotyping came together in Bush's response to the fourth question, "What is expected of us?" In describing the meaning of patriotism, Bush assimilated the U.S. economy into the symbolic meaning of the World Trade Center: "Terrorists attacked a symbol of American prosperity." Religiosity also came into play when Bush implored Americans "to continue to pray," as "prayer has comforted us in sorrow and will help strengthen the journey ahead." Dark and light imagery again were used as points of opposition when Bush stated, "Our nation, this generation, will lift the dark threat of violence from our people and our future." He concluded with his own request: "God grant us wisdom and may he watch over the United States of America."

January 29, 2002: State of the Union Address

By the time of this important address, the enemy was fully constructed, infused by more than twenty years of media and popular culture images equating Muslims/Arabs as terrorists. The United States was firmly positioned, at least in the minds of the Bush administration, as a global caretaker supported by faith in God. The enemy was a dirty, dehumanized animal that scurried to "caves" and dark places. Anyone or any country that empathized or harbored the enemy became the enemy. "They" clearly were no longer individuals but rather demonized as evildoers "who send other people's children on missions of suicide and murder. They embrace tyranny and death as a cause and a creed," and it is "equaled by the madness of the destruction they design."

In this speech, identification with evil was evident when Bush identified the nations of North Korea, Iran, and Iraq as the "axis of evil," a collection of countries that were "arming to threaten the peace of the world" with their "weapons of mass destruction." While going into detail about what these countries have done to their own and other countries' people, he pointed out, "This is a regime that has something to hide from the civilized world. States like these, and their terrorist allies, constitute an axis of evil, arming to threaten the peace of the world."

Economy as sign/symbol and power was apparent with his pronouncement of the new budget, one that nearly doubled "funding for a sustained strategy of homeland security" designed to protect the "economic security for the American people." War, the goals of an impending war, and economics were conflated when Bush stated, "We will prevail in this war, and we will defeat this recession." He assured the nation that "we can overcome evil with greater good"; that "evil is real, and it must be opposed"; and that "God is near." "Our enemies believed America was weak and materialistic, that we would splinter in fear and selfishness. They are as wrong," Bush said, "as they are evil." By this point in time, America's enemy was fully constructed and retaliation fully justified.

CONSTRUCTING THE ENEMY

The purpose of this study was to examine post–September 11, 2001, presidential rhetoric to see if the use of particular words, phrases, and allusions fit Spillman and Spillman's (1997, 50–51) enemy image construction model. In this case, while some of the characteristics (stereotyping and deindividualization, identification with evil, and zero-sum thinking) played a stronger role than others did, it is clear that the carefully chosen, mostly scripted words in President Bush's speeches were grounded in powerful connections to universal notions of enmity. In particular, historical as well as current popular culture portrayals of people of Arab/Middle Eastern descent were coupled with a rhetoric that was able to draw upon collective consciousness in order to revivify, reinforce, and ratify the Arab-as-terrorist stereotype.

Preexisting stereotypical media portrayals and presidential verbiage consistent with dominant ideology about Arabs provided the context for rigidifying the constructed Arab terrorist stereotype in a way that made such associations seem normal and logical. As a born-again Christian, Bush's crusade against terror through domination and cleansing helped fuel the persistence of anti-Arab sentiment. For him, "Evil is real," and "The evil ones must be fought" (Knickerbocker 2002, 11). Combined with verbal and visual portrayals that consistently construct Arabs as terrorists, the tragic events of September 11 gave a real face and, for many Americans, a real reason to retaliate. Presidential propaganda thereby became a powerful hegemonic tool in the organization of public support and energy in the "Hunt for bin Laden," investment in homeland security, and the "Search for Saddam."

The construction of all Arabs as terrorists and all Muslims as Arab terrorists—through political rhetoric, reducing vast populations into a single dark image—has significant consequences not only for the civil rights of individuals living in the United States but also for other citizens of the world. Early rhetoric lubricated the mechanisms through which both policy makers and the media were able to transfer targets and methods for mobilizing public support for war in Iraq. The virtually invisible process distracted the public from substantive discussions of the merits (or lack of merits) of war because of the logic inherent in constructing an enemy. The power to wage war in Iraq was not a given. Rather, consent was constructed from a combination of words and images, from nearly 1,000 films (Shaheen 2001), Gulf War cartoons (Artz & Pollock 1995), and other popular culture portrayals as well as political rhetoric, as analyzed in this chapter. The combination of this (mis)information provided the sociocultural-symbolic material, catalyzed by Bush administration rhetoric and distributed by the media, yielding support for war in Iraq.

We did not see the end of enemy image construction with the war in Iraq. The stereotype was carried from the Taliban, bin Laden, and terrorists to the axis of evil and Hussein. Since the occupation of Iraq, the evil Arab image shifted to Shiite Muslim cleric Muqtada al-Sadr and "crazed" Iraqis opposed to U.S. occupation. When such images appear, it is not simply an issue of imbalance and unfair representations (although it is that, too); rather, it is a question of why such images are necessary and prevalent. Construction of enemy images is a crucial part of the process of justifying an unjust war. It is also necessary if power elites want to move military and diplomatic policies forward without full disclosure but with maximum public support. Ultimately, such patterns have consequences for organizing citizen support for government operations and for discrimination. The ultimate consequence is, of course, loss of Arab and American lives, as has been the case in the Iraq war, and the simultaneous global cost of the loss of humanity.

Television programming largely omits Arabs from stories, and movies continue to rely upon a monolithic Arab stereotype "complete with glinty eyes and a passionate desire to kill Americans" (Said 1997, xxvii). In the absence of a continuum of roles, characters, and occupations, there are very few alternative media sources for non-Arabs to draw upon in their understanding of Arab cultures. Considering how all but European Americans are identified by some level of hyphenation, differences serve as constant reminders of "otherness" to some imaginary real American. If the United States truly is a democratic nation and Arabs and Muslims are truly "our friends," then it is important to reflect this not only in media content, but also in the hiring of writers and producers who can work in cooperation with television, news, and movie executives. Delivery of a more balanced, informed, and fairer image of Arabs (and all other minorities, for that matter) to viewers is a pedagogically crucial, long overdue move toward professional respect and responsibility to all persons in the United States and elsewhere in the world. Perhaps, then, in an odd twist of fate, the experiences of Arab Americans after September 11, 2001, will ironically serve as a crucible for our times.

REFERENCES

Artz, L., & Pollock, M. (1995). Limiting the options: Anti-Arab images in U.S. media coverage of the Persian Gulf crisis. In Y. R. Kamalipour (Ed.), *The U.S. media and the Middle East: Image and perception* (pp. 119–135). Westport, CT: Greenwood Press.

Chandler, D. (2002). *Semiotics: The basics*. London: Routledge.

False bombing suspect sues U.S. government. (1995, November 13). *Milwaukee Journal Sentinel*, 6.

Feehan, J. (2003, April 25). Patriot Act erodes freedom, activists say. *The Eugene Register-Guard*, C1.

Feldstein, F. P., & Acosta-Alzuru, C. (2003). Argentinean Jews as scapegoat: A textual analysis of the bombing of AMIA. *Journal of Communication Inquiry* 27, 152–170.

Fiebig-von Hase, R. (1997). Introduction. In R. Fiebig-von Hase & U. Lehmkuhl (Eds.), *Enemy images in American history* (pp. 1–42). Providence, RI: Berghahn Books.

Fish, S. (2001, October 15). Condemnation without absolutes. [Electronic version]. *New York Times*, A19.

Gandy, O. H., Jr. (1998). *Communication and race: A structural perspective*. London: Arnold.

Gavrilos, D. (2002). Arab Americans in a nation's imagined community: How news constructed Arab American reactions to the Gulf War. *Journal of Communication Inquiry* 26, 426.

Ghareeb, E. (Ed.). (1983). *Split vision: The portrayal of Arabs in the American media*. Washington, DC: American-Arab Affairs Council.

Goffman, E. (1974). *Frame analysis: An essay on the organization of experience*. Cambridge, MA: Harvard University Press.

Green, M. (1993). Images of American Indians in advertising: Some moral issues. *Journal of Business Ethics* 12, 323–330.

Hall, S. (1975). Introduction. In A. C. H. Smith (Ed.), *Paper voices: The popular press and social change, 1935–1965* (pp. 11–24). London: Chatto & Windus.

————. (1997). The spectacle of the "other." In S. Hall (Ed.), *Representation: Cultural representations and signifying practices* (pp. 223–279). London: Sage.

Hamada, B. I. (2001). The Arab image in the minds of western image-makers. *Journal of International Communication* 7 (1), 7–35.

Hathout, M. (1999, March 29). Group looks to bridge gap. In. C. Jones (Ed.), *View*. Retrieved April 20, 2003, from www.viewnews.com.

Hopcke, R. H. (1989). *A guided tour of the collected works of C. G. Jung*. Boston: Shambala.

Hyde, M., & McGuinness, M. (1994). *Introducing Jung*. New York: Totem Books.

Jackson, N. B. (1996). Arab Americans: Middle East conflicts hit home. In P. M. Lester (Ed.), *Images that injure: Pictorial stereotypes in the media* (pp. 63–66). Westport, CT: Praeger.

Kates, S. M., & Shaw-Garlock, G. (1999). The ever-entangling web: A study of ideologies and discourses in advertising to women. *Journal of Advertising* 28 (2), 33–49.

Keen, S. (1986). *Faces of the enemy: Reflections of the hostile imagination*. San Francisco: Harper & Row.

Kibbey, A. (2003). Editorial: Gender and the American ideology of war. *Genders Online Journal* 37. Retrieved March 6, 2003, from www.genders.org

Knickerbocker, B. (2002, February 6). As "evil axis" turns, Bush sees no blur of right, wrong. *Christian Science Monitor*. Retrieved March 20, 2004, from www.csmonitor .com/2002/0206/p01s01-ussc.html

Lasswell, H. D. (1934/1995). Propaganda. In R. Jackall (Ed.), *Propaganda* (pp. 13–25). New York: New York University Press.

Lind, R. A., & Danowski, J. A. (1998). The representation of Arabs in U.S. electronic media. In Y. R. Kamalipour & T. Carilli (Eds.), *Cultural diversity and the U.S. media* (pp. 156–167). New York: State University of New York Press.

Lippmann, W. (1922). *Public opinion*. New York: Harcourt, Brace.

Lyman, R. (2001, October 3). Bad guys for bad times: Hollywood struggles to create villains for a new climate. [Electronic version]. *New York Times*, E1.

Max, D. T. (2001, October 28). [Electronic version]. The speech. *New York Times*, 32.

Merskin, D. (2001). Winnebagos, Cherokees, Apaches, and Dakotas: The persistence of stereotyping of American Indians in American advertising brands. *Howard Journal of Communication* 12, 159–169.

Pagels, E. (1996). *The origin of Satan*. New York: Vintage.

Pilon, R. (2001, December 10). *Right, center, & left support free & open debate in wartime: Dissent does not give aid, comfort to enemy*. Remarks delivered at the National Press Club meeting, Washington, DC, by the vice president for legal affairs and director, Center for Constitutional Studies, Cato Institute, Washington, DC.

Said, E. S. (1997). *Covering Islam: How the media and the experts determine how we see the rest of the world*. New York: Vintage Books.

Shaheen, J. G. (1988). Perspectives on the television Arab. In L. Gross, J. Katz, & J. Ruby (Eds.), *Image ethics: The moral rights of subjects in photographs, film, and television* (pp. 203–219). New York: Oxford.

———. (1990, August 19). Our cultural demon—the "ugly Arab": Ignorance, economics create an unshakeable stereotype. *Des Moines Register*, A7.

———. (1995). TV Arabs. In P. Rothenberg (Ed.), *Race, class, and gender in the United States* (pp. 197–199). New York: St. Martin's.

———. (1998). We've seen this plot too many times. *Washington Post*, C3.

———. (2001). *Reel bad Arabs: How Hollywood vilifies a people*. Northampton, NY: Olive Branch Press.

Spillman, K. R., & Spillman, K. (1997). Some sociobiological and psychological aspects of "images of the enemy." In R. Fiebig-von Hase & U. Lehmkuhl (Eds.), *Enemy images in American history* (pp. 43–64). Providence, RI: Berghahn Books.

Spyrou, S. (2002). Images of the "other": "The Turk" in Greek Cypriot children's imaginations. *Race, Ethnicity, & Education* 5, 255–272.

Suleiman, M. W. (1988). *The Arabs in the mind of America*. Brattleboro, VT: Amana Books.

———. (1999). Islam, Muslims, and Arabs in America: The other of the other of the other . . . *Journal of Muslim Minority Affairs* 19, 33–48.

Takaki, R. T. (1993). *A different mirror: A history of multicultural America*. Boston: Little, Brown.

Terry, J. J. (1985). *Mistaken identity: Arab stereotypes in popular writing*. Washington, DC: American-Arab Affairs Council.

Valbrun, M. (2003, April 15). More Muslims claim they suffer job bias. *Wall Street Journal*, B1.

Zinn, H. (1995). *A people's history of the United States 1492–present*. New York: Harper Perennial.

9

The Political Rhetoric of Sacrifice and Heroism and U.S. Military Intervention

Timothy Cole

We're a peaceful nation and moving along just right and just kind of having a time, and all of a sudden, we get attacked and now we're at war, but we're at war to keep the peace.

Bush (2002b)

After the terrorist attacks of September 11, 2001, the Bush administration initiated a "global war on terror" and chartered an aggressive foreign policy course that would lead to military action and "regime change" in Afghanistan and Iraq. In this essay, I examine presidential rhetoric in a selection of national press conferences and major foreign policy addresses, from September 11, 2001, to the January, 2003, State of the Union message, in order to determine the contribution to the war effort the president has asked of the American public.

Presidential addresses of September 11, September 20, September 27, October 7, October 23, and November 8, 2001; January 29 (State of the Union message), June 1, September 11 (Ellis Island and the Pentagon), October 5, October 7, and November 25, 2002; and the January 28, 2003, State of the Union message were examined. Press briefings/conferences of September 16, September 18, and October 11, 2001; March 13, 2002; and January 2, 2003 were also examined. Each was accessed through the White House website (www.whitehouse.gov/index.html). These addresses and comments provide a good sample of President Bush's rhetoric on the war on terror. The speeches were searched for by key word (sacrifice, loss/lose, death, danger, obligation, duty, public, hero/heroism, volunteer, voluntarism, unselfish, forfeit, cost, deny/denial, risk, security, and service) in order to determine the context and tone for the president's mobilization efforts.

In the wake of the trauma of 9/11, the public might well look to President Bush to be "interpreter in chief" (Stuckey 1991; Tulis 1987), to make sense of what had happened to the nation and how it might properly respond. In bringing its attention to Iraq, Bush rhetoric relied on potent images of a nation defending itself against the predation of a malevolent savage. As Entman notes (2003, 417), with "the Bush administration's recurring use of words such as evil and war in framing September 11, paired in many media reports with searing images of the burning and collapsing World Trade towers" a culturally resonating frame was established. The frame's potency was arguably reinforced by the absence of any emergent counterframe from the media or nonadministration elites (Entman 2004). The president's remarks amounted to a rhetorical crusade, and called on a tradition of heroic American action.

But upon whom will the mantel of heroism and sacrifice rest? Are the American people being called upon to sacrifice? What this analysis will show is a nearly textbook case of rhetorical mobilization for war, *without* any concomitant requirement that the public must contribute to and sacrifice for the cause beyond "supporting the troops" and trusting the administration to aggressively protect the citizenry. In simultaneously seeking public support and quiescence, Bush rhetoric assured the public that its role would be no more than an ancillary one. In an age where media, politics, and popular culture are increasingly intertwined, the Bush administration's principal rhetorical frame could find a significant level of congruence (Entman 2003, 422) with elements of popular culture that promise results without effort, cost, or sacrifice (see, for example, Schultz 2000).

FOREIGN POLICY RHETORIC: BASIC PREMISES

A number of basic premises seek to reveal the dynamic and contestable nature of foreign policy rhetoric. First, rhetorical argument is used in order to justify political action, and to frame the circumstances or situations to which political action is responding (Stuckey 1995; Trout 1975). As Thomas Hollihan notes (1986, 382), one of the more obvious characteristics of foreign policy rhetoric is that it is "an instrumental response to the situations in which nations find themselves"; as such, a rhetorical model constitutes a central organizing argument for presenting foreign policy to the public. In this sense, it is part of the effort by political elites to shape public opinion for their own strategic purposes (Fried 1997). Consequently, this study assesses President Bush's rhetoric in order to establish the motives, or justifications, for the global war on terror, particularly as it was directed against the Taliban regime and al Qaeda in Afghanistan and Saddam Hussein's Iraq.

Second, the president has significant resources that enhance his efforts to persuade the public, in choosing the facts, events, relations, and other phenomena that are relevant in a situation, and in naming or characterizing them (Bitzer 1968; Consigny 1974). In his attempts to mobilize the public through direct rhetorical appeals, the president can invoke constitutional and "prestige" prerogatives as commander in chief and head of state, he enjoys considerable control of the foreign policy agenda, and he has access to privileged information that helps shape expectations about presidential initiatives. Further, the public's remoteness from a direct role in foreign policy enhances opportunities for policy makers to define political situations to their advantage, which emphasizes the expressive and symbolic dimensions of politics (Edelman 1988, 1993; Wander 1984). Since most people lack independent means to check definitions of situations presented to them against their immediate environment, cues from government sources frequently encounter few competing images. Presidential powers derive in significant part, then, from the techniques of direct rhetorical appeals to the people, a technique so routine as to be an essential feature of governance in American politics (Medhurst 1996; Tulis 1987, 1996). Provided that rhetorical appeals meet their expectations, the listening public *may* come to identify with presidential portrayals of reality (Ivie 1986, 91).

Third, foreign policy dramas must set into context the events to which policy is responding, by providing credible historical accounts and visions of the future. The dramatic form must also account for the behavior and motives of foreign policy actors (Hollihan 1986; Stuckey 1995). The persuasive power of a rhetorical model is not automatic. The rhetor's task is to align his or her intentions with audience expectations; images presented to advance policy interests and justify action must resonate with public values, even as they attempt to shape them. Audiences bring to the rhetorical situation their own beliefs, value judgments, and interests, which inform their expectations for, and evaluation of, rhetoric. Presumably, dissonance created by implausible dramatic accounts will fail to persuade. Framing alternatives through rhetorical arguments thus is an attempt to maximize consonance with public values (Medhurst 1996; Miller 1972). I am not suggesting that a president *merely* responds to the public voice, but even if an effort is made to shape the public's outlook by identifying policy with those values, a president has real incentives to gauge accurately the public's mood so that the clear rhetorical opportunities and advantages he enjoys are not squandered and the policies he advocates gather sufficient public support (Fried 1997).

Fourth, as Ivie has skillfully detailed (1980, 1982, 1987), metaphor is fundamental to rhetorical invention. Metaphorical entailments establish the argumentative and contestable character of political reality, and thus indicate the emphases, intentions, and interpretations of reality of the rhetor. In the invitation to the rhetorical audience to identify with particular rhetorical motives, Ivie discusses the "ever-present temptation of literalizing one metaphor to the exclusion of others . . . whenever 'a similarity is taken as evidence of an identity,' it behooves us to understand how the inference is effected" (Ivie 1982, 240, 241), for the process of literalization seeks to exclude competing perspectives. In outlining President Bush's rhetoric on the war on terror, then, it is therefore useful to identify its principal or "master" metaphors that comprise the essential terms of his argument (Ivie 1987; Lakoff & Johnson 1980; Osborn 1967).

FACING A NEW KIND OF ENEMY: PRESIDENTIAL MOTIVES FOR WAR AGAINST AFGHANISTAN AND IRAQ

President Bush's advocacy of a war against terror reveals significant continuities with the history of presidential prowar discourse, particularly the "basic appeal of a rhetorical genre that simplifies the complexities of culpability through imputations of savagery" (Ivie 1980, 294). The image of savagery is "literalized" through the use of a variety of decivilizing vehicles, or a vocabulary that portrays the "enemy's coerciveness, irrationality, and aggressiveness" (Ivie 1982, 250). The rhetorical argument that one is defending oneself against the predation of the malevolent savage, Ivie (1982) argues, is the performance of a "victimage ritual": "Voices of belligerence, disguised in the overtones of pacific ideals, promise salvation to those who would vanquish satan's surrogate" (241).

As Entman (2003) adds, "Reminding the public of the 'evil' helped to maintain their support; merely mentioning the word could cue a whole series of conscious and unconscious thoughts and feelings about September 11" (416). Moreover, by resorting to a rhetoric with significant historical continuity, and by relying on rhetorical vehicles that had framed foreign policy discourse during the Cold War (particularly the metaphor of war, the use of decivilizing vehicles, Manichean imagery, and the ritual of victimage), the administration's words and images were "highly salient in the culture, which is to say *noticeable, understandable, memorable, and emotionally charged*" (417; emphasis in original). The administration's rhetoric turned to images and terms with powerful potential to resonate emotionally with the public (Entman 2003, 416–417, 423–424).

However, the victimage ritual performed in the president's rhetoric has a particular character. As Mackin has noted (1998), "When a violent death is a symbolic sacrifice, the meaning lives on after the body is dead. Sacrifice is a particular type of victimage in which the victim is made holy." Benedict Anderson writes (1991, 144) that the

> idea of the ultimate sacrifice comes only with an idea of purity, through fatality. . . . Dying for one's country, which usually one does not choose, assumes a moral grandeur . . . from the degree to which it is felt to be something fundamentally pure.

But blood and toil from the public to win the war on terror are not components of Bush rhetoric. The victims of the 9/11 attacks, of course, gave their lives, and the basic structure of Bush rhetoric builds on the victim/scapegoat (savage) dichotomy, but the price of restoring order disrupted by terrorist violence is not, in this argument, to be paid by the public. The theme of sacrifice—to forfeit one's life for the good of the larger body politic—does not become part of the presidential motives for the war against terrorism. It could be otherwise: Jean Bethke Elshtain has argued (1992, 147) that

> a state cannot survive if it attempts to embody a universalistic ethic of *caritas*, (but) without *some* such ethic, coercion alone reigns. Hence, the importance of the "consecrated meaning" of the warrior's death. But many of the deaths, the civic sacrifices, in our own epoch have not been those of warriors but of civilians, the noncombatant sacrifices of total war. Noncombatants are molded from the same civic stuff as war fighters. And it is this shaping to and for a way of life that needs to be tended to if we are to assess the power civic identification retains to construct individual and collective identities.

The 9/11 attacks paved the way for President Bush to tap enduring themes of foreign policy rhetoric—of America as an exceptional nation destined to lead, of its victor status in the Cold War, of the economic and military capability that make the United States too powerful to abstain from a major role in the world, and now of its embarking on a global war against terror—all become part of the structure within which the victimage ritual is performed. However, the public is not being asked to pay the price of the conflict. In this, the administration at least tacitly recognized constraints against which it chose not to struggle. The president did not call "for sacrifices from the civilian population, propos[e] tax increases to cover costs, or (bolster) the Veterans Administration," notes Entman (2003, 416). Indeed, "He did the very opposite, urging Americans to consume more, asking Congress to cut taxes and VA services" (416). President Bush's rhetoric acknowledges the limits of the public's acceptance.

President Bush's rhetorical response was fundamentally ordered by the metaphor of war. It is a commonplace statement in virtually all of Bush's foreign policy speeches that the nation is at war. "Our war on terror begins with al Qaeda, but it does not end there. It will not end until every terrorist group of global reach has been found, stopped, and defeated" (Bush 2001b). As he argued in the 2003 State of the Union message (Bush 2003), "This global war against a scattered network of killers . . . goes on, and we are winning."

The confrontation with terrorist enemies is replete with Manichean imagery and themes of savagery. Bush argued on September 16, 2001 (Bush 2001a), that "this crusade, this war on terrorism, is going to take a while." In his ultimatum to the Taliban regime (Bush 2001b), the president argued,

> This is not . . . just America's fight. And what is at stake is not just America's freedom. This is the world's fight. This is civilization's fight. This is the fight of all who believe in progress and pluralism, tolerance and freedom.

And in this global contest, Bush asserted (Bush 2001d), "Every nation has a choice to make. In this conflict, there is no neutral ground."

America, Bush (2001a) said, faces "a new kind of evil . . . somebody so barbaric that they would fly airplanes into buildings full of innocent people." And

> We are not deceived by their pretenses to piety. We have seen their kind before. They are the heirs of all the murderous ideologies of the 20th century. By sacrificing human life to serve their radical visions—by abandoning every value except the will to power—they follow in the path of fascism, Nazism, and totalitarianism. (Bush 2001b)

This rhetorical frame provides a "firewall" against the practical "on the ground" difficulties of hunting down bin Laden, and (perhaps most importantly for the course U.S. policy was to take) it suggests a *series* of targets. Bush rhetoric would seamlessly transition to a principal focus on Iraq and Saddam Hussein. Osama bin Laden is mentioned only once by name (on September 20, 2001; see Bush 2001b) in Bush's remarks, even when reporters posed questions directly about him. Al Qaeda is mentioned with some frequency by Bush, but the terms "evildoers," "evil folks," "evil ones," and "evil acts" are used far more frequently. As President Bush announced military action against the Taliban regime, he noted that "today we focus on Afghanistan, but the battle is broader" (Bush 2001d), and he made clear that, while the war on terror would begin with al Qaeda, "It does not end there. It will not end until every terrorist group of global reach has been found, stopped and defeated."

As the president's attention turned to "rogue" nations (a term that dates back to the Clinton administration, and whose members included Libya, Iran,

North Korea, and Iraq) that presumably sponsor terror, the appearance of the "axis of evil" phrase in the 2002 State of the Union message takes on important connotations, reminding the public that action is required against foes who cannot be deterred or appeased:

> States like these, and their terrorist allies, constitute an axis of evil, arming to threaten the peace of the world. By seeking weapons of mass destruction, these regimes pose a grave and growing danger. They could provide these arms to terrorists, giving them the means to match their hatred. They could attack our allies or attempt to blackmail the United States. In any of these cases, the price of indifference would be catastrophic. (Bush 2002a)

Though several other states had also been identified as rogue states, by the fall of 2002 Bush rhetoric and policy were clearly directed at what was portrayed as a grave and growing threat to national security from Iraq. Bush rhetoric moves from al Qaeda to the Iraqi regime by arguing that "mad terrorists and tyrants" are equally undeterrable; just as the president indicated that the policy response to the terrorist strikes would make no distinction between those who commit acts of terror and those who harbor the terrorists, neither does the rhetoric distinguish between likely actions and motivations of al Qaeda and the Iraqi regime (Gaddis 2002). This argument is made explicitly in President Bush's 2003 State of the Union message (Bush 2003):

> Today, the gravest danger in the war on terror, the gravest danger facing America and the world, is outlaw regimes that seek and possess nuclear, chemical, and biological weapons. These regimes could use such weapons for blackmail, terror, and mass murder. They could also give or sell those weapons to terrorist allies, who would use them without the least hesitation.

The American public figures prominently in the victimage ritual that features the inhuman, savage other. The 9/11 attacks created a rhetorical situation that persuasively grounded the use of this ritual in the expectations of the public that Americans might be victims *again* in this long twilight struggle against evil; in that sense, the public may sacrifice.

The answer to the awareness that we face continuous danger is a call to vigilance. The president's call, though, is accompanied by a promise of protection. The president promised, "I will not wait on events, while dangers gather. I will not stand by, as peril draws closer and closer." President Bush's rhetoric invokes "America's duty" to undertake a global war against a far-flung enemy. We must, the president asserted in the 2003 State of the Union message, "remember our calling as a blessed country" and that our duty is "to make this world better" (Bush 2003).

WHO SHALL BEAR THE BURDEN?

Who, though, will undertake the mission? From whom is sacrifice being called? These questions bring us to the heart of the matter. The first, and most direct, answer to these questions is that the U.S. military will undertake the mission to protect and defend the American people and the American homeland. This "serve and protect" imagery may not be very surprising, but its rhetorical effect is to diminish any suggestion that the American public will be asked to directly sacrifice anything. "I gave our military the orders necessary to protect Americans, do whatever it would take to protect Americans," the president told the press after 9/11 (Bush 2001a). "And tonight, a few miles from the damaged Pentagon, I have a message for our military: Be ready. I've called the Armed Forces to alert. . . . The hour is coming when America will act" (Bush 2001b).

The response, then, will mobilize and involve the full resources of the American military and intelligence capabilities. Americans are right to be concerned, and it is understandable that many feel fear, but the president argued that "our government is taking strong precautions. All law enforcement and intelligence agencies are working aggressively around America, round the world and around the clock" (Bush 2001d). The sacrifices are clear, but the members of the armed forces are bearing them. The president's rhetoric frequently invokes the language of pain, risk, and loss, but apart from the victims of the 9/11 strikes and the psychic blow to the nation, this language is made in direct appeals to the Armed Forces:

> Today, those sacrifices are being made by members of our Armed Forces who now defend us so far from home. . . . We ask a lot of those who wear our uniform. We ask them . . . even to be prepared to make the ultimate sacrifice of their lives.

In his West Point speech, Bush told graduating cadets that "you will stand between your fellow citizens and grave danger" (Bush 2002c).

The president's admonition "to know that your government is on high alert" (Bush 2001g) emphasizes where primary responsibility for American defense lies. In arguing that terrorists would not change the American way of life, President Bush called not on the best efforts of American citizens, but on *Washington's*, to defeat the enemy. "I want to assure my fellow Americans that our determination—I say 'our,' I'm talking about Republicans and Democrats here in Washington—has never been stronger to succeed in . . . protecting our homeland" (Bush 2001f).

Washington's best efforts were intended to make the War on Terror a military undertaking fought away from the home front. The president frequently argues that, because one cannot anticipate all possible attacks on American soil, the best defense is a good offense. President Bush said on November 8, 2001:

> A lot of people are working really hard to protect America. But in the long run, the best way to defend our homeland—the best way to make sure our children can live in peace—is to take the battle to the enemy. (Bush 2001g)

The "idea of denying sanctuary is vital to protect America" (Bush 2002b). The president told the graduating class at West Point that

> the war on terror will not be won on the defensive. We must take the battle to the enemy . . . and confront the worst threats before they emerge. In the world we have entered, the only path to safety is the path of action. (Bush 2002c)

The promise of unilateral, even preemptive, action beyond the response to al Qaeda (and linking Iraq to al Qaeda) helped establish the rationale for war against Iraq: as noted earlier, by the fall of 2002 Saddam Hussein was clearly the focus of administration rhetoric.

WHAT PRICE FROM THE PUBLIC?

Perhaps this argument is not very surprising. Certainly, President Bush draws on prowar discourse with significant continuity in American history (Ivie 1982). Then, too, since the United States was struck horrifically, and since the battle is portrayed as a global war against terror, the American military should be called upon to bear the hardship of the battles to come might be expected. However, it is reasonable to ask if the president intended to steel the American public for its own sacrifices. This President Bush does not do. While aspects of the rhetorical argument suggest that life cannot be the same after 9/11, ultimately the president argues for a return to normalcy.

President Bush invokes the memory of those who died in the attacks, and lauds their courage in the face of imminent death, but what the public is asked to take away from that memory is carefully circumscribed. In his address to a joint session of Congress, Bush argued that the state of the union after the terrorist strikes is seen "in the courage of passengers, who rushed terrorists to save others on the ground" (Bush 2001b), and in his November 8, 2001, address he noted that "some of our greatest moments have been acts of courage for which no one could have prepared" (Bush 2001g). In his commemorative comments at the Pentagon on September 11, 2002, he said,

The 184 whose lives were taken in this place—veterans and recruits, soldiers and civilians, husbands and wives, parents and children—left behind family and friends whose loss cannot be weighed. The murder of innocence cannot be explained, only endured. And though they died in tragedy, they did not die (in) vain. . . . Their loss has moved a nation to action, in a cause to defend other innocent lives across the world. (Bush 2002d)

The question, though, that might logically follow—one, indeed, that the president directly asks at various points—is what does the public owe to their fellow fallen citizens? One response echoes the above discussion:

Americans are asking: How will we fight and win this war? We will direct every resource at our command—every means of diplomacy, every tool of intelligence, every instrument of law enforcement, every financial influence, and every necessary weapon of war—to the disruption and to the defeat of the global terror network. (Bush 2001b)

Americans should return to their lives, be resolute, and live the values that exemplify American exceptionalism. To the question, "What is expected of us?" the president counsels Americans to "live your lives, and hug your children," and he asks them "to be calm and resolute," to "uphold the values of America," to be patient "in what will be a long struggle," and to "continue praying for the victims of terror and . . . for those in uniform."

Another example was given in Chicago, when he exhorted the public (before an audience of airline employees) to "get on the airlines, get about the business of America" (Bush 2001c). The president argued that a primary goal of the War on Terror was to restore public confidence and "to tell the traveling public: Get on board. Do your business around the country. Fly and enjoy America's great destination spots. Get down to Disney World in Florida." The American people "have got to go about their business. We cannot let the terrorists achieve the objective of frightening our nation to the point where we don't—where we don't conduct business, where people don't shop" (Bush 2001e). Given an explicit question in the October 11, 2001, press conference about whether the public would be called upon to sacrifice, the president said, "Well, you know, I think the American people are sacrificing now. I think they're waiting in airport lines longer than they've ever had before. I think . . . there's a certain sacrifice when you lose a piece of your soul." Asked again explicitly about required sacrifice in the form of activating the draft, the president soft-pedaled any such suggestion. "Well, the country shouldn't expect there to be a draft . . . the volunteer army is working. . . . So I don't worry about, and people shouldn't worry about a draft" (Bush 2002b).

The public may live in a different world after 9/11, but the president's conclusion is not a call for *direct* action or sacrifice by the public. The president argued in Atlanta on November 8, 2001, "We're . . . a nation awakened to service" (Bush 2001g). He added that "this new era requires new responsibilities, both for the government and for our people." But what are those responsibilities, and what sort of "service" does the president suggest? As the president put it, "Many ask, what can I do to help the fight." He notes in his November 8 comments, "A terrorism alert is not a signal to stop your life. It is a call to be vigilant—to know that your government is on high alert." The president's extended use of "service" and "volunteer" in these same remarks, moreover, makes it clear that the public's role is ancillary.

The president's conclusion, to "call on all Americans to serve by bettering our communities and, thereby, defy and defeat the terrorists," is at least a step removed from a call to sacrifice; it counsels Americans to stake their claim as an "exceptional people" while the battle is waged elsewhere.

The president's 2002 State of the Union message carefully delimits what sacrifice might entail. The president notes fiscal sacrifice will be required, since "it costs a lot to fight this war"; he argues, "My budget includes the largest increase in defense spending in two decades—because while the price of freedom and security is high, it is never too high" (Bush 2002a). But this suggestion is softened as he adds, "We will win this war; we'll protect our homeland; and we will revive our economy." Juxtaposing the call to combat the "axis of evil" with promises to protect the "economic security" of citizens moves to make (through an extension of the war metaphor to the economy) a seamless connection between any number of domestic and international dimensions of "security," but it simultaneously, if implicitly, rejects putting the economy on a war footing and any suggestion that important "peacetime" priorities would have to await successful conclusion of this global war.

Similarly, in the 2003 State of the Union message, President Bush discusses the War on Terror, which by now principally targeted the Iraqi regime, only after emphasizing "normalcy" issues and telling all that they should not deny or delay meeting their daily needs or do anything more than support administration policy.

The routine invocation of the selfless heroism at "ground zero," of the airline passengers who defied the hijackers, and of the members of the armed forces who have given their lives leads directly to the question of what the surviving public owes to their sacrifice and memory. "We resolved a year ago to honor every last person lost. We owe them remembrance and we owe them more," Bush said (Bush 2002e). What more do we owe beyond remembrance? "We owe them, and their children, and our own, the most enduring monument we can build: a world of liberty and security made possible by the way America leads, and by the way Americans lead our (sic) lives." The loss of life on 9/11, the president argued, "left us to examine our own." Our "days should be filled with things that last and matter: love for our families, love for our neighbors, and for our country; gratitude for life and to the Giver of life."

POST-9/11 RHETORIC AND THE LIMITS OF PERSUASIVENESS

Given the enduring premises of the American political culture, the significant historic continuities in rhetorical motives for war employed by American presidents, and the shocking events of 9/11, perhaps it is not surprising that President Bush would resort to what can be considered a standard portrayal of the requirements of U.S. foreign policy, and that that portrayal would certainly have a ring of plausibility and persuasiveness to the American public. The drama of 9/11 and beyond perhaps reinvigorated the rhetorical advantages in being commander in chief that had been diminished by the end of the Cold War. However, to the extent that events subsequent to the initial military actions in Afghanistan and Iraq point to the United States being bogged down in a military quagmire or reveal the difficult and lengthy tasks associated with nation-building, the president's rhetoric is fraught with political risks (Cole 1999).

The image of enemy savagery, central to the victimage ritual employed by proponents of war, is meant to subvert alternative explanations for foreign policy action (and thus literalize its portrayal) by inviting the public to regard the policy response as one that must inevitably be taken. Ivie (1987) argues that the victimage ritual is enacted with generic regularity, and not only sanctifies American values but legitimizes utter victory over a foe "who is totally uncivilized and therefore perfectly evil" (178).

Two essential constraints may well limit the effectiveness of this rhetoric. First, as Ivie (1980) notes, reliance on the rhetorical pattern of victimage is a potentially unstable justification for war,

> with no guarantee of a permanent grant of public adherence. . . . As a mode of symbolic action, it depends upon the tactic of direct and indirect suggestion, on the omission of balanced and potentially conflicting information about the adversary's character, conduct, and/or condition, and ultimately, on the credibility of the administration in power. Should any of these supporting links be challenged, the spell of the ritual . . . can be weakened momentarily. (293)

The president employed a rhetoric that asked the public for support and prayer—and little else. In the days before the war against Iraq, neither the media nor nonadministration elites offered a compelling counterframe to the administration's culturally resonant images. But the weak link in the support of the administration's argument is the emergence of situations that challenge the administration's credibility. In postwar Iraq, the administration may be encountering the limits of its rhetorical persuasiveness. Mounting casualty rates, increasing reliance on National Guard and reserve units, growing insurgency, acts of terrorism in Iraq against U.S. occupation forces, and uncertainty about any meaningful international support (LaFranchi & Chaddock 2003; Tyson 2003) all raise this specter. Rhetoric used to justify the war with Iraq did not raise the issue of nation building and postwar occupation. Additionally, the continuing failure to find WMDs and the absence of evidence of an al Qaeda–Iraq link could now threaten the administration's credibility and provide the elements for the emergence of a media or elite counterframe and create the dissonance with public values that undermines the persuasiveness of its rhetoric.

The potential emergence of a counterframe and the creation of dissonance suggest a second fundamental constraint on Bush rhetoric. Let me suggest, without fully elaborating here, that the president's *not* calling for public sacrifice in the rhetoric for war was a strategic decision. President Bush's appeal for public support *and* quiescence was motivated in part by the limits of political tolerance from the American public. The administration neither received nor sought a mandate to move the public beyond its wariness (that is a legacy of the "Vietnam syndrome") of intractable conflicts, significant American casualties, and nation building that previous administrations have had (with only mixed success) to grapple with (Cole 1996, 1999). It is unclear whether, for all the ways in which the world supposedly changed after 9/11, that mood had dramatically shifted with respect to questions of the use of American armed force. What's more, media coverage tended to advance the administration's perspective by distributing metaphors from the popular culture that portrayed the conflict with Iraq as "clean, successful, largely painless, exciting, and suffused with the good feelings of potency and solidarity alike" (Hallin & Gitlin 1994, 162). What the administration asked for in its prewar rhetoric was a mandate from the public to accept its leadership to wage war against Iraq and others. The constraints that led the administration to frame its rhetoric in particular ways to achieve that prewar mandate, however, have led to significant dilemmas in the postwar situation that make it an open question whether the president's rhetoric can find acceptance. The use of a rhetorical frame that assumed public wariness and that found congruence with elements of the popular culture that promise results without effort, cost, or sacrifice (Schultz 2000) has perhaps now found the limits of its persuasiveness in the turbulence of postwar Iraq.

REFERENCES

Anderson, B. (1991). *Imagined communities: reflections on the origin and spread of nationalism.* London: Verso.

Bitzer, L. (1968). The rhetorical situation. *Philosophy and Rhetoric* 1, 1–14.

Bush, G. W. (2001a, September 16). President: Today we mourned, tomorrow we work. www.whitehouse.gov/news/releases/2001/09/20010916-2.html

——. (2001b, September 20). President declares "freedom at war with fear." www.whitehouse.gov/news/releases/2001/09/20010920-8.html

——. (2001c, September 27). At O'Hare, president says "get on board." www.whitehouse.gov/news/releases/2001/09/20010927-1.html

——. (2001d, October 7). Presidential address to the nation. www.whitehouse.gov/news/releases/2001/10/20011007-8.html

——. (2001e, October 11). President holds prime time news conference. www.whitehouse.gov/news/releases/2001/10/20011011-7.html

——. (2001f, October 23). President says terrorists won't change American way of life. www.whitehouse.gov/news/releases/2001/10/20011023-33.html

——. (2001g, November 8). President discusses war on terrorism. www.whitehouse.gov/news/releases/2001/11/20011108-13.html

——. (2002a, January 29). President delivers state of the union address. www.whitehouse.gov/news/releases/2002/01/20020129-11.html

——. (2002b, March 13). President Bush holds press conference. www.whitehouse.gov/news/releases/2002/03/20020313-8.html

——. (2002c, June 1). President Bush delivers graduation speech at West Point. www.whitehouse.gov/news/releases/2002/06/20020601-3.html

——. (2002d, September 11). President's remarks at the Pentagon. www.whitehouse.gov/news/releases/2002/09/20020911.html

——. (2002e, September 11). President's remarks to the nation. www.whitehouse.gov/news/releases/2002/09/20020911-3.html

——. (2003. January 28). President delivers "state of the union." www.whitehouse.gov/news/releases/2003/01/20030128-19.html

Cole, T. (1996). When intentions go awry: The Bush administration's foreign policy rhetoric. *Political Communication* 13, 93–113.

——. (1999). Avoiding the quagmire: Alternative rhetorical constructs for post–cold war American foreign policy. *Rhetoric and Public Affairs* 2, 367–394.

Consigny, S. (1974). Rhetoric and its situations. *Philosophy and Rhetoric* 7, 175–186.

Edelman, M. (1988). *Constructing the political spectacle.* Chicago: University of Chicago Press.

——. (1993). Contestable categories and public opinion. *Political Communication* 10, 231–242.

Elshtain, J. B. (1992). Sovereignty, identity, sacrifice. In V. S. Peterson, (Ed.), *Gendered states: Feminist (re)visions of international relations theory* (pp. 141–154). Boulder, CO: Lynne Rienner.

Entman, R. M. (2003). Cascading activation: Contesting the White House's frame after 9/11. *Political Communication* 20, 415–432.

———. (2004). *Projections of power: Framing news, public opinion, and U.S. foreign policy.* Chicago: Chicago University Press.

Fried, A. (1997). *Muffled echoes: Oliver North and the politics of public opinion.* New York: Columbia University Press.

Gaddis, J. L. (2002, November/December). A grand strategy of transformation. *Foreign Policy* 133, 50–57.

Hallin, D. C., & Gitlin, T. (1994). The Gulf War as popular culture and television drama. In W. L. Bennett & D. L. Paletz (Eds.), *Taken by storm: The media, public opinion, and U.S. foreign policy in the Gulf War* (pp. 149–163). Chicago: Chicago University Press.

Hollihan, T. A. (1986). The public controversy over the Panama Canal treaties: An analysis of American foreign policy rhetoric. *Western Journal of Speech Communication* 50, 368–387.

Ivie, R. (1980). Images of savagery in American justifications for war. *Communication Monographs* 47, 279–294.

———. (1982). The metaphor of force in prowar discourse: The case of 1812. *Quarterly Journal of Speech* 68, 240–253.

———. (1986). Literalizing the metaphor of Soviet savagery: President Truman's plain style. *Southern Speech Communication Journal* 51, 91–105.

———. (1987). Metaphor and the rhetorical invention of cold war "idealists." *Communication Monographs* 54, 165–182.

LaFranchi, H., & Chaddock, G. R. (2003, September 12). Architects of Iraq war put on the defensive. *Christian Science Monitor.* www.csmonitor.com/2003/0912/p02s01-usfp.html

Lakoff, G., & Johnson, M. (1980). *Metaphors we live by.* Chicago: University of Chicago Press.

Mackin, J. A. (1998). Sacrifice and moral hierarchy: The rhetoric of Irish Republicans, 1916–1923. *American Communication Journal*, 1. http://acjournal.org/holdings/vol1/iss3/burke/mackin.html

Medhurst, M. J. (1996). Introduction: A tale of two constructs: The rhetorical presidency versus presidential rhetoric. In M. J. Medhurst (Ed.), *Beyond the rhetorical presidency* (pp. xi–xxv). College Station: Texas A&M University Press.

Miller, A. (1972). Rhetorical exigence. *Philosophy and Rhetoric* 5, 111–118.

Osborn, M. (1967). Archetypal metaphor in rhetoric: The light-dark family. *Quarterly Journal of Speech* 53, 115–126.

Schultz, D. A. (Ed.). (2000). *It's show time! Media, politics, and popular culture.* New York: Peter Lang.

Stuckey, M. E. (1991). *The president as interpreter-in-chief.* Chatham, NJ: Chatham House Publishers.

———. (1995). Competing foreign policy visions: Rhetorical hybrids after the cold war. *Western Journal of Communication* 59, 214–227.

Trout, B. T. (1975). Rhetoric revisited. *International Studies Quarterly* 19, 251–284.

Tulis, J. (1987). *The rhetorical presidency*. Princeton, NJ: Princeton University Press.

———. (1996). Revising the rhetorical presidency. In M. J. Medhurst (Ed.), *Beyond the rhetorical presidency* (pp. 3–14). College Station: Texas A&M Press.

Tyson, A. S. (2003, October 9). US "empire" and its limits. *Christian Science Monitor*. www.csmonitor.com/2003/1009/p02s01-usfp.html

Wander, P. (1984). The rhetoric of American foreign policy. *Quarterly Journal of Speech* 70, 339–361.

10

"The Great American Bubble": Fox News Channel, the "Mirage" of Objectivity, and the Isolation of American Public Opinion

Adel Iskandar

While academics contest whether the tragic events of September 11 are indeed a historical precedent, much of the public discourse about this day has already branded it as the day that changed the world. Without reaffirming the self-fulfilling prophecies of the naïvely misinformed "clash of civilizations" thesis, I instead argue that the conceptual creation of "two worlds"—seemingly separate entities—is reflected primarily through the prisms of mediated public opinion in the United States and the rest of the world rather than through dogmatic ethnic, racial, linguistic, or economic categories. As the rift between the views on foreign policy in the United States and the rest of the world grows, the American public finds itself more misunderstood than ever before, effectively isolated from world public opinion by barriers perhaps more expansive than the two oceans that flank this nation.

Since the end of World War II and the advent of modern communication technology such as mass media, public opinion on international affairs and foreign policy in the United States has undergone a gradual yet radical transformation that has made it significantly different from public opinion elsewhere in the world. A canonical dearth on the impact that American and international network news coverage has on public perceptions of foreign policy has left these issues virtually unexamined. The U.S.-led war on Iraq in March 2003 serves as a classical and illustrative example of this phenomenon. Illustrated by the juxtaposition of images of millions demonstrating worldwide against the war with reports revealing an overwhelming support for the war among the majority of Americans, the year 2003 is evidence of the most diametric polarization of U.S. and world publics in recent memory.

In much of the international press during the war in Iraq, reports of distinctive and contrasting coverage repeatedly proclaimed that the American and world publics were watching "two different wars," reflecting a further polarization of public opinion. In the United States, the televised view of the war was provided to American households by a number of corporate national cable networks—CNN, NBC, ABC, MSNBC, and most prominently the recent trendsetter Fox News Channel (FNC). During the war in Iraq, Fox News Channel—the notorious network with a brief yet controversial history—was able to consolidate more viewers than any other cable news network. This made it the most popular among Americans, subsequently confirming it as the indispensable source of news and as a major opinion maker in the United States.

With the objective of revitalizing an interest in political communication for the study of cable news coverage of war and comparative public opinion, this chapter outlines how FNC's history and its institutional characteristics have helped bring about the "Fox Effect," in the process confirming the station as America's favorite news channel. Part of FNC's success is attributed to its brand of reporting, "news commentary," and journalistic standards. This chapter offers an analysis of objectivity as an aspiration and often-mythologized ideal—the "mirage of objectivity"—in the news industry and assesses the validity of FNC's controversial claim of "fairness and balance." The last section of the chapter outlines the impact of both the station and its reinvented approach to journalism on public opinion in the United States, and argues that the station's coverage before and during the war on Iraq may have contributed to the isolation of American public opinion from that of the rest of the world. The cognitive shift in collective public opinion, likely produced by exposure to mediated political messages that resulted in the domestic public's isolation, is referred to here as the "Great American Bubble."

THE "FOX EFFECT"

In late 1996, FNC and MSNBC were the latest additions to the cable news station roster. This happened around the same time that another channel, Al-Jazeera, was starting to make its mark in the Arab world (el-Nawawy & Iskandar 2003). FNC was the brainchild of both Rupert Murdoch and Roger Ailes. Rupert Murdoch, an Australian national who is now a U.S. citizen and global media mogul, is the primary stockholder in News Corp., an Australian corporation that owns 99 percent of FNC. Ailes, a former Republican political operative, had served as a campaign consultant for the presidential campaigns of Richard Nixon, Ronald Reagan, and George H. W. Bush (Collins

2004). Contrary to its current stature, FNC had a very humble beginning. It started with a "small, inexperienced staff and virtually no foreign presence" whatsoever (Farhi 2003). To compensate for this disadvantage, Ailes and Murdoch instead resorted to a marketing approach that eventually proved to be successful—segmentation strategy. Fundamentally, the only way that FNC could compete with its rival stations was for it to offer a "flashier" television product than other news channels. This brought forth brighter graphics, crisper presentation, and more opinionated and combative personalities—a more tabloid-style edge than any other news network on U.S. cable.

Although the station's success has been gradual, its popularity seemed to spike in the months following September 11, eventually peaking in January 2002 when FNC's audience first surpassed that of the news colossus CNN. Some had attributed this success to the post-9/11 national climate in the United States. It was then that FNC captured over 200,000 more viewers than CNN every day. Furthermore, market research has revealed that in addition to winning the daily ratings race against other U.S. news channels, FNC's viewers tend to tune in longer than those of any other network. Fundamentally, Ailes's recipe seems to have created a sense of loyalty among FNC viewers that doesn't seem to exist for its competitors.

IDEOLOGICAL MISSION

This left other news providers keen to learn the mechanism by which FNC was able to outmaneuver them. It would be naïve to assume that the station's popularity is a product of anything besides its "opinions-talk brand"—a brand that FNC transformed into a clear marketplace advantage over its competitors. Hence the station's success came as a consequence of its journalistic approach and overtly right-leaning editorialism. Public discussion and chatter about FNC's conservative sway in news coverage dates back to the controversy surrounding the 2000 presidential election, when the network's executives appointed soon-to-be-president George W. Bush's cousin, John Ellis, in charge of the station's election night vote-counting operation (Poltz 2000). It was during this time that on the night of the ballot count, FNC was the first network to declare that Bush had won the state of Florida, while other networks were still undeclared or predicted a victory by Gore. Many believe that this choice on the part of the station affected the national climate tremendously. Additionally, FNC's coverage of the election recount that ensued was definitive, making it clear that the station's executives and staff favored a particular candidate. Many feel that this and other similar institutional actions by the channel's executives laid the foundations for and helped create a voice for

conservative discourse, one that underlies a majority of the station's programming.

However, accusations that the network espouses an evidently conservative
political leaning in its broadcasts are not based on mere speculation. Instead,
it is now public that the station's executives had devised a strategic plan for
FNC, one that articulated a clearly formulated objective that was carefully
and coherently executed. FNC was constructed with a precise mission and action plan in mind. Arguments stating that the U.S. mainstream media is inherently liberal and biased were taking root, which led to Ailes's self-
described realization that there was a deepening anger among conservatives
in the United States (Collins 2004, 3). This was soon to be the mantra for the
station's programming. Ailes and Murdoch were intent on FNC serving as a
remedy for this perceived "ailment." Murdoch had often referred to CNN as
"too liberal," and Ailes was convinced that FNC should pursue the "hearts of
American viewers who felt abandoned by the mainstream media" (Collins
2004, 3).

Up until that point, according to Ailes, "Conservatives could vent their
frustrations on talk radio, but the rest of the media often ignored or ridiculed
their views" (Collins 2004, 77). Ailes's close relations to conservative talk
show hosts helped him identify a growing hotbed of audience discontent-
ment. This culminated in a poll, commissioned by Ailes, which showed that
between 65 and 75 percent of Americans believe that media in the United
States were left leaning. Whether these statistics were accurate or representative is unimportant; Ailes had discovered his niche audience. He was convinced that he could reach these disenfranchised viewers through FNC. Further, FNC's startup staff very much agreed with Ailes's mission. In one
instance, it is said that during a job interview with a potential employee, Ailes
berated journalism, accusing journalists of being liberals and declaring his
mission: "We must fight that" (73). For Ailes, this mission is one that dates
back to 1967. At a time when anti–Vietnam War sentiments were rising
among the American public, Ailes organized a special programming segment
entitled "Armed Forces Week" on the *Mike Douglas* show in which he acknowledged the military for their heroic acts (Collins 2004, 26). Ailes's position is reflected in FNC's continuing coverage of the Iraq war. FNC criticized
other media's press coverage of Bush's policy on Iraq, claiming it was an "orchestrated campaign to denigrate the Bush administration" (Hart & FAIR
2003, 141). Furthermore, Bob Woodward of the *Washington Post* revealed
that Ailes had himself advised Bush's chief political strategist Karl Rove on
how the war should be conducted (Woodward 2002).

Ailes—a temperamental, sharply witted, uncompromising, and determined
media executive—had dabbled in everything from Broadway theater to polit-

ical campaigns. His unflinching will to make FNC a success drove him to devise politicized programming that can win audiences. Ailes's success in consolidating audienceship has often been described as an ability to convert "everybody to his own church" (Collins 2004, 17). Before inspiring FNC to its astounding success, Ailes helped characterize Nixon's persona and reinvent his image ahead of the elections (Collins 2004, 27; McGinniss 1969), worked some of Reagan's early one-liners, and helped equip George H. W. Bush with enough firepower to win him an election (Collins 2004, 35). At FNC, Ailes is said to be involved in network decision making at every level, from advertising deals to the color of the studio background and the anchors' attire (Collins 2004, 81).

O'REILLY'S TALK SHOW FORMULA

Most criticism of network bias, however, comes with an assumption that these networks give voice to only one side of the political spectrum. This is not the case with FNC. The station doesn't solely invite those who espouse a conservative political leaning on its prime-time programs. ADT Research, a television news consulting firm that tracks the content of news programs, conducted a study that revealed that CNN, FNC, and MSNBC all invited similar proportions of left- and right-wing guests to their chat and interview shows. The fundamental difference, however, was found to lie in the programs' hosts. FNC hosts were found to reveal more of their own personal opinions and interrupted their guests more frequently than anchors on the other two major cable news stations.

Even FNC's chief competitors recognize this difference. Walter Isaacson, the former chairman and CEO of CNN, was quoted as saying that "Fox is driven by opinionated hosts." A good example of FNC's contrast is the striking contradictions between the two networks' leading talk shows and their hosts' personalities. FNC shows that have adopted similar agendized approaches to programming include *Hannity & Colmes* and Greta Van Susteren's *On the Record*. FNC's "boisterous style is coupled with salty conservatism," explained Poltz (2000), and the occasional Democratic guest or host is little more than "window dressing." It is these opinionated hosts whose shows are the bread and butter of FNC, since they are all scheduled during prime-time hours. Officials at FNC have often defended the network's talk shows by claiming that they should be considered the equivalents of newspapers' op-ed pages.

Nowhere is this more obvious than on FNC's *O'Reilly Factor*, hosted by Bill O'Reilly. A combative and wildly opinionated host who espouses a clear ideological line, O'Reilly differs from other network talk show hosts. While nobody watches CNN's *Larry King Live* to discover the views of Larry King (a comparatively sedate and harmlessly passive host with no decipherable political leaning), most of O'Reilly's avid followers are drawn in by his frequent and confrontational liberal-bashing diatribes described as a "bully pulpit to stump against the Clintons, anti-war protesters, and alleged government waste" (Collins 2004, 4).

While O'Reilly's frequent attacks on liberal guests have become a signature part of his show's formula, the sharp-tongued host is also known for his assertive, targeted, and unambiguous commentary. A month into the war in Afghanistan on November 8, 2001, in a discussion about the deaths of innocent civilians, O'Reilly declared: "Civilians killed, no problem. My contention is you have to fight terror with terror" (Hart & FAIR 2003, 123). It is therefore no surprise that O'Reilly publicly reprimands and assaults anyone whose position is antagonistic to his. On June 2, 2001, O'Reilly declared that "violent demonstrations [are] on the rise all over the world as capitalism comes under assault and America's college campuses are being besieged with socialist messages" (Hart & FAIR 2003, 23). This O'Reilly talk show formula seems to be consolidating more audiences for FNC. The *O'Reilly Factor* has the highest ratings of cable television talk shows, surpassing his competitor Larry King by a margin of 2 to 1.

However, there is sufficient evidence to demonstrate that these opinions and similar highly charged content find their way out of the talk shows and onto FNC's news bulletins.

DOGMATIC TRIUMPHALISM

FNC's flagship news show, the *Fox Report* hosted by Shepard Smith, is occasionally treated as a forum in which he and other anchors air their opinions and lambaste liberalism and its proponents. Smith has no qualms about letting viewers know where he stands on an issue featured in a news item. A quick eye roll—or a witty yet invective and spiteful comment—conveys his thoughts on any given issue. One of FNC's staunchest critics, Eric Alterman (1998), described FNC's news formula as a marriage of "sleaze, suck-ups and a fealty to the nuttiest elements of right-wing ideology." This ideology was no more obvious than in the U.S.-led war on Iraq. The military invasion of Iraq became a staging ground for a media battle that would showcase ever more clearly FNC's political position. It seemed that the FNC formula paid off during coverage of the war in Iraq.

The flag-waving FNC—which soon became to many the voice of the Bush administration—has benefited most in overall viewership. In the first nineteen days of the war, FNC averaged 3.3 million viewers, a 236 percent increase from the weeks preceding the war. CNN's audience fell 600,000 viewers below that of FNC. It was very clear throughout the war that the station's talk show hosts, many of its guests, and the overall attitude of its news reports supported the military initiative in Iraq.

Compared to all other stations, FNC upheld a cheerleading approach to the coverage of the war, often toeing the administration's line, both politically and militarily. While objectivity has always been an elusive task for journalists, particularly during times of war, FNC did little to provide a multitude of perspectives on the war. During military engagements in both Afghanistan and Iraq, FNC exuded heavy-handed patriotism, referring to U.S. forces as "our troops" and the enemies with such terms as "terror goons." With these characterizations and an outwardly pro-Bush leaning since September 11, FNC's numbers skyrocketed in the ratings race. This brand of patriotic journalism was coupled with a proficient, concerted, calculated, and sustained attack on all those who opposed the war, effectively defaming dissenters and demanding silence from the "doves." On one night, a FNC correspondent in Iraq referred to war protesters as the "great unwashed." On the day that Saddam Hussein's statue fell in a main Baghdad square, FNC anchor Neal Cavuto had strong vitriolic words for those who opposed the "liberation of Iraq": "You were sickening then, you are sickening now." John Gibson, another FNC anchor, said he hoped Iraq's reconstruction would not be left to the "dopey old U.N."

FNC's Iraq war coverage was reminiscent of a sporting event. Gitlin (2003) quoted FNC's military analyst, David Christian, as openly declaring that "for the military, [an Iraq war would be] the biggest Super Bowl" (44). And a Super Bowl it was. In an April 16 *New York Times* article, Jim Rutenberg stated that "[Fox New Channel's] anchors and commentators . . . skewer the mainstream media, disparage the French and flay anybody else who questions President Bush's war effort" (Rutenberg 2003). In the face of criticism, and as news of an alternative coverage came from the Arab news channels, FNC officials continued to claim that one can be unabashedly patriotic and be an effective and principled news journalist at the same time. However, it remained difficult to justify this in the days before the war began, when FNC's war soundtrack was ready on a CD labeled *Liberation Iraq Music* (Engstrom 2003). It contained theme music reminiscent of the San Francisco Orchestra rendition of the heavy metal group Metallica's hits and a marching beat with loud percussion and guitar chords. Listening to the interlude music between news segments on FNC, it was obvious that the network sought out sounds that will draw most attention—high-pitch choral arrangements, guttural and alerting. It sounds "youthful, impatient and reactionary" with "big brassy timbres" that sound more suited for an NFL intermission (Baer 2003). The music supplemented footage that showcased U.S. military might through aerial shots, motion video from battleships and atop Abrams tanks, and night vision–enhanced paratroopers landing. There was little to no footage of civilian casualties in the news bulletins, and infrastructural damage in Iraq was shown primarily via long-distance footage of smoldering buildings with voiceover military reports proclaiming accuracy in striking strategic targets.

Nonetheless, despite the video game simulator war coverage, Fox's formula has demonstrated, courtesy of the ratings race, that there is a large market for opinionated news with a patriotic twist. Rutenberg (2003) adds that "Fox has brought prominence to a new sort of TV journalism that casts aside traditional notions of objectivity, holds contempt for dissent and eschews the skepticism of government at mainstream journalism's core."

FNC's successful formula is one that most U.S. networks have emulated to capitalize on audience preferences. MSNBC recently hired former Minnesota Governor Jesse Ventura and the flamboyant, hyperconservative radio host Michael Savage in hope of reinvigorating audience interest in the network. Savage on one program declared that antiwar protesters "were committing sedition or treason." His hawkish colleague Joe Scarborough replied, "These leftist stooges for anti-American causes are always given a free pass. Isn't it time to make them stand up and be counted for their views?" (Solomon 2003b, 3). Such commentary is the most apparent and distinct symptom of a new phenomenon that is taking the U.S. news industry by storm—the Fox Effect.

Stubbornly opinionated comments from FNC news reporters, hosts, and anchors—in their singularity—may seem little more than an illustration of the First Amendment. However, in conglomeration, they serve as a political agenda that may effectively displace others, threaten journalistic integrity, and misinform the American public.

THE MIRAGE OF OBJECTIVITY

Fundamentally, modern journalism in the United States has been unequivocally driven to pursue objectivity. While the term "objectivity" itself is used loosely by journalists, media critics, and the public to describe a seemingly linear set of expectations about news coverage, it possesses some deep-rooted meanings that are enshrined in the very ethos of modern journalistic practice. It has served for decades as the invisible altar. To merely question or negate its vitality as a Utopian state that every reporter aspires to in their daily reporting is to threaten the very fabric of a profession and its philosophical underpinnings. Even as it relates to accountability, the symbolic barometer by which journalists are judged has always been this notion of objectivity. Despite this, the debate continues as to whether objectivity is truly attainable, or if is it simply an ideal. Who judges whether or not a news story is objective? Is it the audience or the reporter? During war, objectivity is often the first pillar of journalism that comes crumbling down. Coverage of the war in Iraq illustrated this phenomenon clearly.

Some scholars argue that U.S. media and their operations have changed since 9/11, making FNC's formula of journalistic opinion enmeshed with nationalistic fervor simply more attractive. War and warlike circumstance often prompt an increased sense of nationalism and patriotic fervor, something the FNC has been successful in capitalizing on. These are times when the audience is more likely to embrace the government's spin, leaving little to no room for such civic journalistic responsibilities as the hallmark "watchdog" role.

According to el-Nawawy and Iskandar (2002), "'Objectivity' has come to imply both a media practice of information collection, processing, and dissemination, and an overarching attitude" (1). It signifies the adoption of a position of detachment toward the "object" of reporting, suggesting the absence of subjective and personalized judgment, both as overt opinion and subtle preference. And while media practitioners, namely reporters, and the institutions they work for are often held to a high standard of "objectivity," media audiences, the consumers of print and electronic news, are not expected to be similarly objective in their viewing. Furthermore, it is apparent that objectivity as a mantra for journalism has become unworkable and virtually obsolete except for anecdotal purposes. Objectivity as a core ideal in journalistic practice is simply impossible to attain.

The alternative that emerged during the war on Iraq is the debate around a new conceptualization of journalistic standards. El-Nawawy and Iskandar (2002, 2003) and El-Nawawy (2003) offered "contextual objectivity" as a conceptual framework that both illuminates and reconciles the two seemingly disparate tendencies of journalistic practice: the tensions between instinct and rationality, empiricism and relativism. Contextualization demonstrates a situational perspective, a means of creating collectivism among participants within the same context. This would encompass awareness, sensitivity, and tailoring to cultural, religious, political, and socioeconomic environments. Applied to the work of reporters, it explains the desire to adapt the message to its audience. Within this notion of contextual objectivity, the conceptualization of objectivity is transformed instead from its positivist, reductionist, and fundamentally empirical definition to one where it implies neutrality and a multiplicity of subjectivities. The sum of all opinions is then heralded as the truth. In journalistic terms, this is what media practitioners refer to as fairness and balance. Evenhandedness in war news coverage allows for all sides of the story to be represented and makes it possible for the reporter to speak to the "enemy." When there is equilibrium, the scales of the balance are equal. Objectivity implies that there is no need for the balance since "facts are facts, and truths are truths."

RESURRECTING THE PARTISAN PRESS

While the notion of objectivity is relatively recent in the history of journalism—accentuated by the power and outreach of mass media—it was preceded by generations of partisanship in the popular press. Just sixty years ago, in 1944, the *New York Times* ran a headline declaring, "We Strike at the Japs." Even earlier, during times of relative peace, the print press was filled with opinions and perspectives. In fact, that is how such newspapers as the *Tallahassee Democrat*, the *Arkansas Democrat-Gazette*, and the *Albany Democrat-Herald* got their names. Political alignment and journalism were not irreconcilable. To this day, in other nations with a vast journalistic tradition, news with perspective remains acceptable in the print press. In Britain, for instance, readers are aware of the political leanings of all the major newspapers and make their purchases accordingly. While major dailies in the United States often reflect subtle political sways, their content is always formalized and accented by the absence of agenda or opinion. Instead they are expected to reflect both sides of the political spectrum and answer to a diverse and generalized readership. These ideals have been the underlying principles of news provided by the electronic media.

However, the arrival of FNC has reinvented and reinvigorated partisanship in the press, thereby creating a model for its application in the television broadcast realm. Station officials were smart enough to recognize the potential benefits of returning to a partisan press. This phenomenon is lamented by those network officials who continue to operate on the traditional standard of "objectivity." Andrew Heyward, the president of CBS News, said, "There is a longstanding tradition of middle-of-the-road journalism that is objective and fair—I would hate to see that fall victim to the Fox effect" (Schifferes 2003b).

As a way of reconciling the implausibility of objectivity as a rational ideal for journalistic practice with the journalism's responsibility to the public, contextual objectivity is offered as a novel approach. Instead, contextual objectivity elucidates the importance of an egalitarian incorporation of multiple perspectives in coverage while retaining sufficient context to make content meaningful and relevant to respective audiences. This approach is now being applied by several television networks, including Qatar-based satellite station Al-Jazeera.

FNC's slogans "fair and balanced" and "We Report. You Decide"—products of Ailes's campaign to situate and describe FNC's operations (Collins 2004, 78)—illustrate ideals similar to those of contextual objectivity. However, FNC appears to use these mottos to serve a different purpose. FNC clearly does not present news from multiple perspectives as expressed previously. Instead the terms "fairness" and "balance" are employed specifically not as descriptors of the station's coverage but as an overarching mission that relates to the workings of other media outlets. The belief stated earlier by FNC executives that all mainstream media are tilted to the left has provided the station with a reason to present news from the right. Hence, by providing news and commentary with a conservative twist, FNC would be leveling the playing field by providing "balance" and providing a state of equilibrium.

Accordingly, there seems to be an audience for FNC's news. *Fox Report*, hosted by Shepard Smith, is considered the channel's "impartial" nightly news program. Although less interactive than most FNC programs, there are several patterns that distinguish *Fox Report* from other news programs. Overall, reporters tend to voiceover footage of people speaking for themselves, also choosing sound bites from press conferences over one-on-one interviews (Murry 2001). These choices raise questions of professionalism about FNC's news coverage and cast a shadow over all of FNC's reports.

Collins (2004) interviewed Smith about his jingoistic approach to news and his frequent reference to U.S. troops as "our" troops and the incorporation of an American flag as a graphic in the *Fox Report*. His response, Collins writes, could very well be FNC's creed. "Fuck them," Smith responds to his critics:

> They are our troops. . . . We needed a little something to rally around. I admit
> no apologies. I think the vast majority of Americans are absolutely on board
> with that. They understand we can be credible journalists, fair and balanced
> about everything that we do, and still be on our side. (212–213)

THE GREAT AMERICAN BUBBLE

The irony of FNC claims such as "We Report. You Decide" and "Fair and Balanced" was lamented by many scholars and media critics (e.g., McChesney 2003). Some believe that the only reason why FNC needs to cling to this façade of evenhandedness is because the station's right-leaning audience needs it—they would feel betrayed otherwise. This argument posits that it is vital that such audiences get affirmation that what they are watching is indeed "the truth."

ADT Research found that cable news networks appeal to two distinct types of audiences: highly ideological so-called news junkies whose daily entertainment derives from the overheated debates of the political class, and a less committed group who relies on experienced newsgathering when a global crisis hits the headlines. It appears that CNN's audience can be associated with the latter and FNC's with the former.

In some cases, news, commentary, and talk show programs on FNC offer more than just opinion. In a more engaged, interactive, and some may say populist approach, FNC has taken its political agenda to the people, advocating audience participation in politically motivated actions. Partisanship bordering on populist public mobilization extends far beyond political and social commentary. With persuasive appeal and the intention to enlist and stir up public support and action in favor of the network/anchor's views, FNC places itself in virtually uncharted terrain in terms of standards of journalism. Bill O'Reilly, host of FNC's *O'Reilly Factor*, is a self-proclaimed man of the people who rallies public opinion for the causes he is impassioned about.

In much the same way the military trained its personnel before the launch of the war, FNC employed its coverage to rally populist support for the war. Anchors became political commentators; news bulletins were packed with ideology and political partisanship. The assumption that network coverage affects approval rates for the war is confirmed when rates skyrocketed as Americans saw on their TV sets that the U.S. troops were making progress. However, with Al-Jazeera's airing of a video of U.S. POWs and casualties, in a mere two days, positive perception of the war fell by almost 30 percent among those who were surveyed. For this reason, FNC kept its audience on a strict regimen of positive news throughout the first few months of the war.

FNC's coverage of the war has several characteristics: (1) complete trust and reverence in the Bush administration's decisions, (2) usage of hyperpatriotic rhetoric, and (3) disqualification and marginalization of all alternative narratives—including domestic liberal and dissenting voices, regimes of other nation-states, publics of other countries, and so on. With most Americans going to television for their news, and with FNC's audience increasing exponentially, it is no doubt that the majority of Americans believed that the war was the right decision, before and during the war, and Bush's approval rates were high (Pew Center 2003a). Even before the war, shifts in U.S. public opinion were underway. According to a Pew Research poll from 2002, the political views of those who regularly watch cable news networks shifted strongly to the right (Shafer 2003). The poll also found that 46.4 percent of regular FNC viewers self-identified as "conservative" or "very conservative," while 17.7 percent self-identified as "liberal" or "very liberal." A later survey

(Pew Center 2003b) revealed that two-thirds of those surveyed had clearly positive words in their description of the U.S. President George W. Bush.

Like most U.S. networks' coverage of the war, FNC relied heavily on military informants, Central Command (CENTCOM) press conferences and releases, reports from embedded reporters, in-house military generals, and government officials who relayed a coherent view of the war and how it was progressing. Balance was replaced with hyperpatriotic rhetoric. FNC's formatting and stylistic choices in their coverage of the war, as described elsewhere in the chapter, reflected an unflinching support for American involvement in the war, while reviving and stirring nationalistic fervor.

Since the events of September 11, FNC's success has been deep-rooted in a nation in mourning and fear, needing reaffirmation and security. FNC provided this post-9/11 and through the wars in Afghanistan and Iraq. For instance, following 9/11, FNC was the first station to incorporate the American flag in its coverage (Collins 2004). Although most other American networks soon adopted the flag, FNC considered it the station's trademark. From that point forth, FNC staff had decided that the wars that ensued were not just wars, but their wars. Journalists or otherwise, Americans needed to support the administration's campaign. FNC was determined to turn Americans' fright and confusion into moral certainty and defiance.

However, the most evident complication of hyperpatriotic coverage is its inability to reconcile audience responses to success and failure in the battlefield. Military success in Iraq is greeted with calls of heroism that confirm FNC's coverage. Failures and the human cost of war often create a deep dissonance that FNC cannot manage. In some cases, losses are shrouded either in further hyperbolical patriotism and exaggerated demonization of the "enemy" or in omission or neglect of news stories. In some instances, FNC accused messengers with any negative news from Iraq, including reporters for other stations, Iraqi civilians, guests on the station, and other networks, of working against the U.S.-led coalition. *Fox Report* host Smith explains, "Once we're in this war, it's us against them. . . . And we're going to win" (Collins 2004, 213).

Another characteristic of FNC's coverage of the Iraq war has been the banishing, silencing, and criticism of liberal discourses generally and antiwar voices specifically. The "marginalization and displacement" of such voices has often reached coercive proportions. For example, a month before the launch of the war on Iraq, on February 26, 2003, O'Reilly stated, "Once the war . . . begins, we expect every American to support our military, and if they can't do that, to shut up." He then added, "Americans, and our allies, who actively work against our military once the war is underway will be considered enemies of the state by me" (Hart & FAIR 2003, 144). Only weeks later, he was quoted saying that "any American who commits civil disobedience in this time of war and terror is putting other Americans in danger" (145). On FNC, the attack on all those who opposed the war was even more abrasive for nation-states whose governments did not support the military campaign. In fact, O'Reilly's diatribes on European countries were in full swing even preceding the buildup for war on Iraq. On June 13, 2002, he declared that "the entire European Union is a problem in the war on terror, not just Deutschland." A Pew Center poll also demonstrated that there was growing public antagonism toward antiwar voices. Forty-five percent of those polled said they had heard too much from those who oppose war (Pew Center 2003a), an opinion strongly held and expressed by FNC hosts.

Attitude (Gitlin 2003) and partisanship win audiences. By forcing viewers to take sides at the expense of rationality, FNC's news and commentary often posited "good" and "evil" as binaries in continuous conflict. It allows them to defame anyone, and provides them with the agency to incorporate any issue into public discourse or eliminate any issue from it. Even on the cohosted show, *Hannity & Colmes*, Sean Hannity (the conservative) almost consistently mauls Alan Colmes (the liberal) to illustrate the consistent triumph of conservatism.

THE NEW MEDIA LANDSCAPE

Most troubling about the public opinion on media coverage in the United States is that the networks perceived to be most "reliable" are the least watched. A Pew Center for the People and the Press poll found that while 37 percent of those surveyed thought CNN was the most reliable source for news, compared to 24 percent for FNC, the latter remains the most popular cable news provider in the United States. Hence, to compete, other networks must reprioritize to understate the importance of reliability and focus on the winning formula. If they want a piece of the cake, cable news channels have found themselves needing to emulate FNC's style and approach.

For a period, in an attempt to tap into the growing conservative public sentiment, news networks found themselves trying to "outfox Fox." In February 2003, a month before the start of the war in Iraq, MSNBC decided to discontinue the liberal-leaning talk show *Donahue* while hiring a slew of ideologues who espouse reactionary conservative positions. Two strongly Republican hosts, former U.S. Representatives Dick Armey of Texas and Joe Scarborough of Florida, were now on the station's payroll. The network also hired the fiery-tongued radio personality Michael Savage whose rants about immigrants, gays, and women are known to be outrageous. However, Savage's stint was short, and he was fired six months after his appointment for labeling a caller a "sodomite" and saying that he hoped the caller would die of AIDS. These changes in MSNBC's staff lineup represent a clear political turn to the right. MSNBC even added a special section called "America's Bravest," where viewers could send pictures of their loved ones serving in the armed forces in Iraq.

Even at CNN, it is reported that Isaacson held a meeting with top staff members to discuss the possibility of pushing CNN's news philosophy toward that of FNC News' discussion-opinion style. In the end, those in attendance voted against this transformation, with Isaacson citing that "it's not always about ratings or newsstand sales. Having a sense of mission is important too." The outcome of this phenomenon is the narrowing of mediated and public discourses about politics generally and the war in Iraq specifically, as well as the gradual isolation of U.S. public opinion.

Veteran CNN correspondent Christiane Amanpour, in an interview on CNBC, admitted that her network and others had "self-muzzled." She explained that her station "was intimidated by the administration and its foot soldiers at Fox News" (Zerbisias 2003, A10). She added that this created a climate of "fear and self-censorship" as far as the type of material that was broadcast out of Iraq. She expressed that the problems with the coverage were both in the tone of the reporting and in the avoidance of the most critical questions: "It looks like this was disinformation at the highest levels," she explained (Zerbisias 2003, A10).

While many have accused American media generally and FNC specifically for the gung ho yahooing and outright cheerleading they did during the war in Iraq, conservative media watchdogs in the United States actually claimed that FNC did the best job from a journalistic standpoint. The Media Research Center (MRC), one such organization, released an assessment of U.S. networks' coverage of the war in which they heralded FNC as the best name in news, while sharply criticizing ABC, CBS, and NBC. Throughout the document, poor journalism was exemplified by hosts who presented any opinion that opposed the war. Even interviews with Iraqi civilians asking them about their feelings toward the war were seen as questionable (Brennan 2003). In the report's analysis of FNC's coverage, MRC's Brent Baker and Rich Noyes exclaimed that FNC refused to "embrace the reflexive skepticism of most of the media elite." They added that FNC's audience was "not misled by the unwarranted second-guessing and negativism that tainted other networks' war news." They went on to congratulate those who chose FNC as their preferred source of war news since the station refused to "fall into the standard traps of repeating liberal conventional wisdom as fact" (Brennan 2003, 26).

Carson and Kaye (2003) argue that FNC's war coverage in Iraq is reminiscent of an authoritarian society, where the media would be coerced to cover
news in this fashion; in this case, though, FNC volunteered (Carson & Kaye
2003). Carson and Kaye even compare FNC's approach to the information-
dissemination patterns of the Third Reich: "Demonizing conflicting viewpoints is the channel's polemical specialty even in peacetime, and in wartime
it's pretty much 'Goebbels, bar the door'" (2003, 35).

The end result is that—whether or not FNC is responsible—news audiences in the United States seem to be increasingly conservative. What is clear,
however, is that FNC caters to, encourages, and capitalizes on this trend. As
information becomes more and more centralized and consistent, the narrower
audience perception gets.

RIFT IN PUBLIC OPINIONS

A now-famous audience research study—conducted by the Program on International Policy Attitudes (PIPA) based out of the University of Maryland—
announced results indicating that FNC viewers are more misinformed than
viewers of other network news outlets. For instance, the study found that 80
percent of regular FNC viewers believed one or more of the following misconceptions: that there was evidence of al-Qaeda links in Iraq, that weapons
of mass destruction (WMD) had been found in Iraq, or that world public opinion was favorable toward the Iraq war (PIPA & Knowledge Networks 2003,
13). National Public Radio (NPR) and PBS audiences were least likely to
hold such misconceptions—only 23 percent.

When analyzing FNC's content, it becomes obvious how such misconceptions are ossified. The extent of misinformation presented throughout
FNC's programming is phenomenal. Fundamentally, shifts in public opinion,
however, are not a product of FNC's coverage alone. Instead, the station's
coverage is simply emblematic of a movement in the news media. Even syndicated talk radio is taking a sharp turn to the right. Clear Channel Worldwide Incorporated is the single largest radio station owner in the United
States—running approximately 1,200 stations. Clear Channel stations across
the country orchestrated a ban on songs by musicians such as the Dixie
Chicks and Ani DiFranco for making antiwar remarks and for expressing
anti-Bush sentiments. Clear Channel also organized a couple of hundred
"patriotic rallies" around the country to advocate the prowar agenda and
used their radio power to promote these. Much like FNC's application of the
notion of "balance" described earlier, Clear Channel executives argued that
their promotion of these political rallies is a response to what they expressed

was an attempt by the "liberal" media to "marginalize the voices of patriotic Americans" (Schifferes 2003a)

These views are in sharp contrast to those around the world. Another Pew Center survey conducted in mid-March showed that U.S. favorability ratings had plummeted throughout the world in the six months preceding the war in Iraq: 48 percent in Britain, 31 percent in France, 28 percent in Russia, 25 percent in Germany, 14 percent in Spain, and 12 percent in Turkey (Solomon 2003a). Solomon, like many, believes that the reason for this clear and gaping rift is the media's representation of world public opinion. This is accentuated once the Iraq war issue is presented. In three polls conducted between January and May 2003, citizens of fifty-six countries were surveyed. With the exception of the United States, not a single one showed a majority support for unilateral action in Iraq. Further, survey respondents in thirty-four of thirty-eight countries opposed having their nations support a war in Iraq.

However, among FNC viewers in the United States, 35 percent of them believed that the majority of people in the world favor the U.S. decision to go to war, 7 percent more than the viewers of any other station (PIPA & Knowledge Networks 2003). In fact, taken cumulatively, a total of 56 percent of all those surveyed believed that world public opinion supported the war in Iraq. These and other results illustrating the incongruence of public opinion in the United States with public opinion around the world—as well as the perception of this public opinion—demonstrate the extent of the U.S. public's isolation. Combined with rampant ignorance about international affairs and the workings of intergovernmental institutions, the consistent misinformation of the American public is the responsibility of media outlets whose prime objective is to inform their audience. When 79 percent of those surveyed feel that war coverage in the media was "excellent" or "good," and 83 percent of those who supported the war felt media coverage of the military campaign was "excellent" or "good" (Pew Center 2003a), it is crucial to question the content and approach of journalism in the United States.

This chapter attempted to position the institutional operations and practices of FNC and the communication strategies employed by the station during the buildup to the war on Iraq. It raised crucial questions about the traditional standards and functions of journalistic practice, their applicability during periods of political strife, and their durability in the face of pressures from powers embedded in the military-industrial complex, the nation-state, and the public audience. The chapter also drew attention to the persuasive and pervasive appeals by institutionalized media in their coverage of conflict and its demonstrated impact on public opinion. Like other contributions in this volume, this chapter suggested that a climate of public sentiment was created by some media organizations such as FNC that facilitated support for the war on Iraq.

It is imperative that mass communication research on war coverage engages some of these recent cataclysmic phenomena. From a reevaluation of "objectivity" as a journalistic standard to a dramatic transformation of the U.S. news media as illustrated by FNC, there is an urgent need for thorough and responsible examinations of the impact these have on an increasingly solitary American public. It is vital that news media in the United States are held accountable and required to both fulfill their obligations of informing the public and exercise their constitutionally protected rights. Only then can the "Great American Bubble"—whose shielding opacity has kept the U.S. public in solitude—be burst.

REFERENCES

Alterman, E. (1998, March 23). Murdoch kills again. *Nation*, 6.

Baer, A. (2003, April 17). The sounds of war: Rating the news networks' music. *Slate*. Retrieved July 18, 2003, from slate.msn.com/id/2081608/

Brennan, P. (2003, April 24). ABC's war coverage worst, Fox's best, analysis shows. *NewsMax.com*. Retrieved July 17, 2003, from www.newsmax.com/archives/articles/2003/4/24/164833.html

Carson, T., & Kaye, C. (2003, July 1). Collateral damage: War coverage to make a good American proud. *Esquire*, 34–37.

Collins, S. (2004). *Crazy like a fox: The inside story of how Fox news beat CNN*. New York: Portfolio.

El-Nawawy, M. (2003, April 8). Whose truth is being reported? *Christian Science Monitor* 95, no. 92: 9.

El-Nawawy, M., & Iskandar, A. (2002, Fall/Winter). The minotaur of "contextual objectivity." War coverage and the pursuit of accuracy with appeal. *Transnational Broadcasting Studies Journal*. Retrieved July 22, 2003, from www.tbsjournal.com/Archives/Fall02/Iskandar.html

———. (2003). *Al-Jazeera: The story of the network that is rattling governments and redefining journalism*. Boulder, CO: Westview.

Engstrom, N. (2003). The soundtrack for war. Columbia Journalism Review, 42 (1): 45–47.

Farhi, P. (2003, April). Everybody wins: Fox news channel and CNN are often depicted as desperate rivals locked in a death match. *American Journalism Review* 25 (3): 32–36.

The first casualty of war. (2003, May 3). *Economist*, 66.

Gitlin, T. (2003). We disport. We deride: It's all attitude, all the time at FOX News. *American Prospect* 14 (2): 43–45.

Hart, P., & Fairness & Accuracy in Reporting (FAIR). (2003). *The oh really? factor: Unspinning Fox News Channel's Bill O'Reilly*. New York: Seven Stories Press.

McChesney, R. (2003). Foreword: The golden age of irony. In P. Hart & Fairness & Accuracy in Reporting (FAIR), *The oh really? factor: Unspinning Fox news channel's Bill O'Reilly* (pp. 7–10). New York: Seven Stories Press.

McGinniss, J. (1969). *The selling of the president.* New York: Trident Press.

Murry, B. (2001). Fox news, fair and balanced—not. *St. Louis Journalism Review* 32 (242): 4–5.

Pew Research Center for the People and the Press. (2003a, March 25). *Public confidence in war effort falters: But support for war holds steady.* Retrieved July 27, 2003 from http://people-press.org/reports/display.php3?ReportID=177

———. (2003b, April 9). *War coverage praised, but public hungry for other news.* Retrieved July 27, 2003, from http://people-press.org/reports/display.php3?Report ID=180

Poltz, D. (2000, November 22). Fox News Channel: It's not fair. It's not balanced. So what? *Slate.* Retrieved July 22, 2003, from http://slate.msn/toobar.aspx?action= print&id=93999

Program on International Policy Attitudes (PIPA) & Knowledge Networks. (2003, October 2). Misperceptions, the media and the Iraq war. Retrieved October 21, 2003 from www.pipa.org/OnlineReports/Iraq/Media_10_02_03_Report.pdf

Rutenberg, J. (2003, April 16). Cable's war coverage suggests a new "Fox effect" on television. *New York Times*, B9.

Schifferes, S. (2003a, April 1). Analysis: U.S. media under fire. *BBC News.* Retrieved July 27, 2003, from http://news.bbc.co.uk/go/pr/fr/-/1/hi/world/americas/2904073.stm

———. (2003b, April 18). Who won the U.S. media war? *BBC News.* Retrieved July 17, 2003, from http://news.bbc.co.uk/1/low/world/americas/2959833.stm

Shafer, J. (2003, February 26). Donahue never had a chance: Don't blame Phil or MSNBC for his failure. Blame the cable audience. *Slate.* Retrieved July 22, 2003, from http://slate.sn.com/toolbar.aspx?action=print&id=2079326

Solomon, N. (2003a May 9). Introspective media not in the cards. *Znet.* Retrieved July 27, 2003, from www.zmag.org/content/print_article.cfm?itemID=3593&sectionID=15

———. (2003b, October 2). Unmasking the ugly anti-American. *Media Beat.* Retrieved April 30, 2004, from www.fair.org/media-beat/031002.html

Woodward, B. (2002). *Bush at war.* New York: Simon & Schuster.

Zerbisias, A. (2003, September 16). The press "self-muzzled" its coverage of Iraq war. *Toronto Star*, A10.

11

Preemptive Strikes on the Cultural Front: Big Radio, the Dixie Chicks, and Homeland Insecurity

Matthew A. Killmeier

On March 10, 2003, on the cusp of the U.S. invasion of Iraq, the lead singer of the country band the Dixie Chicks made a remark that triggered spectacular displays of the resonance and power of popular music in American society. Before an audience in London, Natalie Maines said, "Just so you know, we're ashamed the president of the United States is from Texas." The remark became the basis for the band's thirty-day ban on Cumulus Media Inc.'s country music stations; a similar ban on Clear Channel Communications, Inc. stations; staged demonstrations; and death threats. Cumulus' action, and its Chairman Lewis W. Dickey Jr., became the subject of pointed questions by U.S. Senator John McCain during a July 2003 Senate Commerce Committee hearing underscoring criticism of media concentration and its power. Like the near-ubiquitous support for the invasion by mainstream news media, and the accompanying active disciplining of dissenters, the radio industry worked to police the broadcasting of popular music to contribute to a cultural climate favorable to the "preemptive" attack on Iraq. An increasing concentration of power in large, corporate radio groups; right-leaning management and ownership; and the need to actively "preempt" cultural dissent combined to vigorously discipline the Dixie Chicks.

This chapter aims to unpack the larger meaning of the reactions to this rather benign remark; what it suggests about the relationship between politics and popular music in general, and country music in particular; and how this relationship is impacted by the increasing power of big radio vis-à-vis the recording industry, artists, and listeners. The flap following the remark has less to do with its content or the perceived conservative cultural politics of country music per se, but is a manifestation of vigorous attempts to police the fragile articulation between the hegemonic political bloc of the new right and the popular culture it's worked to co-opt and incorporate. Country music, the most popular American music with a close association and appeal to the demographic and regional strongholds of the new right's base, is a site of struggle for the cultural work of hegemony and the manufacture and reinforcement of consent. This fragile, tenuous linkage is made, reinforced, and policed in the processes of mediation between the work of country artists and its interpretation by listeners, and recent changes in the radio industry have given it greater power over the processes of mediation. Before exploring pertinent elements of country music and changes in the radio industry, I will explore some theoretic underpinnings of my arguments and approach.

POPULAR CULTURE AND POLITICS

For cultural theorists, popular culture is a site of struggle over meaning and identity, as well as a site where the culture industries in capitalist societies attempt to co-opt expression toward hegemonic ends. Popular culture's importance lies not only in its widespread influence—the market definition of "popular"—but also as it is a key space for working-class expression and interpretation; that is, popular culture taps real elements of social experience in the process of creating cultural commodities (Hall 1981). It is therefore fraught with contradictions.

> If the forms of provided commercial popular culture are not purely manipulative, then it is because, alongside the false appeals, the foreshortenings, the trivialization and shortcircuits, there are also elements of recognition and identification, something approaching a recreation of recognizable experiences and attitudes, to which people are responding. (Hall 1981, 233)

Particularly for the working class, popular music is a key cultural entity contributing to understanding the past and the present and a key linkage to the hegemonic bloc of the new right.

There is an assumed, implied, and oftentimes explicitly stated belief about the conservative cultural politics of country music, an oversimplification that rests on the assumption that artists, audiences, and the broad and deep collection of work encapsulated in the industry genre "country" are homogenous in political terms. A number of considerations obviate any simplistic linkage between a political bloc and popular music. The polysemic nature of popular music, partly a function of its generic encoding and commodity status, precludes homogenous interpretation and any simplistic linkage to a hegemonic culture. Furthermore, it is a product of concentrated, rationalized cultural industries and forms—recording labels, distributors, retailers, radio stations, radio conglomerates, and music videos—that intervene at various levels between the production of songs and albums and their interpretation by listeners. The country industry generally situates overtly political music as commercially nonviable; thus, support is limited. Bands and musical artists may espouse political viewpoints in their songs, or support political platforms, parties, or candidates; however, in country music, particularly since its construction as a viable, commercial genre in the 1950s, this is generally the exception (Malone 1985). In addition, the social status of popular music as entertainment in a rather depoliticized society means that most listeners will not interpret music or musicians as inherently political. As Negus (1996) notes, straightforward "readings" of popular music are fraught with problems: "They are based on a simplistic model of how the meaning of popular music is produced and communicated; they are based on the idea that a song has a straightforward 'message' that is then transmitted, received and understood" (193). While the song's lyrics and producers' intentions provide some of the material from which meanings are drawn, the processes of mediation and articulation and the social, historical, and cultural contexts in which audiences make meaning are key elements of the process of constructing a cultural politics of popular music. Country music exhibits the "double-stake" in popular culture, "the double movement of containment and resistance," in particular as it is one of the key cultural forms that explicitly and consistently draws upon elements of the popular reservoir of the American past for contemporary meanings about the past and present (Hall 1981, 228).

Gramsci's (1971) concept of hegemony describes the processes through which political actors and blocs gain and maintain power through consent. When a particular hegemonic bloc is dominant, its ideas, values, and sociopolitical practices, Gramsci argues, are seen as common sense and as relatively safe from question, challenge, or critique. Williams (1977) stressed the increasing importance of cultural forms in cultivating and sustaining hegemony, supplementing hegemony in political economy and civil society in culture. Hegemony, or hegemonic culture, links the conceptualization of culture as a whole way of life to power and domination in capitalist societies (Williams 1977). A key way in which popular culture contributes to a hegemonic culture is through drawing upon elements of the past through what Williams describes as "incorporation" (1977, 115) and Hall as "transformation" (1981, 228), and reworking them to create what Williams terms a "selective tradition" (115) that resonates in the present. Selective tradition is constructed "in the interest of the dominance of a specific class" and provides "a version of the past which is intended to connect with and ratify the present" (Williams 1977, 116). The selective tradition of country, explored below, provides generative material for hegemonic processes; however, the chapter is also concerned with the construction and maintenance of hegemony at the macro level of society.

Negus's (1996) arguments about the concept of mediation are instructive for understanding how popular music is linked with or encompassed by a cultural politics. Mediation comprises intermediary actions, which refer "to the practices of all the people who intervene as popular music is produced, distributed and consumed" (Negus 1996, 67); transmission, which is the "way that media technologies have been used for the distribution of sounds, words and images of popular music" (68); and the mediation of social relationships, which refers to "how power and influence [are] exercised through such mediated relationships [intermediary activity and transmission] and how this has a direct impact on the creation and reception of manufactured objects" (69). The processes of mediation occur where attempts are made to link popular music with particular political meanings that are neither wholly prefigured in the content nor stable over time.

Linking popular music with political values—the attempt to craft a cultural politics—can be further understood from a political economy perspective as a process of articulation. According to Negus (1996),

> For a song to be fully realized, for it to have any social meaning, then its production has to be connected to consumption, to an audience for the song. In this way artist and audience can be said to "articulate," in the sense that articulation involves a process whereby elements are connected that do not necessarily have to belong together. (134)

Negus is drawing upon Hall's (1986) elaboration on Marx's (1973) theory of the dialectic relationship between production and consumption and the processes in between—distribution and exchange—that comprise "distinctions within a unity" (Marx 1973, 99). For Marx, while production is the determinative moment, it is partly constituted by distribution, exchange, and consumption. However, with commercial popular music, the initial creation of music and songs is a distinct type of production.

> The production of popular music can be called "industrial" only in its promotion and distribution, whereas the act of producing a song-hit still remains in a handicraft stage. The production of popular music is highly centralized in its economic production, but still "individualistic" in its social mode of production. (Adorno 1990, 306)

As a distinct type of cultural commodity, popular music—with the initial production distinctly separated from later rationalized and industrialized processes—the processes of distribution, circulation, and consumption, mediations, are critical moments for articulating it with political inflections. As differentiated audiences labor to construct meaning, and owing to the processes of mediation, the artifacts of popular culture are inflected with preferred meanings and political significance in the processes of distribution and circulation. As with the world of art, popular culture does not simply "arrive" on the listener's radio, but is also articulated by impresarios—disk jockeys, critics, reviewers, and so on—who contribute to its social, cultural, and political resonance (Bourdieu 1993). In the processes of mediation, songs, artists, and genres are articulated with a political platform or ideology, which is part of a larger, cultural process of co-optation, adoption, or incorporation that contributes to constructing and maintaining hegemony.

For example, the Reagan administration's attempt to articulate Bruce Springsteen's song "Born in the U.S.A." to its new right bloc was contested by Springsteen. Similarly, the Conservative Party in the United Kingdom attempted to articulate John Lennon's song "Imagine" with its bloc. Both examples seem to belie the meanings of the songs—progressive, left-leaning lyrics for many listeners—however, they are instructive of the ways the processes of mediation and articulation can work in attempting to link popular culture with a hegemonic bloc, and how cultural politics are not encoded solely in lyrics. The case of the Dixie Chicks differs somewhat, particularly in regard to the larger context of country music.

COUNTRY'S HISTORY AND SELECTIVE TRADITION

The history of modern, commercial country music, from the early 1950s onward, involves the construction of a selective tradition characterized by a number of salient characteristics that artists and the recording industry tap as a well of source material in the production of songs. For Peterson (1997), this allows artists to reproduce new derivations on established, resonant themes, providing a "renewable tradition"—an ongoing recreation of the country "tradition" that was established in the 1950s when country became a viable, commercial genre with attendant formations.

Peterson (1997) traces the origins of roots of commercial country music to two main strains of American popular music: "hard core" and "soft core." Peterson sees in these two strains the main sources for "tradition" constructed by the country music industry, radio, writers, and artists; this "tradition" is mined and effectively reworked throughout the history of commercial country music for generative themes in song lyrics. The lyrics of the hard-core strain are characterized by "concrete situations, simple vocabulary; references are concrete and evoke specific personal experiences; singers perform songs that express a wide range of emotions, and these change with their own life experiences" (Peterson 1997, 151).

The characteristics of the soft-core lyrics are "general situation or specific situation stated in general terms; sets a mood; third-person voice, or if first-person, evoking feelings shared with the listener. Performers sing songs that fit their media persona as this changes with the musical fashions" (Peterson 1997, 151). For Peterson (1997), the success of country music as a commercial genre, and of individual artists and songs, is predicated upon the reworking of these strains in the production and reproduction of music that is seen as "authentic" and "original"—akin to Adorno's (1990) observations about the "pseudo-individual" characteristics of popular music. While the "new," "authentic," and "original" are valued in country and popular music, they are reproduced from a limited repertory that underscores the "traditional" in country music's selective tradition.

As with any history, the work of selective tradition is an active process that parses from available sources materials it uses to construct its account. While necessarily partial, it is partly a function of the documentary record; it is dependent upon what has been preserved and recorded. Owing to the work of early folklorists, such as Alan Lomax, and early commercial recording pioneers, such as Ralph Peer, the dominant strains that Peterson cites—those recorded and published in the early twentieth century—that were later drawn upon to craft the commercial genre of country music only tapped certain characteristics of American popular music. The folklorists and early commercial recording pioneers focused on the rural South at a time when forces of modernity—mass production/consumption and new technologies of transportation and communication in particular—were contributing to rapid changes in the nation. They were actively seeking out artists and songs that were "original" or "authentic." For the commercial recorders, "original" was the preeminent concern, as songs that had not been published or recorded, and hence copyrighted, were the most commercially desirable. Folklorists were looking for remnants of a disappearing "authentic" America, the ways and mores of a simple, rural "folk" encapsulated in music.

The predominant thematic characteristics of country music reflect these strains, their selection from the larger field of American popular music, and the guided interests of early intermediaries (folklorists and recording pioneers). One key thematic characteristic of country music is tradition, more specifically tradition as "a rustic alternative to urban modernity" (Peterson 1997, 55). The theme of tradition often hearkens to disappearing, if not lost, rural areas and small towns, and their attendant norms and values—community, simplicity, informality, and the perceived homogeneity of "Middle America." While this element of tradition overemphasizes the perceived unities of the rural/small town, it complements in binary form the perceived unities of urban modernity, and both draw upon powerful myths and ideologies, with deep historical roots, running through much American literature, film, and popular culture. The theme of the traditional rural/small town has resistant as well as reactionary dimensions. The idealization and valorization of the traditional rural/small town offer alternatives to the encroachment of horizontal forms of power—the federal government, industrial capitalism, media, and the invasion of small-town trade by the likes of McDonald's, Wal-Mart, and transnational corporations that export profits and have little ties to the community. It can also be used in reactionary ways to reinforce certain dimensions of vertical power—actively excluding Others, contributing to anti-immigration sentiment, augmenting and reproducing racism, and underscoring and reinforcing patriarchy.

The theme of tradition also has religious and cultural dimensions that map the continuum of one element of American popular music in general: the sacred and the profane. Country music's tradition of the sacred draws from gospel music, hymns, and the Protestant religious sects that dominated the non-urban South, in particular the evangelical sects. Country draws upon these roots in the construction of a moral, social tradition steeped in the influence of evangelical Protestantism.

> The emphasis is on . . . the cooperation of basic institutions, like the family, the school, and the church. The basic commitment is not to liberty but to a religious and socio-moral world. Traditional life does not encourage the pursuit of self-interest but instead focuses on the restraint of self-interest and the solidarity of the community . . . the basic threat is not the loss of liberty, but moral decay. (Sample 1996, 93)

This theme of moral tradition in country music, however, exists in a dialectic relationship to the profane, which is equitably represented in country music, with some artists and their work drawing heavily upon both for generative themes (i.e., Johnny Cash), as "personal morality, while often preached as a virtue, was just as often violated in practice" (Malone 1979, 130). The tapping, and oftentimes celebration, of the corporeal—drinking, drugs, sex, and violence—resonates throughout the thematic history of country music, most visibly in so-called honky-tonk music that rose to popularity in the 1940s. As with the theme of tradition as a rustic, small-town alternative to modernity, however, the sacred and the profane (or corporeal) in country music are not just thematic wells, but also tap key contradictions of working-class life that are refracted, rather than reflected, in popular culture.

Another derivation on the theme of tradition can be found in country music's invocation of region, in particular the South as a geographic and cultural place situated in distinction to the rest of the country. Part of the emphasis on the

South, and to a lesser extent the West, is a way of connecting with the selective tradition established by the early intermediaries and as a means of establishing a song or artist's "authenticity" or "originality"—as the industry consciously "accentuated the regional and rustic nature of the music, its performers, and its audience" (Peterson 1997, 51). The South as the place most bound to and supportive of tradition is a generative theme that highlights a complex relationship between identity, region, and nation. According to Malone (1979),

> The relationship between country music and "Americanism" is a tenuous one, but one that is rooted in the South's ambivalent relationship to the nation at large—the sense of being both out of the mainstream and at the same time more "American" than other regions of the nation. . . . It is conscious of its "southerness," [sic] and therefore presumably of its uniqueness, but it is also convinced that it embodies the best in the American character as a whole. (130)

This is also a theme that, to a lesser extent and with differing emphases, characterizes the West.

The theme of tradition is encapsulated by two powerful, mythic figures in country music: hillbillies and cowboys. As Peterson (1997) shows, these figures manifest other derivations of the theme of tradition in contradistinction to modernity.

> Both hillbilly and cowboy suggest a self-reliant (most often male) child of nature, unfettered by the constraints of urban society. . . . Both depended on friends and family rather than on written law and officialdom. Both find little use for formal education in their environment, relying on knowledge that comes from a oneness with nature and its creatures. Finally, both feel at a loss in an urban environment, not only unschooled in its appropriate ways of behavior, but also unrefined in dress, speech, and manners. (Peterson 1997, 67)

The theme of tradition and its derivations—the rural/small town, the moral and social dialectic of the sacred and profane, and its invocation of place in the South and West—provide the base for, and sources of, the rather loose and unstable elements with which a cultural politics can be assembled. These elements comprise materials for an inchoate cultural politics; however, the work of articulating the contradictions and antinomies into a seemingly univocal cultural politics is a process we need to look to political economy and the mediations between artists and listeners to understand further.

RADIO'S CHANGING POLITICAL ECONOMY

Changes in the political economy of the radio industry have made the articulation of a cultural politics encompassing country music to the hegemonic bloc of the new right much easier, as the variability of the processes of mediation are lessened in general, with more of the processes subject to the "command and control" power of the dominant radio interests. The rapid concentration of ownership in radio, following the removal of ownership caps with the Telecommunications Act of 1996, has led to centralized decision making, playlists, and personnel/management, giving an unprecedented amount of power to large radio corporations over the mediations between artists and the recording industry on one hand and listeners on the other.

At the macro, industry level, there has been a reconfiguration of the power relationship between the recording and radio industries; what had been a relatively stable, mutually beneficial, and equitable interrelationship for approximately fifty years has begun to change following the Telecommunications Act. Beginning in the late 1940s, as the networks left radio for TV, and their national programming and advertising revenues vanished, radio needed inexpensive, reliable, and popular content to replace the network fare. Radio found in the recording industry a complementary partner—the recording industry would provide gratis or discounted disks that would advertise and promote their product, and radio would pay blanket royalties to the recording and publishing industries for inexpensive content they used to sell audiences to advertisers. This relationship, with some variations, has existed with remarkable stability until quite recently. As radio station ownership has concentrated, the balance of power in this relationship has changed.

The Telecommunications Act spawned unprecedented concentration of ownership in the radio industry, with radio becoming more powerful in relation to the recording industry, artists, and listeners. Giant radio corporations, such as Clear Channel Communications, Inc. (approximately 1,200 stations), and Cumulus Media, Inc. (approximately 270 stations), have centralized decision making and playlists, which constrict opportunities for the music industry and what listeners hear. One example of how big radio corporations' power is increasing are the intermediaries known as independent promoters. In the wake of the payola scandals of the late 1950s, Congress banned the pay-for-play practice whereby the recording industry would pay disk jockeys or programming directors in exchange for favorable treatment of their recordings; however, it did not ban money from going to station owners. The recording and radio industries reconfigured payola through legal intermediaries called independent promoters (IP)—individuals and organizations that labels pay to push their songs. Following the post–Telecommunications Act rise of big, corporate radio groups, the groups began restricting the number of IPs they work with and charging the IPs centralized fees for exclusive "affiliations" with a number of their stations, which makes it harder for the recording industry to "influence" playlists. This situation is further exacerbated by other developments unique to big, corporate radio groups: the centralization of playlists, personnel, and decision making. Unlike the relatively decentralized and local character of the radio industry pre–Telecommunications Act, the radio industry is increasingly centralized and national (McChesney 2004).

The post–Telecommunications Act reconfiguration of the radio industry has resulted in an environment where a smaller number of owners wield "command and control" power over content and the industry is increasingly allied with the political bloc of the new right. The banning of the Dixie Chicks by Cumulus and Clear Channel, and Clear Channel's earlier "recommendations" for appropriate (and inappropriate) songs post–September 11, epitomize the command and control power wielded by big corporate radio; however, this power isn't only exercised during times of perceived national crisis. The centralization of big radio produces a "conservatism" in its risk aversion that eschews an organizational culture that would seek out a wide range of new artists and music; instead, it looks for derivations of proven successes, institutionalizing a conservative and self-fulfilling definition of viable programming that delimits artists and listeners (McChesney 2004). In this respect, big radio is following the well-established institutional conservatism and blandness of such enterprises as McDonald's (Ritzer 2004) and network TV (Gitlin 2000). The increasing alliance between the owners of big radio and the political bloc of the new right is partly a function of another dimension of the Telecommunications Act. The provision requiring the FCC to revisit existing regulations, coupled with an aggressively industry-oriented FCC under Chairman Michael Powell, has created a situation whereby big radio, somewhat concerned if not fearful of increasingly well-organized concentration critics, sees its interests as consonant with the hegemonic bloc of the new right (McChesney 2004). In addition to guarding their concentration spoils, big radio and big media are interested in further relaxation of regulations preventing cross-ownership and single-market ownership caps, and see in a Republican-dominated FCC, chaired by the neoliberal Powell, their best chances. And, given the slim hold the new right holds on political power in the executive branch, the unprecedented antiwar actions in advance of the attack on Iraq, and a less than unified public, big radio likely sees its aggressive pro-Bush and prowar stances as prudent preemption:

> The concentrated world of radio was seen as being particularly hostile to all who did not support the Bush administration. Clear Channel DJs led pro-war rallies, [and] fired the South Carolina 2002 "Radio Personality of the Year" allegedly for her anti-war politics. (McChesney 2004, 279)

Big corporate radio, on an acquisition binge post–Telecommunications Act, is more of a structure of dominance in relation to the recording industry, creating a situation where single corporate entities wield command and control over artists and the industry. The attendant centralization of decision making, personnel, and playlists and the conservative corporate culture of big radio are exceedingly constrictive. The toady trinity between big radio, the FCC, and the political bloc of the new right has created a context in which dissident ideas, music, and views are efficiently stymied.

HEGEMONY AND CULTURE

Hegemony and its cultural dimension are processes that require constant reinforcement and maintenance in order to maintain and reproduce the consent necessary to maintain a ruling political bloc in liberal societies. Popular culture, perhaps equal to if not more important than news media, particularly for the working class, is a key site where hegemonic struggles are waged, and country music with its large, politically important audience is one of the most important cultural fronts. And as popular culture increasingly becomes a key circuit for gaining and maintaining consent, and its ownership, control, and distribution are controlled by fewer corporate entities, its "enclosure" by and articulation to political power are easier operations.

As Lessig (2004, 12) wrote,

> There has never been a time in our history when more of our "culture" was as "owned" as it is now. And yet there has never been a time when the concentration of power to control the uses of culture has been as unquestioningly accepted as it is now.

Hence, in times of domestic and international crises it is vigorously policed, and the case of the Dixie Chicks places in relief the backlash when artists cross the real delimitations of an articulated cultural politics.

Popular culture in general, and country music in particular, however, are not firmly articulated with a political bloc, nor are its artists and listeners politically homogenous; rather, the link is fragile and requires maintenance. Furthermore, the history of country music, its selective tradition, and its attempted co-optation by the new right make it a particularly salient case for understanding the linkages between media practices and political power. Its uniqueness is highlighted in cases similar to the Dixie Chicks prior to the Iraq invasion. Actors such as Tim Robbins, Susan Sarandon, Janeane Garofalo, and Sean Penn; director Michael Moore; and musical artists such as Sheryl Crow and John Mellencamp spoke out stridently against the war, in terms much more damning than Maines's remarks. While these celebrities were criticized in mainstream media, they were not targets of the aggressive policing that the Dixie Chicks received, the central difference being that the Dixie

Chicks were firmly situated in the country genre. Furthermore, the recent history of country music during the Vietnam era, with several successful songs "protesting the protestors," augments its selective tradition, providing further cultural fodder for a successful articulation with the hegemonic bloc of the new right (Malone 1985, 318). Additionally, country music has long been associated with stability during periods of perceived cultural and social upheaval: with jazz in the 1920s and rock in the 1950s and 1960s (Malone 1979). The generative themes of country music provide some of the materials for a cultural politics of the new right, although their antinomies and contradictions do not guarantee this particular political inflection, nor is it fixed.

> It seems strange indeed for a region and a people that have always taken great pride in their intense individualism to make such a fetish today of national conformity. The tradition of the drifter, the rounder, and even the lawless man, preceded the period of commercialization and has been a continuing thread in the music of Jimmie Rodgers to Waylon Jennings. . . . The contemporary endorsement of the status quo in country music, a mood which often assumes rather mindless bland, and homogenized forms—directed as much toward the pocketbook of Middle America as toward its mind or heart—obscures the facts of the music's historic diversity. Despite the abundance of songs stressing the domestic virtues and the sense of place, country music, as much as anything, has been the music of an uprooted people with an acute consciousness of a world of shifting values. Country music is indeed "American," but its Americanism is broad rather than narrow, deriving from many sources and presumptions. (Malone 1979, 130–131)

The successful construction and maintenance of a cultural politics comprising country music is crafted in the processes of mediation where attempts are made to articulate the culture of country music to the political bloc of the new right, processes made much easier due to changes in the political economy of radio. Thus, the flap over the Dixie Chicks singer's comments is more than simply a reaction in a less than united country on the verge of war, but rather an active policing of culture—a sort of boundary work necessary to maintain consent (or perhaps a cultural variant of the domino theory, as Vietnam is a fashionable metaphor). And given the marginal hold on consent of this political bloc, this may not be disproportionate. Not the comment of the Dixie Chicks, but the potential dis-articulation between country music and a cultural politics of the new right that it portends, is what the fuss is about.

REFERENCES

Adorno, T. W. (1990). On popular music. In S. Frith & A. Goodwin (Eds.), *On record: Rock, pop and the written word* (pp. 301–314). New York: Pantheon.

Bourdieu, P. (1993). The production of belief: Contribution to an economy of symbolic goods. In R. Johnson (Ed.), *The field of cultural production: Essays on art and literature* (pp. 74–112). New York: Columbia University Press.

Gitlin, T. (2000). *Inside prime time*. Berkeley: University of California Press.

Gramsci, A. (1971). *Selections from the prison notebooks* (Q. Hoare & G. N. Smith, Ed. & Trans.). New York: International.

Hall, S. (1981). Notes on deconstructing "the popular." In R. Samuel (Ed.), *People's history and socialist theory* (pp. 227–240). London: Routledge & Kegan Paul.

———. (1986). On postmodernism and articulation: An interview with Stuart Hall. *Journal of Communication Inquiry* 10 (2), 45–60.

Lessig, L. (2004). *Free culture: How big media uses technology and the law to lock down culture and control creativity*. New York: Penguin.

Malone, B. C. (1979). *Southern music/American music*. Lexington: University Press of Kentucky.

———. (1985). *Country music, U.S.A.*, rev. ed. Austin: University of Texas Press.

Marx, K. (1973). *Grundrisse: Foundations of the critique of political economy* (M. Nicolaus, Trans.). London: Penguin.

McChesney, R. W. (2004). *The problem of the media: U.S. communications politics in the 21st century*. New York: Monthly Review.

Negus, K. (1996). *Popular music in theory: An introduction*. Hanover, NH: University Press of New England.

Peterson, R. A. (1997). *Creating country music: Fabricating authenticity*. Chicago: University of Chicago Press.

Ritzer, G. (2004). *The McDonaldization of society*, rev. ed. Thousand Oaks, CA: Pine Forge.

Sample, T. (1996). *White soul: Country music, the church, and working Americans*. Nashville, TN: Abingdon Press.

Williams, R. (1977). *Marxism and literature*. New York: Oxford University Press.

12

The Mass Media, Politics, and Warfare

Christian Fuchs

MEDIA, SOCIETY, AND KNOWLEDGE

A medium is an entity that helps organize a relationship between two other entities. Via a medium, a relationship between parts of a system and/or a system and its environment is produced in order to enable the self-organization of the whole system. Etymologically, the term medium stems from the Latin *medius*, which means in the *middle*, or the *middle one*. Media have to do with mediation. Social media mediate the social relationships of human beings. They are employed in social relationships of living, social actors.

Social structures can be found in all societal areas: in technology, ecology, economy, polity, and culture. *Tools* are means employed for reaching defined goals, *natural resources* organized by humans are necessary in order to reach these goals, and *property* enables the production of use values and the satisfaction of needs. *Decision power* is necessary in order to orient processes and achieve decision-based results; *definitions* (norms, values, knowledge) serve as means of reflection and assessment of concrete human existence. That is, in society we find technological, ecological, economic, political, and cultural structures that mediate the relationships of human beings and hence the reproduction of social systems. They are both medium and outcome of social actions; they constrain practice, but also enable practices that result in new structures and the differentiation of already existing ones (Fuchs 2002, 2003a, 2003b; Giddens 1984). Media can be found with different characteristics in all complex, self-organizing systems. The basic characteristics of social media are:

- Media store and fix social knowledge and simplify human action because due to their existence, certain foundations of actions don't have to be permanently (re)produced, but can be accomplished by making use of media. Media reduce the complexity of society. They are carriers of knowledge and a foundation of the spatial and temporal extension of social systems.

- Media enable the continuity of social reproduction over space and time; they result in a spatial and temporal distancing of social relationships without loss of continuity. But media also produce special modes of proximity and hence sublate distance by reembedding spatio-temporally disembedded relationships.
- Media are a foundation of practice and enable a certain degree of mobility.
- Media mediate, organize, and coordinate social relationships, communication, knowledge management, production, cooperation, competition, domination, decision processes, the discursive establishment of norms and values, and the production and materialization of ideologies.
- Media connect actors, individuals, and groups.
- Special skills, rules, organizational forms, and norms are necessary for using media (media literacy). Media put forward certain forms of usage and exclude others.
- Media mediate and change human perception.
- Media are symbolic systems and referential systems (e.g., technologies refer to purposes, property refers to material possibilities and positions, power to decisions, and definitions to lifestyles and taste).
- Media have material-substantial and ideational aspects; for example, in computer-mediated communication (CMC), the technological distribution as well as the produced content are important.
- Media make possible new experiences and ways of experience that transcend the immediate experience of corporeal presence.
- Media dissolve on the one hand temporalities and spaces, but on the other hand also produce new spaces and temporalities.
- Media don't come into existence by chance, but in certain historical situations and due to certain social and cultural needs and interests. Media have their own history.
- Media are referring to objective reality, but these references are not simply reflections and mappings of reality, but also contain new meanings and contents. Media unite different contexts, for example different subjective value schemes in face-to-face communication or different cultural contexts in virtual discussion boards. Mediation means frequently that realities are disembedded from their context of production and reembedded into new contexts, for example in the Internet; and in a film montage, elements that stem from different contexts can be embedded

into a new context that contains new, emergent meanings that can't be found in one of the single elements.

- Media employ principles of order; for example, linearity is a principle of order of the book, networking and linking are order principles of hypertext, and precision is one of the principles of the medium of money.
- Media contain certain meanings, ideologies, myths, and worldviews.

In modern capitalistic society, media play a particular role. The development of technological media has been advanced in order to organize economic production more efficiently. Capital accumulation is a driving power of the development of new technological media. As the scope of technological media (railway, telegraph, public transport, mass transport, telephone, radio, automobile, airplane, TV, fax, computer, and so on) expands, the flexibility of social relationship increases. Economic and military interests are present in the genesis of technology; the globalization of capitalism is medium and outcome of the development of new technological media. Anthony Giddens (1985) has shown that the emergence and expansion of capitalism are connected to the emergence and development of means of surveillance controlled by the nation-state (Fuchs 2003b). These are means of organization (census, statistics, public records, and so on) and means of discipline that allow political control of citizens. The development of modern media is connected to political and ideological interests. Military interests play an important role because the enforcement of certain political interests is based on efficient military technologies.

During the Fordist mode of development that was based on mass production and mass consumption, the mass media emerged as a relatively autonomous and functionally differentiated subsystem of society. The beginnings can be found earlier with the establishment of the press; radio, film, and television have propelled the development of the system of the mass media. In this system, ideologies are produced and distributed, and it is a diffusion channel of knowledge, news, ideologies, and views. The mass media form a self-organizing system that is organized around the permanent production of topical news about the state of the world. The mass media don't map objective reality exactly, but construct social realities that distort objective reality due to the subjective views, interests, and complex relationships that are contained in this system. The system of the mass media produces imaginary representations of reality: it doesn't simply construct one of many legitimate realities, as claimed by the constructivist sociologist Niklas Luhmann (1996), but rather produces and distributes various views of objective reality that are different from reality as such to certain degrees. This system can be considered a subsystem of the cultural subsystem of society. Mass media are organized around certain technological media (printing press, radio technology, television, computer, and so on) that are embedded into social institutions. Hence, the term "mass media" doesn't simply denote certain technologies, but also social relationships that make use of technological media in order to organize themselves and to reach certain goals.

The mass media are closely structurally coupled with the economic, political, and technological subsystems of society; they can achieve their goals only by making use of technological, economic, political, and cultural media. Institutions of the mass media frequently (and especially within deregulated social and institutional settings) also pursue economic interests and make use of technological media in order to achieve these aims; that is, they sell knowledge and news as commodities. The commodification of symbolic forms aims at capital accumulation in both a direct and an indirect way. In a direct way, information commodities are sold on the market; the indirect way is constituted by the sale of advertising space (advertisement in television, banner commercials in the Internet). Due to the emergence of the new electronic media that are based on computer technology, new forms and ways of capital accumulation such as digital pay-per-view television and online shopping have emerged.

We should employ the term "mass media" because technologies are used in order to reach a large number of people. Audience ratings are an important economic aspect of the mass media. A central characteristic of the existing organization of the mass media is that the main contents are controlled and produced by a relatively small number of people and groups, whereas the number of recipients is much larger. It no longer makes sense to distinguish subsystems of the mass media such as printed media, film, radio, and TV because of the convergence of technologies and media institutions. Due to digitization and technological networks, it is possible to digitally unite several classical media. Such a combination of text, audio, images, video, music, communication, and body enables a multimodal dimension of the mass media. The Internet as a new technological medium is a typical expression of the convergence of technological media. Media organizations make use of technological convergence in order to expand the scope and distribution of their contents. In institutional convergence, one can find a convergence of different markets and institutions. Monopolization is an important aspect of the mass media. Media corporations engage in both horizontal and vertical integration, they try to monopolize existing areas of specialization, but they also try to settle down and expand their influence in other areas of mass media. They aim at both selling content (film, music, videos, books, TV programs, and so on) and acting as providers and distributors (media megastores, TV channels, cinemas, and so on). The production and distribution of media contents are converging. The system of the mass media is technologically multidimensional (multimedia), but institutionally there is an increasing lack of plurality; it is controlled by a few large global players that engage in such different areas as software, Internet, film, broadcasting, music, and other media at the same time. The mass media are dominated by a few, large transnational corporations (AOL Time Warner, Disney, Viacom, Bertelsmann, Murdoch, AT&T, Sony, Seagram, and others). The largest one has been Time Warner Inc., which was been a result of the fusion of Time and Warner in 1989 and of Time Warner and Turner Broadcasting in 1996. In 2000 AOL, the largest Internet provider, merged with Time Warner, the largest media and entertainment corporation, in order to create AOL Time Warner. The system of the mass media is coined by capitalist interests and to a certain extent pursues economic goals. Hence, Dieter Prokop (2002) speaks of "media capitalism"; the media world market would be an oligopoly.

The example of multimedia corporations shows that social media don't operate fully separated from each other. Human beings make permanent use of different media (also at the same time) in order to organize their daily lives and to reach certain goals. Technologies, organized natural resources, property, decision power, and definitions don't exist fully autonomous from each other, but rather as a totality constitute the structural characteristics of all social systems. In order to exist, the human being must make use of different media: technological ones (language, text, computer, and so on), cultural ones (norms, values, knowledge), economic ones (goods, money, and so on), and political ones (laws, elections, rules, and so on). The system of the mass media embeds technological media institutionally, but it is also based on economic, political, and cultural media. Its aim is the production and distribution of knowledge and topical news that frequently take on ideological and economic forms and are coined by economic, political, and ideological interests.

POLITICS AND THE MASS MEDIA

The borders between media, politics, and economy are increasingly diffusing and becoming blurred today. Polity is increasingly organized around a logic that corresponds to the economy and the mass media. Modern democracies have emerged in coevolution with the modern economy; the two systems have never been independent. Hence, the principle of competition is not only an economic, but also a political principle. Decision processes have a competitive character in modern society, but the degree of competition has thus far been low concerning the mode of presentation of political issues. Due to the rising importance of the mass media, this area of polity is increasingly influenced by the economic logic of the media industry. This economization and mass-mediazation of politics result in several tendencies (Fuchs & Hofkirchner 2003). The first four principles stem from Dieter Prokop (2002); I have added the latter three.

- *Staging*: Politics is today frequently a staging without issues (issueless politics); concrete political actions and political programs have become rather unimportant issues. Politics is confronted with the exertion of pressure for staging, and it answers with self-staging. Personal competence in staging and entertainment is today one of the most important qualities of a good politician. Politicians are associated with certain images, and these images are created by the media and marketing experts. Advertisement, communication, and PR experts—so-called spin doctors—actively plan the appearance, strategies, and images of politicians.
- *Personified Politics Instead of Party Politics*: We are witnessing a change of the role of political parties, which define and present themselves via leadership figures staged in the mass media. Long-term strategies are no longer of much interest for the mass media, resulting in a loss of the importance of parties in politics.
- *Pressure Exerted by Topicality*: The political process time is much longer than the one of the media, because news is of value only for a very short time in the media business. Political parties orient their policy on media time; hence they are oriented on short-term political strategies. The mass media present politics to the viewers as a fast-moving flux that doesn't include more permanent processes, but constitutes itself as a fast juxtaposition of relatively independent singular events and topics that will be forgotten after a short time.
- *Political Events*: Politics gains an event character, and contacts between politicians and citizens are staged and organized as important mass events (e.g., party congresses). Political coverage in the mass media is organized around such events. Party congresses are used for the self-staging of political leaders and for attracting public attention.
- *Political Coverage in the Mass Media*: Political coverage is increasingly based on the simplification of complex political processes; on visualization, personification, short reports, statements, and articles; and on enlargement of the degree of entertainment by integrating "light," unambitious topics, dramatizing, scandalizing, problematization of the unproblematic, emotionalizing, concentration on single examples and private persons, conflicts, scandals, celebrities, and surprise effects. There is a tendency that ambitious, demanding, substantial contents are substituted by commerce, sex, and scandals. The political is frequently marginalized and extremely simplified by the mass media. Visual im-

ages dominate texts and words. Jean Baudrillard (1983), in this context, speaks of simulation, the substitution of the real by the fictitious resulting in self-referential sign systems that don't have fixed, but flexible, contents and meanings. Images are made up of iconographic signs that directly resemble the represented object. This is not the case with symbolic signs, which make up written and spoken language. Hence the video images presented by the mass media seem to be directly insightful, although they frequently don't represent reality. A difference between essence and mediated appearance of reality shows up that can't be recognized easily. There is a false appearance of authenticity and immediacy. Politics is presented as a fast sequence of images, symbols, and pseudo-events by the mass media. The concentration on fast sequences of images and statements results in a tendency of anti-intellectualism. Bad journalism is based on a positivistic practice that discards critical thinking. Tactics employed include the *concentration on facts* (external contexts, backgrounds, and larger coherence are ignored), *limitation to the methodical* (concentration on the search for evidence on certain assertions; the usefulness and meaningfulness of the employed strategies and the contents aren't reflected), *demonstrative harmlessness and inoffensiveness* (harmful and dangerous processes are presented as harmless; the meaning of the harmful is not questioned), and *classificatory thinking* (certain social affairs are presented as self-evident although they are not; there is a lack of differentiation; existing orders are described and classified, but not questioned; existing phenomena are presented as being without alternatives; and possible alternatives are discarded). Another methodological process one can find is *decontextualization*: images from certain contexts are embedded into other contexts without taking over the whole contextual information; a new mosaic that consists of different images and descriptions is created, characterized by a lack of contextual information. New meanings emerge from and are produced by this mosaic of disconnected pieces of information. Due to the interlinked, decontextualized, fast-flowing character of information that is transmitted by the mass media, it is sometimes hard to judge whether or not meanings correspond to factual reality. The principle of *emergent meaning* is very important in modern mass media: a media report is more than the sum of its elements; it has symbolic and emergent contents, and puts forward certain implications indirectly. Frequently, meanings are not articulated and coded directly in the media, but *recoded* into other symbols.

- *Politics and Entertainment*: Politicians make use of entertainment strategies in order to enlarge their electorate. The entertainment industry to

some extent makes use of political topics and figures (in films, TV serials, and so on) in order to increase their attractiveness. Politics can be a topic on the level of the characters, the characters' practices, or the employed topics (i.e., the issues and contents that the characters talk about).
• *Interactivity*: Political correspondence is increasingly employing interactive elements such as Internet discussion boards, live chats with politicians, and so on.

EXAMPLES: MEDIA COVERAGE OF THE GULF WAR

War coverage in the mass media is especially interesting for exemplifying some of the tendencies mentioned above because these are situations where the media are especially important for the public and are getting very large amounts of attention from both the public and political actors. I want to point out some aspects of coverage of the Iraq war in U.S. media in order to show that political interests and media coverage are interrelated. This coverage has, as I will try to show, sometimes been extremely one-sided, manipulative, and unbalanced; however, Americans don't seem to worry about media distortion and seem to be satisfied with the coverage. On March 22–23, 87 percent of the interviewees in a CNN/*USA Today*/Gallup Poll said the media are doing a good or excellent job.

The war coverage of eleven important U.S. mass media institutions was observed from March 21 until April 3: CNN.com, *Chicago Tribune, Los Angeles Times, New York Post, New York Times, Newsweek* magazine, *San Francisco Chronicle, Time* magazine, *USA Today, Washington Post*, and *Washington Times*. The first two weeks of war seem to be of particular interest for observing new tendencies in war coverage. I concentrated on articles on war protests and the role of the media in order to find examples for the theoretical assumptions mentioned above.

In 1991, coverage of the attacks on Iraq was dominated by pictures broadcast by CNN that mainly showed Baghdad by night illuminated by flashes and radar images, as well as military analyses. Almost no dead bodies were shown; the media created the image that this was a clean, surgical war without civil casualties. For many observers, these pictures seemed realistic because they were broadcast live; the observers took what they saw as representing the reality of war. But the decisive question in war correspondence is not what is shown, but what is not shown, and it seems strange when there are no reports on casualties and the horrors of warfare. This war was the first hyperreal war: the images broadcast consisted mainly of simulated, fictitious, virtual reality detached from the real world of war. Media coverage changed the public perception of war; war became a media event that entertains people and that one can watch live on TV for twenty-four hours:

> The Gulf spectacle was "postmodern" in that, first, it was a media event that was experienced as a live occurrence for the whole global village. Second, it managed to blur the distinction between truth and reality in a triumph of the orchestrated image and spectacle. Third, the conflict exhibited a heightened merging of individuals and technology, previewing a new type of cyberwar that featured information technology and "smart weapons." (Best & Kellner 2001, 73)

The situation was a little bit different in 2003: the Internet as a new medium for alternative coverage was present, and there were websites where independent journalists and alternative agencies reported directly from Iraq. This can help in establishing a plurality of sources from which observers can choose and compare in order to create their own opinions. This time also, many European countries along with large media institutions opposed the war and hence provided alternative sources of information. Six hundred reporters were "embedded" with British and U.S. troops and reported directly from the front. All of these journalists had to sign an agreement that defines "ground rules" and set strict limits for coverage. The coverage directly from the front has further transformed the media coverage of warfare into a spectacle that excites and thrills the viewers—dead soldiers, dead civilians, and other horrifying effects of horror were not shown. One can question whether it makes sense to embed journalists and whether this results in a more balanced coverage. These journalists face all the dangers that the fighting soldiers are facing, and hence their reports might be distorted and might reflect their subjective fears and angers more than in traditional coverage. Can "embedded" journalists report independently and impartially on warfare they are involved in personally? Can they adequately maintain distance from their objects of coverage? Which stories are shown on TV, and which ones are missing? Do twenty-four-hour live coverage and reports directly from the front democratize and pluralize media coverage, or do they create yet a new dimension of hyperreality, media spectacles and simulated, false, one-dimensional realities? The reality of death and destruction might get lost amid the high-tech imagery delivered by the mass media. Was the embedding experiment really "a demonstration of democratic values and freedom of speech in action" (Katovsky & Carlson 2003, xix), or rather an integrative strategy of manipulation?

"When the American military goes to war, so does American journalism," said Marvin Kalb, fellow at the Shorenstein Center on Press, Politics and Public Policy at Harvard and former CBS and NBC correspondent. "The American soldier is trained to accomplish his mission, and it's a narrow mission. He has to take that hill, and so does journalism. It often has difficulty showing you the full terrain" ("With media in tow" 2003).

The Department of Defense *Embedment Manual* (Katovsky & Carlson 2003, 401–417) defined precise "ground rules" for embedded journalists and their coverage: it says, for example, that the media will be briefed in advance about what information is sensitive and "what the parameters are for covering this type of information"; after exposure to sensitive information, the media should be briefed "on what information they should avoid covering." In instances where a unit commander decides that coverage of a story will involve extremely sensitive information, "The commander may offer access if the reporter agrees to a security review of their coverage." If, in such a security review, sensitive or classified information is found, "The media will be asked to remove that information." Another rule says that "embargoes [of certain media] may be imposed to protect operational security." Embedding is an integrative strategy of dealing with the mass media that allows influencing coverage by close contact and precisely defined rules. The ground rules enabled the filtering of coverage.

Due to Vietnam experiences, the U.S. government in subsequent decades tried to keep the mass media out of the war zones and the invaded countries. This was, for example, the case in Grenada and Panama. Since the 1990s and starting with the Gulf War in 1991, a different strategy was employed, one that focuses on integration instead of repression. This shift is an expression of a larger ideological shift in society from "disciplinary society" to the "society of controls." The disciplinary regime that dominated during the area of Fordism operated with the help of disciplines and disciplinary milieus. Disciplines are methods that secure the submission to external forces by surveillance and punishment (Foucault 1977). They are inherent in modern institutions such as schools, prisons, families, universities, hospitals, corporations, and so on because these milieus try to enclose the individual. Disciplines were also incorporated into the Fordist apparatuses of mass production, especially into assembly lines. These aspects still exist today to a certain extent, but concerning the disciplinary regime there is also a shift from the disciplinary society (Foucault 1977) to what Gilles Deleuze (1992) calls the society of control. Controls are internalized disciplines, forms of self-discipline that present themselves as liberating and operate in a more subtle manner:

> Enclosures are molds, distinct castings, but controls are a modulation, like a self-deforming cast that will continuously change from one moment to the other, or like a sieve whose mesh will transmute from point to point. . . . The old monetary mole is the animal of the space of enclosure, but the serpent is that of the societies of control. We have passed from one animal to the other, from the mole to the serpent, in the system under which we live, but also in our manner of liv-

ing and in our relations with others. The disciplinary man was a discontinuous producer of energy, but the man of control is undulatory, in orbit, in a continuous network. . . . The coils of a serpent are even more complex than the burrows of a molehill. (Deleuze 1992, 4–5)

The mole as a symbol of disciplinary society is faceless and dumb, and monotonously digs his burrows; the snake is flexible and pluralistic. The repressive political strategy tried to discipline the mass media; the integrative strategy in addition tries to provide a certain degree of flexibility (such as embedding journalists), and freedom of movement that is kept within clearly defined limits. It tries to produce identity between the mass media and political strategies. This strategy is one of ideological integration. The ground rules were a discipline, but in many cases there was no need to apply them due to the ideological identity established by the practice of embedding that dissolves distance. This ideological shift can not only be observed in the mass media, but also in the area of production where strategies of participative management aim at the ideological integration of the workforce into corporations. Bonus systems, teamwork, share options, corporate identity, attractive design of the workplace, construction of a community between management and workers, advancement of spirit of enterprise within the workforce, and so on are part of this strategy that constitutes new qualities of the disciplinary regime.

The Project for Excellence in Journalism (PEJ) Research Center (2003) concluded that "the overwhelming majority of the embedded stories studied, 94%, were primarily factual in nature." That the reports were to a large degree according to facts doesn't mean that they all told the entire truth about the war. Decisive questions that one would also have to cover in such a study are, Which facts are shown, which ones are not shown or omitted? Which language and symbols are used for describing both U.S. and Iraqi troops and people? Is the context of the shown pictures adequately presented? Which emergent meanings do the reports put forward? Are there indications that the reports can manipulate or influence public opinion into a certain direction? Do the embedded journalists have enough distance from prowar arguments, and are they able to keep such a distance from the action in their reporting? To which extents do the reports represent the subjective views and experiences of the embedded journalists? The PEJ study quantified a report as factual if it is not an analysis, opinion, or commentary, but this means that the decisive question of whether the reported "facts" represent or misrepresent reality wasn't researched. Facts were simply understood as those that are presented by the media as facts, not as coverage that corresponds to objective reality. The study doesn't take into account that one of the main aspects of information management in the media society is that facts and fiction, reality and simulation, essence and appearance are increasingly harder to distinguish. Another result of the PEJ study was that "while dramatic, the coverage is not graphic. Not a single story examined showed pictures of people being hit by fired weapons," indicating that the selection of the pictures is a decisive criterion for representing or misrepresenting reality. The extent to which the media can report the truth about the war can't be answered easily by researching whether certain selected pictures represent certain aspects of reality. Reality is multidimensional and interlinked. Especially complex sections of reality like war zones have a high degree of networked, interlinked, multidimensional causality and events. Media coverage always and necessarily reduces this complexity because it can't show all dimensions at the same time. But in order to represent reality adequately, it is necessary not to focus on single events, but to embed single reported events into larger contexts and dimensions. Hence, coverage should not focus on single events, but try to represent as much of the complexity of reality as possible. This is especially a problem for war correspondence because there are multiple limits of coverage. In short, media studies on war coverage should take into account how the various complex variables, aspects, and dimensions, as well as how they interlink, are represented in reports.

In 2003 there was no longer a CNN monopoly on war coverage, Murdoch's FOX TV heavily competed with CNN, and there were alternative press institutions that mainly made use of the Internet in order to provide alternative sources of war information. The competition for topical news and ratings between large channels such as Fox, CNN, ABC, CBS, and MSNBC didn't automatically result in a more democratic and pluralistic type of coverage. Driven by the run for ratings, such competition can easily result in a media competition for who can present the war in the most sensationalistic and spectacular way. The result won't be the representation of alternative views, but mass one-dimensional coverage. The problem that alternative media are facing is that they are hardly recognized and hardly known, and that the war-waging parties try to control and influence information and war coverage. A study on two weeks of U.S. media prewar coverage concluded that the networks are megaphones for official views.

Seventy-six percent of all sources were current or former officials, leaving little room for independent and grassroots views. Similarly, 75 percent of U.S. sources were current or former officials. At a time when 61 percent of U.S. respondents were telling pollsters that more time was needed for diplomacy and inspections, only 6 percent of U.S. sources on the four networks were skeptics regarding the need for war. Sources affiliated with anti-war activism were nearly non-existent. On the four networks combined, just three of 393 sources were identified as being affiliated with anti-war activism—less than 1 percent. Just one of 267 U.S. sources was affiliated with anti-war activism—less than half a percent. (FAIR, 2003)

When comparing media coverage of the first Gulf War in 1991 with war coverage in 2003, one sees that the sanitization of war has remained, but a new humane touch—an emotionalization—has entered. Embedded journalists show staged pictures of hard-working British and U.S. soldiers who risk their lives for liberating the Iraqi people from Saddam Hussein and helping them. Pictures of explosions are shown in order to present the alleged superiority of the allied forces, and so-called psy-ops (psychological operations) against the enemy are waged by making use of the mass media. War has become a spectacle media event—a twenty-four-hour live coverage, which is sold as a home entertainment commodity.

TV networks like CNN have established special filtering systems:

A new CNN system of "script approval"—the iniquitous instruction to reporters that they have to send all their copy to anonymous officials in Atlanta to ensure it is suitably sanitized—suggests that the Pentagon and the Department of State have nothing to worry about. (Fisk 2003, 1)

The mass media make use of the blurring of the boundaries between truth and fiction, making it hard for the viewer to decide what is right or wrong, what corresponds to reality and what does not. "On September 7, 2002, Bush cited a report by the International Atomic Energy Agency (IAEA) that he said proved that the Iraqis were on the brink of developing nuclear weapons. . . . Actually, no such report existed" (Rampton & Stauber 2003, 86). In autumn 2002, U.S. media reported that Iraq bought special aluminum tubes for its nuclear weapons program. In January 2003, the IAEA reported that the size of the tubes shows that they are not suited for uranium enrichment. Meanwhile, the speculations about the tubes had influenced the opinion of Congress members on voting for an authorization of war. A few weeks before the start of the war, Colin Powell announced that Saddam Hussein tried to buy nuclear material in Africa, and he presented a letter as evidence. Many observers, among them IAEA head Mohammed El Bardei, questioned the authenticity of this letter. In February 2003, Powell also presented other material purporting to show that Iraq was producing weapons of mass destruction in violation of UN sanctions. He included a report of the British MI6. However, this dossier wasn't an authentic work, nor was it accurate (Rampton & Stauber 2003, 96).

The main argument for justifying the war was that Iraq possessed weapons of mass destruction. But no such weapons were found. This fact sheds critical light on the presented arguments. In his speech on the Interim Progress Report on the Activities of the Iraq Survey Group (ISG) on October 2, 2003, the head of the ISG David Kay admitted that "despite evidence of Saddam's continued ambition to acquire nuclear weapons, to date we have not uncovered evidence that Iraq undertook significant post-1998 steps to actually build nuclear weapons or produce fissile material." Instead of objective facts that could prove the existence of mass weapons, Kay presented purely subjective intentions as solid results of the survey: "Saddam, at least as judged by those scientists and other insiders who worked in his military-industrial programs, had not given up his aspirations and intentions to continue to acquire weapons of mass destruction." After resigning in January 2004, David Kay said, "My summary view, based on what I've seen, is we're very unlikely to find large stockpiles of weapons. . . . I don't think they exist" ("No evidence Iraq stockpiled WMDs" 2003). Being confronted with such hard facts, Colin Powell now argued that because Iraq *intended* to develop weapons, the invasion was justified.

Clearly, depending on government pronouncements and corporate media makes it hard to judge whether information corresponds to reality or not. Speculation often influences important decisions. When symbolic content plays an important role, as is the case in media coverage, one is confronted with the fact that symbolic forms can be manipulated and fabricated in order to influence public opinion and to manufacture hegemony and consent. This is especially critical when such images play a decisive role in influencing political decisions and opinions. Critical examination of all alleged facts, critical awareness of the public, and permanent reflection of the contents presented by the mass media and politics seem to be the only ways for managing these complex situations. A pluralistic media landscape that reflects alternative standpoints, methods, and approaches is needed, but especially in times of warfare this is hard to achieve.

A U.S. media center was established in Qatar, and Western media coverage on the war in Iraq depended to a large extent on the information given from U.S. officials to the few hundred journalists present in Qatar. Three press conferences per day had been promised before the war began, but frequently none took place and gagging orders were issued. This shows that Western media coverage to a large degree depends on the information issued by U.S. officials, that censorship and disinformation are military tactics, and that war-waging parties try to influence the mass media in order to mobilize the global public opinion. Going to war also means staging propaganda warfare. The mass media line up frequently with their government on important issues because they are politically influenced and shaped by, and to a certain extent represent, the same economic and political interests as dominating groups.

One can report on events in a manner that tries to invoke positive or negative feelings of the readers; differentiated coverage tries to avoid strongly emotional articles that could influence the reader in one or the other direction. Negative feelings can be invoked by associating events or persons with phenomena or terms that are considered as dangerous, threatening, extreme, and menacing. This is especially true when media connote coverage about certain events with images of violence. Many examples for such an unbalanced, emotional coverage could be found in the coverage of U.S. media on the protests and demonstrations against the war in Iraq.

The *New York Times*, the *San Francisco Chronicle*, and the *Los Angeles Times* had varied in their coverage of antiwar protests, but exhibited several operating principles: concentration on violence and arrests, limitation to the methodical, classificatory thinking, decontextualization, emergent meanings, and recoding. Certain facts that have to do with violence are overemphasized, a simple picture of the protesters is put forward, and there is a lack of differentiation, complexity, and contextual information. There is a limitation to the method of reporting mainly on violence and arrests, the method concentrates on searching for evidence of such behavior, and the method itself is not critically reflected, that is, it is presented as self-evident. Pictures and images presented reality in a positivistic manner, and they were offered as self-explaining reality that doesn't need to be questioned and checked. Different categories and images create a new whole that contains new meanings that can't be found in any single piece or element. The possible invocation that antiwar protest = violence is such an emergent meaning. Frequently, certain acts of violence are presented as isolated facts, many such singular events are decontextualized and accumulated in one article, and a new meaning emerges. Dislike and negative feelings toward protestors are not coded directly, but recoded into images and descriptions of violence.

Stuart Hall (1980) has pointed out that the coding and decoding of the meaning of messages are shaped and influenced by discourses, that is, by knowledge from routines of technological infrastructure, relationships of knowledge production, and institutional frameworks. Coded messages would be significant, meaningful discourses. Subjective aspects that influence coding and decoding would be very important, and hence one couldn't assume an automatic identity of encoded and decoded meaning. In the examples just mentioned, there is information that contains meaning and gains significance by media discourses. There might be certain meanings that shall be decoded in certain intended ways, but there surely are different decoded meanings, that is, there is no absolute identity between coding and decoding—some might see the media coverage as providing good information on the war, whereas others might consider it as highly manipulative. However, Hall mentions that there are dominant/hegemonic codes that try to ensure that recipients decode messages in a certain intended manner.

Employing emotional images of violence, disruption, arrests, and so on is a form of dominant encoding that makes use of the recipients' fears and emotions in order to increase the possibility that the forms of decoding and reading/interpreting a text remain strictly limited.

On March 26, many U.S. newspapers expressed relief that the antiwar protesters seemed to shift their strategy from mass demonstrations to smaller events and raising awareness for the relationship between economic interests and warfare. The *San Francisco Chronicle* reported, "Protests shift to firms. Demonstrators scale back, focus on war's supporters." The *Chicago Tribune* had a headline: "Protesters to cool down a bit, seek to widen support"; and the *Washington Times* reported that "anti-war groups redirect energies." The *New York Times* reported on March 29 that protesters abandoned a plan to disrupt everyday life and "have shifted away from large-scale disruptive tactics and stepped up efforts to appeal to mainstream Americans" ("Antiwar Effort Emphasizes Civility over Confrontation," *New York Times*, March 29, 2003). In many newspapers, the focus of covering protests shifted from describing the protests as violent acts, or ignoring or downplaying them, to expressing that the demonstrations will exhaust themselves.

Many articles created the impression that the international antiwar protests were anti-American. For example, the *New York Times* reported on the first day of protests that American flags were burnt in Athens and that anti-American slogans were shouted ("Wave of Protests, from Europe to New York," *New York Times*, March 21, 2003). *USA Today* listed international protests against the war and described the protesters mainly in negative terms:

> Police clashed with 30,000 anti-war demonstrators Friday outside the U.S. Embassy in Yemen. . . . 10,000 people chanted anti-U.S. slogans. . . . Small groups of protesters hurling rocks and gasoline bombs at officers guarding the glass-and-marble U.S. Embassy. . . . Protesters on bicycles blocked Parliament Square. ("Anti-War Rallies March On," *USA Today*, March 22, 2003)

On March 31, *USA Today* reported protests in Egypt and Morocco, and concentrated on the burning of U.S. flags and on stones and bottles that were thrown. Arab protesters were portrayed by some media as aggressive, violent rioters. The *Chicago Tribune* wrote of "violent anti-American clashes involving tens of thousands" in Jordan ("Simmering Rage Threat to Regimes," March 24, 2003). The *Washington Post* reported that "anti-war protesters were out in force on the streets of cities across the Arab world again yesterday to vent their anger at the U.S.-led assault on Iraq" ("Marchers Object to Assault on Iraq," *Washington Post*, March 23, 2003). The *Los Angeles Times* reported that Arabs derived pleasure from watching U.S. POWs on Iraqi TV and Al-Jazeera:

From the Arab League to the Arab street, television images of Iraqi resistance and American prisoners of war have drawn cheers. Pictures of four dead U.S. soldiers are circulating on the Internet under the words "About Time." Said a Cairo cabby: "The Iraqis are wonderful. I never dreamed they could do this." ("Arabs Take Pride in Iraqi Resistance," March 26, 2003)

Descriptions such as these can distort public opinion and mobilize the public against antiwar protests, and they also have racist implications. There is a concentration on certain facts, others are left out, and pieces of information are decontextualized and create new meanings for the reader. Many journals limit themselves to the method of finding evidence for violent behavior of protestors, and this method is not questioned or reflected. Violent images are presented as self-evident. The decontextualized description of acts of violence in Arab countries joins with terms that describe the events in a drastic way; a new meaning can emerge in the readers' mind, an emergent meaning that implies Arabs = bastards and hence has racist implications. John Fiske (1996) stresses that social struggles that are organized around the lines of class, gender, ethnicity, sexuality, age, and so on are reflected within and are part of the mass media. Social conflicts are slugged out in the media; conflicting discourses are represented by the media in certain ways. "Discourse . . . is always a terrain of struggle. . . . The dominant discourses, those that occupy the mainstream, serve dominant social interests, for they are products of the history that has secured their domination" (Fiske 1996, 5). In these examples, racial meanings are not spoken directly, but indirectly recoded into other discourses about warfare.

CODING AND CONTENT

The examples gathered in the conducted qualitative media observation study indicate that the mass media are prone to a type of political coverage that tends to distort and misrepresent reality. This is especially the case in tense political times. Making use of principles such as emotionalization, concentration on selective facts, limitation to the methodical, demonstrative harmlessness and inoffensiveness, classificatory thinking, decontextualization, emergent meaning, and recoding distinguishes manipulative coverage from high-qualitative coverage. The analyzed coverage on antiwar protests was frequently selective, emotional, unbalanced, misleading, deceptive, disorienting, and one-dimensional. Singular events were frequently decontextualized, overemphasized, and combined with other singular events, descriptions, and images in such a way that emergent meanings were produced that could easily be decoded by readers so that the coverage heavily influenced their views.

Many articles were heavily recoded with connotative images of violence used to describe antiwar protests; hence, they must be considered as having a strong ideological, manipulative propaganda character. Certain facts were frequently overemphasized, whereas other, more decisive facts at the same time were dropped or underrepresented. One can conclude that many of the analyzed products "indoctrinate and manipulate" (Marcuse 1964, 12) and represent an "attack on transcendent, critical notions" (Marcuse 1964, 85) as well as a mainstream media universe of "one-dimensional thought and behavior in which ideas, aspirations, and objectives that, by their content, transcend the established universe of discourse and action are . . . repelled" (Marcuse 1964, 12). The mass media are not a neutral, fully autonomous subsystem of society; they are closely linked to both the political and economic systems. They shape public opinion and are shaped by external social interests. Mass media are a territory of propaganda warfare; they compete for steering public opinion into certain directions. The mass media encode certain meanings, views, and ideologies into symbolic content; they make use of hegemonic codes in order to increase the possibility that the recipients will decode the content in intended ways. In times of heavy social struggles, hegemonic codes and strategies gain special importance. Due to the one-dimensional character of many war reports, alternative, independent media and information sources are very important for trying to compensate the imbalance of represented views and information.

In conclusion, one can say that the relationship of media and warfare in the Iraq War of 2003 can be characterized by a series of continuities and discontinuities that are characteristic for media coverage of warfare in the social formation of informational capitalism/media capitalism. Comparing the war in 2003 to the one in 1991 shows similar elements such as hyperreality, derealization, high-tech warfare, the presentation of high technology by the media instead of the horrors of war, the mass media's avoidance of showing and reporting about dead bodies, and the war's coverage as a global media spectacle. But one can also find new elements:

- *Internet*: War coverage making use of the Internet, interactivity, and twenty-four-hour live coverage with the help of Internet streams, War-Blogs, and alternative net media.
- *End of Monopoly*: The CNN monopoly in war coverage has been ended by the rise of FOX TV, Al Jazeera, and a European form of differentiated, balanced coverage.
- *Embedded Journalists*: An expression of the transition toward the "society of control" that relies on an integrative form of ideology.

REFERENCES

Baudrillard, J. (1983). *Simulations*. New York: Semiotext(e).

Best, S., & Kellner, D. (2001). *The postmodern adventure: Science, technology and cultural studies at the third millennium*. New York: Guilford Press.

Deleuze, G. (1992). Postscript on the societies of control. *October* 59: 3–7.

Fairness & Accuracy in Reporting (FAIR). (2003). *FAIR study: In Iraq crisis, networks are megaphones for official views*. www.fair.org/reports/iraq-sources.html

Fisk, R. (2003, February 25). How the news will be censored in this war. *Independent*, 1.

Fiske, J. (1996). *Media matters: Everyday culture and political change*. Minneapolis: University of Minnesota Press.

Foucault, M. (1977). *Discipline and punishment*. New York: Vintage.

Fuchs, C. (2002). *Krise und kritik in der informationsgesellschaft*. Norderstedt, Germany: Libri BOD.

———. (2003a). The role of the individual in the social information process. *Entropy* 5 (1), 34–60. www.mdpi.org/entropy

———. (2003b). Structuration theory and social self-organisation. *Systemic Practice and Action Research* 16 (2), 133–167.

Fuchs, C., & Hofkirchner, W. (2003). *Studienbuch informatik und gesellschaft*. Vienna: Libri BOD.

Giddens, A. (1984). *The constitution of society*. Berkeley: University of California Press.

———. (1985). *A contemporary critique of historical materialism. Vol. 2: The nation-state and violence*. Cambridge: Polity Press

Hall, S. (1980). Encoding/decoding. *Media, Culture and Society* 2, 57–72.

Katovsky, B., & Carlson, T. (Eds.) (2003). *Embedded: The media at war in Iraq*. Guilford, CT: Lyons Press.

Luhmann, N. (1996). *Die realität der massenmedien*. Opladen, Germany: Westdeutscher Verlag.

Marcuse, H. (1964). *One-dimensional man: Studies in the ideology of advanced industrial society*. London: Routledge.

No evidence Iraq stockpiled WMDs. (2003, October 2). Interview with David Kay. Retrieved April 24, 2004, from www.cnn.com

Project for Excellence in Journalism Research Center. (2003). *Embedded reporters: What are Americans getting? PEJ looks at embedding*. Washington, DC: PEJ Research Center. www.journalism.org

Prokop, D. (2002). *Der medien-kapitalismus: Das lexikon der neuen kritischen Medienforschung*. Hamburg: VSA.

Rampton, S., & Stauber, J. (2003). *Weapons of mass deception: The uses of propaganda in Bush's war on Iraq*. New York: Tarcher/Penguin.

13

Might Makes Right: News Reportage as Discursive Weapon in the War in Iraq

Mike Gasher

Language is one of the most powerful weapons of war. If U.S. President George W. Bush can be criticized for oversimplifying the conflict as a clear case of good versus evil, mainstream news coverage adopted its own comic-book discourse in framing the 2003 Iraq war. In the last stages of buildup and the first weeks of fighting, reportage in *Time* and *Newsweek* depicted the war as a decided mismatch between the formidable U.S.-led coalition and an Iraq divided between a dictatorial regime ill-equipped to resist invasion on the one hand and, on the other, a beleaguered Iraqi people desperate for liberation from the evil dictator Saddam Hussein.

A central element in this depiction was the repeated recitation of the U.S. military's technological sophistication, with particular emphasis on its devastating yet precise weaponry. These accounts of the American forces' clean, accurate, and efficient armaments stood in contrast to the far more opaque references to Iraq's "weapons of mass destruction," a menacing label that implied imprecision, indiscriminate devastation, and a reckless regard for human life (including Iraqi lives), the frightening last resort for an army otherwise described as unkempt, inept, and disinclined.

This assertion of American technological superiority was neither merely bravado nor technophilia. It was closely allied to the claims of moral superiority proffered by George W. Bush (and Tony Blair), who argued that the war in Iraq would not be a war *on* Iraq, but a dramatic and necessary first step in freeing both the Iraqi people and Western democracies from the persistent threat posed by Saddam. Nancy Franklin (2003) neatly summarized the sentiment in the *New Yorker*: "If today's weapons really are as microsurgically precise as we have been told they are, perhaps we will see that it's possible to conduct a war with little collateral damage, and perhaps we will be less likely in the future to question those who get us into wars" (32).

But if Franklin was circumspect, *Time* and *Newsweek* reporting uncritically subscribed to this premise. The breathless and reverent cataloguing of high-tech firepower, described in such specific detail that even the brand names of the weapons became familiar, foregrounded a decidedly technocratic theme in the war coverage. The automated, long-range capacity of these expert weapons systems, supported by equally sophisticated intelligence and sur-veillance networks, tied the notion of power to precision and accuracy, a kind of responsible, even moral, military might, the same kind of responsible po-litical power the U.S. and allied governments maintained they were employ-ing to depose Saddam Hussein. The theater of war was thus rendered a sani-tized operating theater for the careful, studied, and surgical removal of a cancerous regime.

The prospect of going to war must be sold and, in democracies at least, must be sold on grounds of military, political, and economic logic as well as moral claims. One frame for the sales pitch for this war was "unfinished business"—the unfinished business of the 1991 Gulf War, in which the Al-lied forces settled for expelling the Iraqis from Kuwait rather than expelling Saddam from power; the unfinished business of the subsequent UN-sanctioned weapons inspections; and the unfinished business of the September 11, 2001, terrorist attacks on New York City and Washington, D.C. (see Thomas 2003). President Bush succeeded in selling his "War on Terror" to allies will-ing to take on the Taliban in Afghanistan, but convincing countries like France, Germany, Russia, and Canada to carry the fight into Iraq proved much more difficult.

If the Bush administration mustered an argument for a preventative or pre-emptive war based on the danger that Saddam Hussein posed to his own peo-ple (and the outside world), Iraq's ties to the al-Qaeda terrorist network, and its biological and chemical weapons stores, news coverage delivered a re-markably similar message, depicting American-led military action as a rela-tively benign solution to a threat taken very seriously by an American news audience traumatized by September 11, feeling vulnerable to the very real prospect of future terrorist attacks on U.S. soil, and already familiar with the demonized Saddam Hussein.

Through a close, textual analysis of *Time* and *Newsweek* reporting in the two weeks preceding the war and the first two weeks of the invasion, this chapter seeks to demonstrate that the message these newsmagazines delivered conformed to that of the Bush administration. But rather than argue that their journalists were merely parroting White House and Pentagon statements, this chapter instead asserts that their reportage tapped into deeper ideological currents of U.S. exceptionalism, Orientalism, and cultural superiority. These currents provided a cognitive context in which Iraq could be readily understood and in which government policy decisions could be perceived as sensible and appropriate. In such a context, journalists covering those policy decisions could be seen as reporting the factual, the newsworthy, and the commonsensical, when in fact what they were doing was granting legitimacy to partisan political interests and goals.

The particular emphasis on technology in this reportage—weapons systems, related military hardware, and surveillance and intelligence techniques—not only reassured readers of U.S. military hegemony, but also framed this technology as the product of a superior culture and served to minimize the damage war would do. When, in the first weeks of the war, a surprising number of American and British soldiers were killed in helicopter accidents and so-called friendly fire mishaps, as civilian casualties began to mount, as military intelligence shortcomings became evident, and as the U.S. invasion strategy came into question, considerable ideological work was necessary to maintain the simple equation between might and right. Analysis of *Time* and *Newsweek* reportage reveals some of the techniques involved in this work.

JOURNALISM AS REPRESENTATION

Journalism is a practice of representation, which Stuart Hall (1997) defines as "the production of meaning through language" (16). Rather than simply mirror or reflect reality, as many journalists still stubbornly insist, news reportage selectively deploys words, images, and sounds to depict newsmakers and news events, constructing stories through which we come to know about the world around us. If these stories are always partial depictions and share cognitive space with other sources of knowledge and information, they nonetheless help to define, or give meaning to, people, places, institutions, and events.

In no area of journalism is this more true and more significant than in war reporting, because the stakes are so high; individual lives, political regimes, and even the future of nation-states depend on whether, and how, the war is fought (see MacMillan 2003). Combatants who know full well the role of news in the formation of public opinion, both at home and abroad, use every propaganda technique they can muster and shield journalists from direct access to knowledge and information (see Alter 2003; Poniewozik 2003). Even when embedded reporters had access to the battlefields of Iraq, they did not always know what they were witnessing, nor were they completely free to report it. The particular meanings produced in war reportage play an important role in defining the conflict and contribute to questions of legitimacy and illegitimacy—even legality and illegality—so central to public debate. The words that reporters use to describe things ("collateral damage" or "civilian deaths"), the people they seek information from (Americans or Iraqis, generals or soldiers, politicians or civilians), and the metaphorical frames they employ ("liberation" or "occupation") take on considerable significance in this process.

Public opinion was especially important for the United States in late 2002 and early 2003, when it sought both international approval and military allies for its Iraq campaign. The news media provided terrain upon which beliefs about Iraqi and American motives could be explored, ideas about how to resolve the "Iraq problem" could be debated, and, ultimately, mandates could be forged and won.

A source of endless fascination for communications scholars is how news terrain, from the time of the Crimean War to the present, has been demarcated and employed (see Knightley 1975). How wide a range of views have been identified and included? How have those views been represented? Who gets to speak with authority, and who doesn't? What aspects of the conflict are foregrounded, which are backgrounded, and which are ignored? What meanings are attributed to the various possible outcomes? As Jaap van Ginneken (1998) notes:

> Certain repertoires [sic] of discourses are implicitly treated in the news as falling within the consensual, common-sensical, acceptable realm. They are actively made to seem obvious, logical, coherent. Others are thought to be outside "the limits of acceptable discourse." They are actively made to look silly, irrational, weird. (164)

While each news medium will provide its own specific answers to the questions posed above, *Time* and *Newsweek* are being singled out here on the basis of their mainstream status within the larger U.S. mediascape. *Time* and *Newsweek* are the clear circulation leaders among newsmagazines in the United States; *Time* has a weekly circulation of 4.1 million (which translates into 22 million readers) and *Newsweek* sells 4 million copies each week (i.e., 21 million readers). Both magazines are available at newsstands around the world and on the World Wide Web (*Time* 2004; *Newsweek* 2004). Analysis was conducted on the two editions of each magazine immediately preceding the war (March 17 and 24, 2003) and the two editions of each covering the opening weeks of the war (March 31 and April 7, 2003).

PUTTING THE POWER IN FIREPOWER

Readers of *Time* and *Newsweek* had plenty of opportunity to be shocked by the specter of Iraq's chemical and biological weapons stores and awed by the power and sophistication of U.S. military capabilities by the time the bombing campaign began on the night of March 19–20, 2003. Readers could be forgiven, however, for wondering why U.S. munitions were not also described as "weapons of mass destruction," given their evident capacity for such.

In excited prose, *Time* emphasized the scale of the attack, the magnitude of American firepower, and the "intelligence" of its weapons in an article outlining U.S. war plans (Thompson 2003). The war would be like "the Big Bang—hundreds of towering explosions all across Iraq all at the same time," employing "unprecedented numbers of smart, satellite-guided bombs." The story noted, "Pentagon planners suggest that more targets in Baghdad would be hit in the first 24 hours of Gulf War II than were hit in all 43 days of the first war" (Thompson 2003, 26). If only 10 percent of the bombs dropped in 1991 were "smart bombs," this time almost 80 percent would be. "And unlike the laser-guided bombs of 12 years ago, these satellite-guided weapons, known as joint direct-attack munitions (JDAMs), should be able to find their targets automatically, unimpeded by smoke or bad weather" (26). If this wasn't enough, *Time* assured its readers, the U.S. Air Force could deploy 9.5-ton, satellite-guided "massive ordnance air-bust bombs (MOABs)" with the power of a small nuclear weapon "complete with mushroom cloud" (27).

To minimize "collateral damage"—an estimated 3,500 Iraqi civilians were killed in the 1991 war—U.S. military planners were using a computer program called Bugsplat to estimate the "blast pattern" of bombs and thereby adjust aircraft approaches to minimize civilian casualties (Thompson 2003, 28–29). The principal targets of the plan were presidential palaces, government buildings, and military installations:

> If things went as planned, key civilian sites like bridges and water and power systems would largely be spared, bringing home the message that the U.S. target is Saddam, not the Iraqi people. Such a strategy would make reconstruction easier when the war ended. (Thompson 2003, 29)

Time expanded on the inventory in its March 31 edition. Superimposed on a graphic illustration of Iraq were depictions and detailed descriptions of bombers, bombs, and missiles ("Weapons of War" 2003), with an emphasis on their power, precision, and long-range capabilities. The Tomahawk Cruise Missile RGM/UGM-109, for example, could be launched from ships and submarines, was equipped with a global positioning system, flew at low altitude and high speed to evade radar detection, and carried a 1,000-lb. warhead. The Joint Stand-off Weapon (JSOW), a 1,000-lb. air-to-surface guided missile, could carry a single warhead, armor-piercing "bomblets," or a "soft bomb containing filaments" to short-circuit power lines. Four of the bombs dropped on the bunker where Saddam was believed to be staying the first night of the war were Enhanced Guided Bomb Unit-27s, which could be directed by either laser or GPS, "making it ideal for any weather condition" ("Weapons of War" 2003, 26–27).

The two-page, full-color spread entitled "High-Tech Brute Force" in *Time*'s March 31 edition ("High-Tech" 2003), looked like a still from a video game and read like an advertisement for the battlefield technology depicted. Accompanying an illustration of the M270 tank, for example, was this description: "Without leaving the cab, the crew can fire up to 12 surface-to-surface rockets in less than a minute, then move on." Beside an illustration of the M1 Abrams tank, the caption read, "With thermal imaging, night vision, laser rangefinders and computerized targeting, this is the world's most advanced— and most lethal—tank." The Apache Longbow helicopter could conduct "war at warp speed" ("High Tech" 2003, 30–31).

Newsweek similarly catalogued the American military's "enormous" array of weapons, but also underscored how few soldiers were required to guide this technology. The Abrams tank carried just four crew members, and the $45 million F-117A stealth bomber needed only a pilot (Ulick & Sparks 2003). Such weaponry was testament to "the American way," *Newsweek* noted: "The American way of war has always been to overwhelm the enemy with superior firepower—more, bigger and better guns, ships, planes and tanks. (It was often said that World War II was won in the factories of Detroit)" (Thomas & Klaidman 2003, 28). The war itself, it seemed, could be run by remote control. This story was illustrated with a photograph of Defense Secretary Donald Rumsfeld (at the Pentagon) and General Tommy Franks (at Central Command in Qatar) discussing the opening days of the invasion by videoconference (Thomas & Klaidman 2003, 22–23).

Only later, when it appeared the war would become mired in guerilla warfare in the streets of Baghdad, were the disadvantages of the U.S. military's high-tech weaponry noted. *Newsweek* informed readers that the Abrams tank, for example, "has enormous firepower, but limited visibility and cannon range—making high and low targets hard to hit" ("Taking It to the Streets" 2003).

American soldiers were depicted as veritable cyborgs, highly trained and loaded down with gadgetry to enhance their vision, their killing capacity, and their safety. A graphic illustration in *Time*, under the aggressive headline "Strike Force," showed an infantryman equipped with a night vision scope; a Kevlar helmet; a backpack full of food, water, and "supplies"; a first-aid pack; an M4 carbine rifle with a daytime telescopic sight and a laser sight; a mask in case of chemical or biological attack; a grenade belt; and a uniform available in various camouflage colors—tan for the desert and green for other areas (Dykman & Bradford 2003, 30–31). Later in the war, American soldiers could draw on special equipment for urban warfare. *Time* illustrated a soldier equipped with a lightweight ladder and rope with grappling hook, a GPS tracker, a small mirror to see around corners and under doors, a portable light, tape and paint for marking targets, a flare, a biohazard suit, elbow and knee pads, and an M16 rifle (Tweeten, Gabel, & Orecklin 2003, 30–31). In case of the dreaded attack by biological or chemical weapons, U.S. ground forces were equipped with protective clothing "but only a few minutes to put it on before it's too late." Beneath the headline "Lethal Weapons," *Time* showed a soldier dressed in Joint Service Lightweight Integrated Suit Technology, essentially "a hooded jacket and trousers made of special lightweight fabric" with a water-repellent shell and carbon layers (Tweeten, Adams, & Bradford 2003, 29).

Both *Time* and *Newsweek* added to this formidable picture by alluding to the long military history of a number of U.S. fighting units and the credentials of their obviously competent commanders. The 3rd Infantry Division, for example, carried the nickname "Rock of the Marne" for its fighting in France during World War I and saw "heavy action" in Kuwait during the 1991 Gulf War. Its commander was Major General Buford C. Blount III, a thirty-two-year Army veteran. The 173rd Airborne Regiment was led by Colonel William C. Mayville Jr., who had an M.A. in aerospace engineering, and the 101st Airborne Division was commanded by Major General David H. Petraeus, a West Point graduate with a Ph.D. in international relations from Princeton ("Guide" 2003, 22–23). *Newsweek* noted that the First Armored Division "fought Rommel's tanks in World War II and Saddam's Republican Guard in 1991," and the 101st Airborne "famously jumped into Normandy on D-Day" (Piore 2003, 8).

The American troops were supported by the latest in battlefield medical technology, a benefit equally available to Iraqi military and civilian casualties. *Time* carried a two-page photograph of U.S. and British medics treating two Iraqis burned during the bombing of Safwan ("Casualties of War" 2003, 16–17), and later ran an article describing the American military's Forward Resuscitative Surgical Suite, designed to provide surgery at the front lines, "a ground-breaking approach to battlefield medical care" (Gupta 2003). The *Time* story said that 70 percent of the sixty-four patients treated over a six-day period were Iraqis (Gupta 2003, 51). But perhaps the greatest medical marvel available to U.S. troops were sperm banks "offering to give military couples a year's free storage, in case a chemical attack destroys the husband's fertility or an older wife wants to keep trying to have a baby and can't afford to wait a year while her husband is gone" (Gibbs 2003, 29).

If *Time* and *Newsweek* revered well-equipped U.S. troops, they were equally enthusiastic in their denigration of Iraqi military preparedness. Stories repeatedly

called into question the willingness of Iraq's conscripted soldiers to fight, referred constantly to their penchant for quick surrender, and at one point noted
their "almost medieval" tactic of filling moats with oil and setting them alight
(Thomas & Barry 2003a, 27). In the *Time* photo spread "Inside Iraq" (2003),
readers saw Iraqi civilians transporting their belongings in rickety wagons (38),
a boy practicing with his father's AK-47 assault rifle (38), and children playing
on sandbags in Baghdad (40–41). In *Newsweek*, readers saw an old man with a
rifle peering through a sandbag barricade and read of Iraqi soldiers filling "moats
of oil" to foil U.S. attacks (Liu 2003a, 34). Iraq's defense depended to a great extent on "tribal loyalties," as three-quarters of Iraq's 24 million people belonged
to one of 150 tribes (Liu 2003b, 31).

In contrast with the boundless U.S. weaponry, a one-by-seven-inch box in
the March 17 edition of *Newsweek* summarized Iraq's troop numbers and military hardware, with particular emphasis on how the Iraqi military had been
depleted since 1990 ("What He's Got" 2003). No brand names and no high-
tech specifications were mentioned, just "combat aircraft" and "helicopters"
(28). Where detail was provided, readers learned that the troops were "de-
moralized, frightened conscripts" (Thomas & Barry 2003a, 26) who would be
inspired by Saddam to be "good martyrs" (27).

If these descriptions painted Iraq's defense forces as feeble and pathetic,
they also reinforced the prospect of Saddam resorting to "weapons of mass
destruction," maintaining Iraq as a "threat" and tapping into American fears
of terrorist attack. The newsmagazines consistently raised the possibility of
Iraq deploying biological and chemical weapons—against enemy troops and
against Israel. This was the menacing qualifier in an otherwise uninspiring ré-
sumé of Iraq's military preparedness in *Newsweek* (Thomas & Barry 2003a).
"The most pressing—and disturbing—question is whether and when Saddam
will use weapons of mass destruction" (Thomas & Barry 2003a, 28). He
could use poison gas to "cause chaos and possibly panic among support
troops in rear areas," or "he could create mayhem by unleashing biological
agents in the American bases . . . that sprawl over much of northern Kuwait"
(29). If his desperation were to reach a critical point, he could even gas his
own people and blame the United States. "Many Arabs watching Al-Jazeera
would believe him" (30).

TECHNOLOGICAL SUPERIORITY AS MORAL SUPERIORITY

Morality was a central theme of the news coverage in *Time* and *Newsweek*,
even if it was more commonly discussed in terms of fairness. A *Time* column
by Andrew Sullivan (2003), explaining the close relationship between Bush

and British Prime Minister Tony Blair, found common denominators in religious faith and morality.

What brings these two men together is a shared Christian faith. Blair is lampooned in London for having the self-righteous fastidiousness of an Anglican vicar. But his sincere faith forged a bond with a believing president and made Blair more receptive than most nonbelieving Europeans to the clear moral tone in the White House (Sullivan 2003, 37).

Sullivan continued: "Blair not only helped prove that this war was necessary, he also helped show that it was moral. That is no small achievement" (2003, 37). While using different language, *Time* columnist Joe Klein (2003a), too, spoke of America's higher purpose in the "liberation, not conquest" of Iraq. He hoped for the same kind of humility in winning the peace. Describing the United States as "incomparably strong and admirably free, the most benign superpower in history," Klein wrote, "Can Americans learn to use diplomacy as exquisitely as it [sic] does force?" (2003a, 72).

As noted above, the newsmagazines drew a clear distinction between the sophisticated, high-tech, "conventional" weapons of the United States and the crude (rifles, oil, smoke) and "unconventional" (biological agents, chemicals) weapons of Iraq. Not only was it taken for granted that Iraq possessed "poisonous weapons" (e.g., Thomas 2003, 58), but the way they kill was also described in detail. The nerve agent VX, for example, "blocks the transmission of impulses down the body's central nervous system, causing convulsions, respiratory paralysis and death. It penetrates through the skin, eyes or respiratory system" (Tweeten, Adams, & Bradford 2003, 29).

U.S. weapons were never described in this way. In fact, readers were given the impression that their targets were buildings rather than people (e.g., Liu 2003a), and their awesome power was even potentially life preserving. In *Newsweek*, George F. Will (2003, 66) heralded technological advances in U.S. air power to advance a moral argument: "Air power by itself recently won a sort of war—the 1999 *no-casualty campaign* conducted from 15,000 feet, to stop Serbia's depredations in Kosovo" (emphasis added). Air supremacy not only justified U.S. unilateralism "because it becomes increasingly difficult to integrate most other nations' forces into operations," but also "becomes a huge factor in psychological warfare" (Will 2003, 66). That is, awesome U.S. air power could prompt a quick Iraqi surrender, saving the lives—American and Iraqi—that would otherwise be lost in a protracted, and ultimately futile, war.

Related to this, *Time* and *Newsweek* drew clear distinctions between American and Iraqi tactics, especially in the second week of the war. As the name "Operation Iraqi Freedom" suggested, the war was against Saddam, not Iraq, and U.S. soldiers, like tourists who wished not to offend their overseas hosts, carried with them a military guide to Iraqi history, politics, culture, food, and language (Lorch 2003). Soldiers were advised to "maintain eye contact and avoid arguments" and warned *not* to discuss religion, use A-OK or thumbs-up gestures (because these signify obscene gestures in the Middle East), or move away when someone stands close in conversation (13).

More seriously, the newsmagazines contrasted the two countries' styles of warfare, clearly favoring the Americans' upfront approach of conventional air and ground forces to the Iraqis' battlefield deception and, later, urban guerilla warfare. This was part of a larger tendency to humanize American partici-pants—for example, General Tommy Franks (Duffy & Thompson 2003) and a husband-and-wife military couple (Gibbs 2003) in *Time* cover stories, pro-files of heroic *Time* and *Newsweek* journalists (Kelly 2003; Whitaker 2003)—and denigrate Iraqis. The Iraqis never attacked; they always "ambushed" U.S. troops. *Time* and *Newsweek* consistently referred to "sneaky" Iraqis, who, in their worst moments, would pretend to surrender, then open fire on American troops (e.g., Robinson 2003, 34; Thomas & Barry 2003a, 25–26). In an arti-cle entitled, "Who Do You Trust?" *Newsweek* reporter Kevin Peraino (2003) said U.S. officers were learning that trusting Iraqis would get their troops killed. "Enemy soldiers wearing civilian clothes and driving pickup trucks have been conducting guerilla-style attacks." This creates an obvious dilemma for U.S. troops, who don't want to kill civilians. "American soldiers do not aim to kill innocents, and they know that Saddam Hussein could use civilian casualties as propaganda" (Peraino 2003, 31).

As *Time* and *Newsweek* noted, these tactics evoked bitter memories of pre-vious U.S. military campaigns in Vietnam and Somalia. And, certainly, criti-cism of such tactics might be warranted were not for the obvious double stan-dards at play. In the early stages of the war, it was the American forces that were "unfair," but the label was a proud boast rather than a slight. *Time* quoted 1st Marine Expeditionary commander Lieutenant General James T. Conway as saying, "This isn't a fair fight. We didn't intend it to be" ("Guide" 2003, 23). This comment was repeated by a number of armed-services per-sonnel. Major Kevin Dunlop of the 3rd Infantry Division told *Time*, "It's not a fair fight. Trucks with machine guns against tanks and Bradleys can only have one outcome. We are slaughtering them" (Lacey 2003, 46). The last sen-tence of this quotation was used as the headline for *Time*'s April 7 section, "Iraq: With the Troops."

Responding directly to the criticism of unseemly Iraqi guerilla tactics, Michael Elliott (2003) used a column in *Time*, titled "Playing by Mogadishu Rules," to remind readers that such deception is always used by armies that face an overpowering opponent. "In any armed conflict, guerilla tacts can be an equalizer." If "the heroic narrative of American warfare stresses great, set-piece, conventional battles," Elliott noted that Americans invented guerilla tactics during the War of Independence against Great Britain. Today, he argued: "Given the conventional power of the U.S. military, any probable adversary will choose unconventional tactics" (2003, 32). Elliott, however, drew an important distinction between guerilla wars today and those of the past; with the invention of the video camera and global, twenty-four-hour news coverage: "One unarmed Afghan—or Iraqi—killed by a scared soldier can have greater political consequences than a truckload of humanitarian aid" (2003, 32).

The ethics of TV news coverage was a particularly touchy subject, but also underlined a double standard. The U.S. objected to Iraqi TV and the Qatar-based Al-Jazeera showing pictures of dead American soldiers and prisoners of war following the capture of a convoy outside Nasiriya (Alter 2003; Poniewozik 2003). In *Time*, columnist Joe Klein (2003b) wrestled with this issue—"The right to privacy after death in combat should trump all other concerns" (45)—and noted that *Time* had not published the photograph of a dead American soldier that had appeared on Al-Jazeera. What Klein did not mention was the two-page color photograph published a few pages earlier, which featured, close up and in clear focus, a dead Iraqi soldier ("Death in the Desert" 2003, 18–19).

SOURCES OF NEWS KNOWLEDGE

No discourse is totalizing. But the clarity and consistency in the way the two newsmagazines portrayed the war in Iraq were remarkable; dozens of reporters, photographers, and editors at the two magazines systematically elevated U.S. motives and military capabilities at the same time as they denigrated those of Iraq. Once "the cradle of civilization," as *Newsweek* pointed out (see Liu & Underwood 2003), Iraq now awaited rescue by the new guardians of civilization.

This framing of the war conformed to that of the Bush administration; *Time* and *Newsweek*, in effect, served as voices of U.S. political power, lending journalistic authority to a partisan and contentious, not to mention simplistic, worldview. This was critical because these magazines provided a central site upon which information about the war became available to the public, and their interpretations of events were normalized as standard ways for understanding, discussing, and justifying the war effort.

The newsmagazines' extensive coverage gave little serious attention to arguments mustered in opposition to the war, either by protestors, U.N. diplomats, weapons inspectors, or the governments of countries like France, Germany, Russia, and Canada; nor was any serious credence given to the political-economic contention that the Bush administration's obsession with Iraq had more to do with liberating oil than liberating people. The only serious and sustained reflection on U.S. intentions in Iraq and its larger role in international affairs came in a *Newsweek* cover story by Fareed Zakaria (2003) entitled, "The Arrogant Empire." The article maintained that criticism of U.S. foreign policy was a product of the Bush administration's arrogant style, and insisted that the United States was a part of the solution to international tensions rather than part of the problem. "In principle, American power is not simply good for America; it is good for the world. Most of the problems the world faces today—from terrorism to AIDS to nuclear proliferation—will be solved not with less U.S. engagement, but with *more*" (Zakaria 2003, 30).

It would be facile to suggest that the newsmagazines' reporting was strictly a case of centralized editorial control—whether by U.S. military authorities or *Time* and *Newsweek* management—or journalists simply being faithful to the commander in chief in the context of war. Instead, it suggests that there were deeper ideological currents at play, firmly held and widely shared values and beliefs that took on the mantle of common sense and that surfaced in news reports in the form of language choices, definitions, metaphorical frames, and unquestioned assumptions. There were beliefs about diplomatic avenues of conflict resolution as bureaucratic inaction and Orientalist beliefs about the "nature" of Muslims and the Middle East, which construct the Orient as an "ethnic unit" that is inferior to the West (see Said 1979). There were beliefs about where to draw the line between fair and unfair on the modern-day battlefield; beliefs about U.S. exceptionalism, in which the United States was not merely a "benign superpower," in Joe Klein's words, but beneficent; and beliefs about the threat that terrorism uniquely posed to the United States. As *Time* stated in an article analyzing the Bush administration's decision to go to war in Iraq:

> Everyone sensible—French, American, Russian, German—has known for years that Saddam is a dangerous tyrant who brutalizes his people, is prepared to threaten others and bears abiding grudges. But only one nation—the U.S.—has suffered the thousands of deaths that a few people with a deep hatred could inflict. (Elliott & Carney 2003, 51)

If *Time* and *Newsweek*'s particular emphasis on technology in the reportage affirmed U.S. superiority—not only military, but cultural—considerable ideological work became necessary to maintain the simple equation between might and right when, in the first weeks of the war, a surprising number of mishaps cost lives—of American and British soldiers, and of Iraqi civilians—and appeared to call into question the discourse of preeminence. Fatal helicopter accidents, "friendly-fire" incidents, stray bombs, and intelligence failures threatened to undermine the case for technological proficiency and cast doubt on the concept of responsible military action. But *Time* and *Newsweek* coverage was undeterred; invested in their faith in the righteousness of the U.S. cause, the newsmagazines either rationalized these incidents or perceived them as too inconsequential to explain.

U.S. and British claims about Iraq's secret nuclear weapons program were reported to be based on forged documents (Wolffe, Hosenball, & Lipper 2003, 8) and U.S. Air Force planners complained about the intelligence community's inability to locate storage sites for Iraq's biological and chemical weapons (Thomas & Barry 2003a, 30). After just two weeks of war, *Time* ran a feature entitled "3 Flawed Assumptions" (McGeary 2003), which noted that the Bush administration's "Teflon war" was not "quick, easy, relatively bloodless"; ordinary Iraqis did not welcome U.S. soldiers as liberators; and the war plan had seemed to bog down (52–56). While dutifully reported, these intelligence failures were not framed as significant impediments to the larger mission.

Three days into the war, military vehicles were breaking down and getting stuck in the desert sand, stretching convoy lines and creating dangerous traffic jams. After three days of fighting, more soldiers had been killed in helicopter crashes and collisions than by enemy fire. *Newsweek* noted that in the 1991 war, one-quarter of casualties resulted from "friendly fire" (Thomas & Klaidman 2003, 31). When sandstorms weren't creating havoc with the proper functioning of military equipment, they were blinding tank and truck drivers (Campo-Flores 2003, 30). Of the thirty-seven dead who *Newsweek* identified in its April 7 edition, eighteen had died accidentally: seven in a helicopter collision, four in helicopter crashes, two in road accidents, two in a grenade attack by a fellow American soldier, two by drowning, and one in a machine-gun accident (Adler, Kantrowitz, & Cowley 2003, 54–57). None of these mishaps prompted *Time* or *Newsweek* to qualify their commitment to the sophistication of U.S. military technology or the preparedness of U.S. troops.

The U.S. military accepted no responsibility for civilian deaths in the early stages of the war; news coverage in *Time* and *Newsweek* focused on the propaganda points at stake. *Newsweek* reported:

Saddam was no doubt heartened when a blast ripped through a crowded Shiite marketplace in Baghdad on Friday, killing 58 people and creating bloody images, including a severed head, for the cameras of the ubiquitous Arab cable-TV network, Al-Jazeera. The Iraqis blamed an American bomb; the Americans couldn't explain the explosion, except to note that Saddam is not above slaughtering his own people and pointing to the infidels. (Thomas & Barry 2003b, 26–27)

Time contextualized civilian deaths the same way: as part of the propaganda war. "In Baghdad, Iraqi officials claimed last week that U.S. bombs hit a marketplace and a hospital, killing 30 civilians; U.S. commanders said the damage may have been caused by falling Iraqi antiaircraft missiles" (Ratnesar 2003, 28).

When two survivors of a bombing on the Shaab market told *Newsweek* reporter Melinda Liu (2003c) that a U.S. warplane had fired two missiles into an oil tanker parked nearby, her story assigned far more credence to the explanation offered by Brigadier General Vincent Brooks the next day at Central Command. Brooks said it was either the fault of a stray Iraqi missile or a deliberate Iraqi attack (Liu 2003c, 42). Further on in her story, Liu interviewed Dr. Sermed Al-Gailani, who was treating the bombing victims in a Saddam City hospital. Al-Gailani clearly blamed the Americans, but Liu remained doubtful:

> I supposed it was possible that a U.S. pilot could fire on an oil tanker, mistaking it for a missile launcher in the smoke, the dust and the rain. The next day I went back to the site. There was no sign of an oil tanker amid the charred metal. (2003c, 45)

Later that week, a bombing in the Al-Shoala district killed a reported sixty people, and the blame game was resumed. "By the next morning, the scene and its surroundings were effectively sanitized of any bomb fragments or other evidence. For some reason, dump trucks and backhoes were busy removing a fetid mountain of trash from a lot nearby" (Liu 2003c, 42). Liu didn't specify who was cleaning up the evidence. She didn't need to.

PLAUSIBILITY RATHER THAN TRUTH

In the complexity and chaos of war—the prewar diplomacy, the combat, the postwar negotiations—plausibility is more accessible than truth. War correspondents, no matter how hard they work and how conscientiously they seek the factual, more often deal in the plausible, the credible, the conceivable, the logical, the likely. This is a dangerous game, because while plausibility is based to some extent on the evidence provided, it is based on much more besides. Today's news stories belong to a larger inherited discourse, a larger body of texts and talk characterized by recurring themes and tendencies, all of which combine in messy ways to attribute meaning to the people, places, institutions, and events that populate the news. We have been reading for a while news about Saddam Hussein's Iraq, news that has rendered plausible torture, mass killings, biological and chemical weapons, and even the export of terrorism.

Journalists unavoidably engage in the construction of plausibility. When truth and factuality are elusive, the news becomes a site of persuasive speech and news texts become rhetorical, even self-fulfilling, prophecy. Readers faced the 2003 war in Iraq with a considerable number of preconceived notions—about Iraq, about Saddam Hussein, about the United States, about terrorism. *Time* and *Newsweek* coverage of the war constructed a picture of events that remained faithful to those preconceptions and reinforced the framing of the conflict as a simple struggle between good and evil, and the war as a just means, the only sensible means, to eradicate that evil.

REFERENCES

Adler, J., Kantrowitz, B., & Cowley, G. (2003, April 7). I had a terrible feeling. *Newsweek*, 52–57.

Alter, J. (2003, April 7). The other air battle. *Newsweek*, 38–39.

Campo-Flores, A. (2003, April 7). The sand and the fury. *Newsweek*, 30.

Casualties of war. (2003, March 31). *Time*, 16–17.

Death in the desert. (2003, April 7). *Time*, 18–19.

Duffy, M., & Thompson, M. (2003, March 17). Straight shooter. *Time*, 22–25.

Dykman, J., & Bradford, L. (2003, March 17). Strike force. *Time*, 30–31.

Elliott, M. (2003, April 7). Playing by Mogadishu rules. *Time*, 32.

Elliott, M., & Carney, J. (2003, March 31). First stop, Iraq. *Time*, 40–51.

Franklin, N. (2003, March 31). TV goes to war. *New Yorker*, 32–33.

Gibbs, N. (2003, March 24). An American family goes to war. *Time*, 26–33.

A guide to the Allied Forces. (2003, March 31). *Time*, 22–23.

Gupta, S. (2003, April 7). At the front with the devil docs. *Time*, 51.

Hall, S. (1997). The work of representation. In S. Hall (Ed.), *Representation: Cultural representations and signifying practices* (pp. 1–64). London: Sage.

High-tech brute force. (2003, March 31). *Time*, 30–31.

Inside Iraq. (2003, March 24). *Time*, 36–41.

Kelly, J. (2003, March 31). How we cover war and uncover history. *Time*, 5.

Klein, J. (2003a, March 31). America shows its colors. *Time*, 72.

———. (2003b, April 7). The PG rated war. *Time*, 45.

Knightley, P. (1975). *The first casualty. From the Crimea to Vietnam: The war correspondent as hero, propagandist, and myth maker*. New York: Harcourt Brace Jovanovich.

Lacey, J. (2003, April 7). On the road to death at Najaf. *Time*, 46–47.

Liu, M. (2003a, March 31). Live from Baghdad. *Newsweek*, 32–38.

———. (2003b, March 17). The will of the tribes. *Newsweek*, 31.

———. (2003c, April 7). The mind of the Iraqis. *Newsweek*, 40–45.

Liu, M., & Underwood, A. (2003, March 24). Babylonian booty. *Newsweek*, 50–51.

Lorch, D. (2003, March 17). Iraq: Do read this for war. *Newsweek*, 13.

MacMillan, M. (2003). *Paris 1919: Six months that changed the world*. New York: Random House.

McGeary, J. (2003, April 7). 3 flawed assumptions. *Time*, 52–56.

Newsweek. (2004). History of *Newsweek*. MSNBC. Retrieved February 29, 2004, from www.msnbc.com/modules/newsweek/info/nwinfo/_history. asp

Peraino, K. (2003, April 7). Who do you trust? *Newsweek*, 31.

Piore, A. (2003, April 7). Grunt 101: A peri primer. *Newsweek*, 8.

Poniewozik, J. (2003, April 7). The war on TV from both sides. *Time*, 60–61.

Ratnesar, R. (2003, April 7). Sticking to his guns. *Time*, 20–29.

Robinson, S. (2003, March 31). Dispatches from the front: Basra. *Time*, 34.

Said, E. (1979). *Orientalism*. New York: Vintage Books.

Sullivan, A. (2003, March 31). The American prime minister. *Time*, 37.

Taking it to the streets. (2003, April 7). *Newsweek*, 28–29.

Thomas, E. (2003, March 31). The 12 year itch. *Newsweek*, 54–65.

Thomas, E., & Barry, J. (2003a, March 17). Saddam's war. *Newsweek*, 24–31.

———. (2003b, April 7). A plan under attack. *Newsweek*, 25–36.

Thomas, E., & Klaidman, D. (2003, March 31). The war room. *Newsweek*, 22–31.

Thompson, M. (2003, March 17). Opening with a bang. *Time*, 26–29.

Time. (2004). About time. Retrieved February 29, 2004, from www.time-planner.com/planner/about_time/index.html

Tweeten, L., Adams, M., & Bradford, L. (2003, April 7). Lethal weapons. *Time*, 29.

Tweeten, L., Gabel, E., & Orecklin, M. (2003, April 7). Urban warriors. *Time*, 30–31.

Ulick, Josh, & Sparks, J. (2003, March 31). In the air, on the ground. *Newsweek*, 26–27.

Van Ginneken, J. (1998). *Understanding global news: A critical introduction*. London: Sage.

Weapons of war. (2003, March 31). *Time*, 26–27.

What he's got. (2003, March 17). *Newsweek*, 28.

Whitaker, M. (2003, March 31). The editor's desk. *Newsweek*, 4.

Will, G. F. (2003, March 31). The hour of air power. *Newsweek*, 66.

Wolffe, R., Hosenball, M., & Lipper, T. (2003, March 17). The blame game between Bush and the Brits. *Newsweek*, 8.

Zakaria, F. (2003, March 24). The arrogant empire. *Newsweek*, 18–33.

14

Journalists Embedded in Culture: War Stories as Political Strategy

Heinz Brandenburg

One of the distinguishing features of the Iraq war in 2003 was the phenomenon of "embedded" media. This term describes journalists who were assigned by the Pentagon or the U.S. Department of Defense to specific troop units, traveled and lived with these units, and dispatched reports from the front line. This type of war reporting was by no means entirely new. In the United States since the Civil War, and in Europe since the Napoleonic wars, war reporters have often accompanied advancing troops. However, the conceptualization of embedding, the rationale behind it, the scale of it, and also the term "embedding" as such were indeed largely unprecedented.

The purpose of this chapter is to investigate the phenomenon of embedded media in the Iraq war, which means to describe the phenomenon, to explain the military and political rationale behind it, and to draw conclusions about the effects of embedding on the nature of war reporting and its consequence for public perception and mobilization.

THE CONCEPT OF "EMBEDDED MEDIA"

Given that embedded journalists were so dominant a feature of Iraq war coverage, it is surprising that wide sections of the public remained unfamiliar with the concept. When the first surveys were carried out in the United States and United Kingdom, aiming to measure public opinion about the Iraq war in its initial stage, many survey respondents required explanations of what it means to "embed journalists" before they were able to state whether or not they approved of the practice. And even as late as August/September 2003 (that is, about half a year after the war), researchers from the Cardiff School of Journalism, who conducted a study of the embedding process commissioned by the BBC, found that in Britain "despite the currency of the phrase 'embedded reporter' amongst broadcasters, most people—74%—did not know what the phrase meant, and only 20% were able to offer a broadly accurate definition" (Lewis et al. 2003, 28).

It is interesting to note that the broader audiences in the United States and elsewhere remained unprepared for the type of war coverage that would result from embedding, even though the Pentagon had already gone on record with the plan in October 2002 and invited media to send journalists selected for embedding to military boot camps, which were held in November and December 2002. It appears to have been a deliberate strategy of the media in the United States and elsewhere to keep a low profile about the embedding program, with the exception of the odd news story about experiences at those boot camps.

The thought process that eventually resulted in the embed program began in 2002, in the aftermath of the Afghanistan campaign and as part of the larger war preparations against Iraq. The war against Iraq was considered well suited for the embedding of journalists on a comprehensive scale, because it included all branches of the military. In one of the relatively frequent meetings with media bureau chiefs at Pentagon, October 30, 2002, Deputy Assistant Secretary of Defense for Media Operations Bryan Whitman outlined that, although no decision on war with Iraq had been made, "we have been doing public affairs planning right from the beginning alongside all the contingency planning, the military contingency planning being done in this building." On this occasion, he disclosed the plan for "very extensive use of embedded media" (Whitman 2003). According to the Assistant Secretary of Defense for Public Affairs (ASD PA) Victoria Clarke, "It was an extraordinary evolution of a concept that already existed" (Brookings Institution 2003).

And, indeed, the notion of "embedding journalists" had been introduced years earlier, albeit somewhat differently, in two Department of Defense news briefings in June 1996, under the Clinton administration, by then ASD PA Kenneth Bacon and his deputy, Michael Doubleday. With respect to then-ongoing military operations in Bosnia, the Pentagon defined embedding as the situation "where a reporter goes and lives with the unit *for several days or a week* and then writes a story about it" (Bacon 1996; emphasis added). Already back in 1996, the objective was clearly stated, namely, that "with embedded media the whole idea is that the reporter becomes part of the unit" (Doubleday 1996). However, the idea of integrating journalists into military units for the duration of a war was not yet considered.

Once Secretary of Defense Donald Rumsfeld confirmed that embedding media is considered a "core principle" (Whitman 2003), the media were then invited to training courses, so-called boot camps in which their journalists would be prepared for their assignments in the gulf region. These three- to four-day boot camps took place from the second week of November onward and received some low-key coverage in U.S. newspapers. The procedure was then that media outlets were asked to name the number of reporters they wanted to be embedded, and assignments to specific units were administered by the Pentagon.

According to Central Command, which took oversight of the embed program from Pentagon during operations, a maximum of 775 journalists were at one point embedded with U.S. troops; later, 128 British journalists joined UK units. Embedding began just ahead of operations, when in mid-March journalists joined military units for deployment to Iraq. Most embeds left their assigned units after Baghdad was taken, going "unilateral" or returning home, with only 185 journalists still remaining as embeds on April 23. After that point, no new assignments were offered by the Pentagon; however, journalists were encouraged to remain with their assigned units in the aftermath of military operations.

Journalists embedded with U.S. troops were required to sign a "Release, indemnification, and hold harmless agreement and agreement not to sue" (Department of Defense 2003b), which specifies that journalists, their relatives, and their employers cannot hold the government responsible for injury or loss of life, and that the government "may terminate the embedding process at any time and for any reason, as the Government determines appropriate in its sole discretion." In turn, no specification is made as to whether and under what circumstances embedded journalists can terminate their stay with the assigned military unit. Both documents, the PA guidelines and the agreement, specified that the embedding of journalists takes place "for the purpose of providing news media coverage *before, during, and after* military operations" (emphasis added).

THE U.S. MILITARY, THE MEDIA, AND THE POLITICAL RATIONALE BEHIND EMBEDDING

One cannot emphasize enough how significant a departure from previous practice in media treatment by U.S. forces the embedding program was. It constituted the outcome of a long historic process that saw U.S. political and military leaders moving from ignoring to understanding the value of positive military-media relationships, and eventually from understanding the necessity of accommodating the media toward proactive media management.

While during World Wars I and II, military and media enjoyed an almost symbiotic relationship, with media neither questioning the righteousness of war involvement nor their own assigned role as propaganda instruments of their political and military leaders (Hudson & Stanier 1997, 47), the Korean War gave the first indication that media support can be conditional, depending on the nature of the war and the degree of consensus amongst domestic political elites (Hudson & Stanier 1997, 92–99).

Vietnam was to intensify the adversarial nature of media-military relations. In the absence of censorship, the U.S. media were uninhibited in painting a picture of a war that on the one hand exposed all the brutality of war as such and on the other remained far from a straightforward success story for the U.S. forces. Vietnam was not only to intensify the adversarial nature of media-military relations, but also resulted in long-term effects of deep-seated mistrust, especially amongst military leaders. While military officers and politicians often view media coverage as harmful to the U.S. campaign in Vietnam, Herman and Chomsky (1988) have provided a fairly thorough content analysis that debunks the claim that media undercut the war—indeed, news anchors and reporters of major networks and newspapers followed U.S. administration agendas—although news facts often contradicted frames. In the 1960s, of course, there were more independent journalists and much more diversity in media (Bagdikian 2000).

In response to the perceived noncooperation of the media during Vietnam, the Pentagon and military leadership went on the defensive. They took an essentially negative approach to public affairs, trying to contain and control the media. Notwithstanding the widespread understanding that the media were put on a short leash after the Vietnam experience because of distrust (Hall 1995, 7), adversity between military and media can also, at least partly, be attributed to the significant differences in organizational culture between the two professions. To put it bluntly: military operations work on the basis of teamwork, hierarchy, and the integration of the individual into existing structures, while journalists are individualists in competition with one another over who gets the bigger story the quickest.

Frank Aukofer and William P. Lawrence (1995) argue that "by the time of Grenada in 1983, there was an entire generation of military officers who did not think 'public affairs'" (44). Thinking that the military can lose more than gain from interaction with the press, the low-scale invasion of Grenada was military planned, but practically excluded PA officers and hence did not consider accommodating the media. The conclusion was, however, not to rethink media containment but to formalize it by establishing the Department of Defense National Media Pool, which came to structure the relationship with the media largely until the Afghanistan campaign in the aftermath of 9/11.

It was only after the Gulf War that the military began to contemplate working with the media (Hall 1995). Colin Powell, then chairman of the Joint Chiefs of Staff, issued a directive in May 1990 in which he reminded commanders "that military actions in Grenada and Panama demonstrated that otherwise successful operations are not total successes unless the media aspects are properly handled" (Powell 1990).

In 1995, Aukofer and Lawrence reported on the relationship between media and military. Working on the basic premise that "there are wise men and women in both institutions who recognize that their ultimate goal—the preservation of American freedoms—is the same" (1995, viii), they proposed training journalists for combat situations, to involve them in war games and general preparation, to train officers of different ranks systematically in public affairs, and to develop joint programs and seminars between military academies and journalism schools in order to enhance mutual understanding (1995, 3–7).

The new core principle of "positive engagement," which developed during the 1990s, took many of its inspirations from the Aukofer and Lawrence (1995) report and culminated in the embed program in 2003. It is based on the assumption that the media can only be brought back "into the team" by accommodating their needs, developing positive relations with them, granting them access, and trying to bridge the gulf between the organizational cultures of media and military. Embedding is an ideal tool to accomplish these tasks. Embedding increases access, since journalists, story selection, and war coverage in general are no longer centrally directed as they were during the first Gulf war (or at least not apparently so). And integrating journalists into military units serves directly to overcome many of their suspicions about the "esprit de corps," the anti-individualist organizational culture. Since journalists are no longer forming a press corps themselves, but are integrated into established military troop units, they have to adapt. The purpose of boot camps is to make journalists understand the routines and basic necessities of the life among soldiers that they will have to face. In that sense, embedding is a process that physically reintegrates the media into "the team" that, from a military point of view, they quit in Vietnam.

PRACTICE AND CONSEQUENCES OF EMBEDDING DURING THE IRAQ WAR

In February 2003, only a few weeks before the war against Iraq, the Department of Defense published a document containing "public affairs (PA) guidance on embedding media during possible future operations/deployments in the U.S. Central Commands area of responsibility" (Department of Defense 2003a). One might, of course, suspect that these PA guidelines were particularly designed for the impending war with Iraq and that general reference to any future operations had to be made because a military solution had not yet been sanctioned. However, the document provides a paradigmatic outline of the principles of strategic media management, and it is reasonable to assume that these principles are meant to be applied beyond the particular campaign against Iraq. In that sense, the Iraq campaign provided the test case for their application.

Recognizing that "media coverage of any future operation will, to a large extent, shape public perception of the national security environment," a strategic choice was made to depart from previous practices and instead to provide the media "long-term, minimally restrictive access to U.S. air, ground and naval forces through embedding." To embed journalists meant that they will "live, work and travel as part of the units . . . to facilitate maximum, in-depth coverage of U.S. forces in combat and related operations." The declared objective of the embedding process was "to tell the factual story—good or bad—before others seed the media with disinformation and distortions, as they most certainly will continue to do." To that end, "Our people in the field need to tell our story" (Department of Defense 2003a).

From a strategic point of view, as applied on a massive scale in the Iraq war, embedding is an ideal tool to exercise control of the media for public affairs purposes without openly having to contain them and thereby taking story selection away from the individual journalist.

THE STOCKHOLM SYNDROME

The political goal of embedding, and coincidentally the danger to independence and objectivity of the press that many critical observers have warned about, is the integration of the journalist into the troop unit, the bonding between journalist and soldiers, and, as a result of this, a positive bias in the dispatches from the embedded reporter. The notion of the Stockholm syndrome (Lang 1974), even though it originally refers to developing empathy between kidnappers and their hostages, can serve as a suitable model for describing the psychological processes that unfold under conditions of embedding and may result in positive media bias.

Length and intensity of embedding are crucial factors and should be good predictor variables for the presence or absence, and indeed the extent, of positive bias amongst embedded reporters. While embedding in the 1990s in Kosovo referred to periods of 7–10 days during which journalists visited troops, embedding in Iraq meant living together over a prolonged period. Logically, relationships between humans can only develop over time. Social penetration theory, for example, evokes the metaphor of an onion to describe how relationships intensify incrementally, through repeated disclosures of information between partners (Heath & Bryant 2000). The process of mutual communication, information exchange, costs, and rewards leads to the establishment of mutual trust. In order to benefit from the process, to receive support in terms of resources and information, the reporter needs to integrate into the group. And troop units will be the more willing to integrate the reporter if they can expect the coverage to reflect positively on their performance. Irrespective of whether one models the process as a tit-for-tat strategy (supply with resources, transport, information, and so on) for sympathetic reporting, or as a bonding experience between troop units and embedded reporters that culminates in reporters taking the in-group perspective in their dispatches, long-term embedding is likely to and (from the perspective of the Pentagon) intended to produce positive bias in reporting.

Such positive bias does not necessarily mean that embedded reporters give inaccurate and propagandistic accounts of the operations they witness. Notwithstanding the political rationale behind embedding, which may aim at controlling media coverage and receiving the portrayal of the war that helps to maximize domestic support, one also has to take into account the inherent PR dilemma of military operations, and especially so with nonconscript military forces as in the United States. The armed forces and their political leaders need to constantly reinforce public identification with troops in limited wars (Carruthers 2000; Hall 1995)

Shooting, bombing, killing, and breaking things being the essence of military operations, a necessity arises for selling the rightfulness and professionalism in exercising these tasks. Not only do domestic audiences need to know, understand, and appreciate the political reasons for engaging in a war, but it will also help ensure public support if reassurance is given about the manner in which the war is fought—especially if the avowed reasons for war are not the actual reasons (e.g., no weapons of mass destruction, no connections to al Qaeda, no violations of UN sanctions, no Iraqi desire for intervention, and so on).

THE PR EFFECT

In the case of the Iraq war, the political will to pursue a new public affairs strategy coincided with the availability of technological advances that made it possible to implement the embedding program in the intended form. Since most journalists were equipped with digital cameras, they did not have to rely on a larger crew to produce their coverage. Nor did they require as much technical support for transmission as was the case in earlier wars. Even television reporters could be individually placed with troops and function as reporter, cameraman, and editor at the same time.

At the same time, these technological advances explain part of the positive response, if not enthusiasm, of the media about the embed program: this war differed from previous ones both in the amount and the kind of live footage that it produced. A first comprehensive study of Iraq war coverage on U.S. network television, which was conducted by the Project for Excellence in Journalism (PEJ 2003), did provide some insight into this core element of the embed program: live coverage. They found that over 60 percent of embedded reports were live, the vast majority of those audiovisual. This opportunity to report live from the battlefields may explain the particularly strong reliance of TV networks on embedded reports.

At the same time, the content of reporting does support the notion that individual embeds get to see and cover only "small slices" of the larger picture. Since more than 70 percent of the filed stories were combat related, and very few indeed used interviews with service members, one can conclude that embeds were entrenched in and could only report from the day-to-day combat activities on the ground without managing to contextualize these fragmented action sequences.

Also, even though media management differed hugely from Operation Desert Storm, "cleanness" of coverage was achieved just the same. While the firing of weapons was prominently featured, there was no indication of their impact—few images of human targets, human victims, or human consequences were shown in dispatches from embeds. Although over a fifth of the video footage from embedded reporters presented combat action, that is the firing of weapons, only nonhuman impact or the results of impacts were ever shown. Reporting was overwhelmingly factual (93.5 percent), not interpretative. The PEJ (2003) study draws the interesting conclusion that the war in Iraq did indeed fail to "become the ultimate reality TV," mainly because of the lack of editing that produced fragmentation, with sanitized white noise rather than subplots and retraceable story lines.

Embedding does result in the fragmentation of war reporting. This is to some extent the direct result of embedding journalists as isolated individuals into troop units. Not only are individual journalists restricted in their viewpoint by the activities of the units they are embedded in, but they also lack exchange with other members of the press corps.

While this might count as a distinct disadvantage of embedding as opposed to a pool system, journalists from the United States and other countries overwhelmingly approved of the practice of embedding and regarded it as an improvement on media treatment and frontline access in earlier conflicts. A British report on the role of embedding during the Iraq war (Lewis et al. 2003) found that particularly those journalists from Europe and the United States who were embedded with U.S. troops tended to report predominantly positive experiences. Better planning of the embed program and a greater abundance of resources and implementation of the public affairs doctrine at lower levels of the military hierarchy were mentioned as reasons for the comparatively smooth practice. In contrast, more ambiguous experiences were made by embeds with UK forces, who encountered "very little access to military commanders," repeated inability to supply "up-to-date information to confirm stories happening elsewhere," and even at times breakdowns "of trust or co-operation between the journalists and the military" or "deteriorating working relationships . . . culminating in . . . censorship" (Lewis et al. 2003, 5).

Journalists acknowledged the inherent limitations on access that derive from dependence on the units they were assigned to, as well as the fragmented picture of the war that an individual embed could witness and report. Some stated that the absence of more graphic war imagery was part self-censorship "because they knew that the more gruesome scenes that they witnessed would not be shown on British television news" (Lewis et al. 2003, 9).

The reasoning behind embedding and the apparent enthusiasm about embedding amongst political and military leaders before and after the war imply the expectation that embedding does actually produce measurable gains in terms of positive coverage. This is a hypothesis that can be investigated empirically. Lewis et al. (2003) made some attempt at answering it for the UK media but fell short, mainly because they only measured the presence of impartiality with regard to the larger war effort. Embedded journalists were found not to emanate more prowar statements than anchors or correspondents, but this research design does not tap into the essence of attitudinal effects of embedding. Assessing impartiality or political bias in war coverage means to investigate whether media refer to sources of one side in the war more than to the other, what kind of picture of the two sides in the war they present, and so on.

The most likely effect of embedding on reporter attitude is not a change in their attitude toward the war efforts and their explicitly voiced opinions about the war (or a difference between their attitude and those of nonembedded media). Instead, the intended effect of embedding is to alter the attitude of the reporters toward the troop units. Since they are living with them, embedding should result in increased group identification. The measurable effects of such attitude change should be twofold: first, expressed positive feelings toward the troop members that reporters are embedded with; and second, an increased focus on episodic storytelling from life amongst the unit and the war experiences of the members. The latter aspect would mean that the reporting of embedded journalists should use episodic rather than thematic framing.

The only set of studies that has attempted to seriously assess the effect of embedding on the attitudes and behavior of individual journalists was conducted as assignments for the Department of Defense at the University of Oklahoma (Coupaud, Davis, Evans, & Pool 2003; Donnelly, Scott, Gettle, & Warr 2003; Reyes, Samsel, Curtis, Ulmer, & Wilson 2004). And all three studies, which used similar research designs, did indeed find corroborating evidence for the hypothesis that embedding alters reporter attitudes.

Coupaud et al. (2003) found that (1) media coverage in 2003 was on average more positive than during the 1991 Gulf War or during the 1999 Kosovo operations; (2) "troop-focused stories generated more positive feelings toward military members than command-oriented" (9); and (3) embedded reporters showed substantially more positive attitudes and warmer feeling toward the subject of their reports than nonembedded reporters.

In a similar vein, Donnelly et al. (2003) explored tone and framing of stories. They found a difference in attitude and trust between embedded and nonembedded reporters. They also reported that dispatches from embeds tended to be significantly more episodic than thematic in nature.

Finally, Reyes et al. (2004) used a Web-based survey of around 1,400 troops from the Marine Corps and the U.S. Air Force, finding that military members had a positive perception of embedding, especially troops deployed in the Iraq war.

While on the one hand the findings about the effects of embedding on reporter attitudes and content of war coverage remain somewhat inconclusive because of the indeterminate research designed in all the reviewed studies, even the tentative confirmation of some attitudinal effects that can be drawn from these studies still has to be treated with caution. As Lewis et al. (2003) mentioned, a general difference between U.S. and UK media was the more affirmative, patriotic attitude that the Pentagon encountered from their compatriots. And a generally patriotic attitude can be regarded as a factor that helps embedding to achieve the intended results. As Artz (2004) notes:

> Embedding encouraged reporters to identify with the soldiers they were traveling with and photographing, contributing to U.S.-favorable stories. Part of the point of view of any journalistic account depends on the actual location from which reporters witness events. In this war, embedded journalists identified more viscerally with the U.S. troops as "fellow-travelers"; there was almost no U.S. reporting from Iraqi cities. "Sheer genius," commented U.S. public relations consultant Katie Delahaye Paine, saying that embedded reporters "have been spectacular, bringing the war into our living rooms like never before . . .

the tactic is based on the basic tenet of public relations: It's all about relationships. The better the relationship any of us has with a journalist, the better the chance of that journalist picking up and reporting our messages. So now we have journalists making dozens—if not hundreds—of new friends among the armed forces" (in Rampton & Stauber, 2003, 22). It turns out to have been an effective propaganda adjustment: in 2003, news media outlets certified the Gulf War according to Pentagon outtakes—few photos showed actual fighting, as one might expect from previous war photojournalism. Indeed, the predominant message in news photos from the first weeks of the war was that of a giant training exercise: sophisticated weaponry in the setting sun; determined soldiers on scouting patrols; photogenic boys and girls in desert fatigues just wanting to have fun.

Positive media engagement, and the particular practice of embedding, are intended to assure patriotism and improve voluntary propaganda activity from the national media. And even though U.S. media in 2003 might have had a largely positive attitude toward the war effort, this was also the case with the Gulf War in 1991. But there, media treatment by the U.S. military proved to be counterproductive by alienating correspondents and journalists in the media pool. In contrast, embedding is intended to reinforce positive attitudes toward military operations by making the reporter a participant who shares experiences with troop units. Professional isolation and social integration of embedded journalists are likely to impact on the type and content of their dispatches from the front line. In the larger picture, the intention of the military is to fill increasing amounts of airtime with episodic stories, the actors of which are individual soldiers with whom domestic audience can easily identify. The reporter serves as the public representative who integrates and identifies with these soldiers on a daily basis and introduces them to the domestic public. This way, the question of domestic support for war operations is removed from the abstract, rational arena of political justification to the social arena of personal identification with the troops.

REFERENCES

Artz, L. (2004). War as promotional "photo-op": The *New York Times*' visual coverage of the U.S. invasion of Iraq. In Nancy Snow and Yahya Kamalipour (Eds.), *War, Media, and Propaganda*. Boulder, CO: Rowman & Littlefield (2004).

Aukofer, F., & Lawrence, W. P. (1995). *America's team: The odd couple, A report on the relationship between the media and the military*. Nashville, TN: Freedom Forum.

Bacon, K. (1996). Department of Defense news briefing. Retrieved May 7, 1996, from www.defenselink.mil/news/May1996/t050796_t0507asd.html

Bagdikian, B. H. (2000). *The media monopoly*, 6th ed. Boston: Beacon.

Brookings Institution. (2003). *Assessing media coverage of the war in Iraq: Press reports, Pentagon rules, and lessons for the future.* Brookings Iraq Series Briefing. www.brook.edu/comm/events/20030617.pdf

Carruthers, S. L. (2000). *The media at war: Communication and conflict in the twentieth century.* Houndsmills, UK: Macmillan.

Coupaud, P., Davis, B., Evans, R., & Pool, J. (2003). *Embedded media with the military.* Capstone Project 03C, Department of Defense Joint Course in Communication, University of Oklahoma. www.ou.edu/deptcomm/dodjcc/groups/03C2/index.htm

Department of Defense. (2003a). *Public affairs guidance on embedding media during possible future operations/deployments in the U.S. central commands area of responsibility.* www.cpj.org/Briefings/2003/gulf03/embed.html

——— (2003b). *Release, indemnification, and hold harmless agreement and agreement not to sue.* www.defenselink.mil/news/Feb2003/d20030210embed.pdf

Donnelly, M., Scott, G., Gettle, M., & Warr, D. (2003). *Embedded journalism: How war is viewed differently from the frontlines versus the sidelines.* Capstone Project 03D, Department of Defense Joint Course in Communication, University of Oklahoma. www.ou.edu/deptcomm/dodjcc/groups/03D1/INDEX.htm

Doubleday, M. (1996). Department of Defense News Briefing, Tuesday, May 7, 1996. Retrieved March 3, 2004, from www.dod.mil/news/May1996/t050996_tbrfg 050.html

Hall, T. M. (1995). *The military and the media: Toward a strategy of engagement and enlargement.* Research report. School of Advanced Airpower Studies, Air University, Alabama.

Heath, R., & Bryant, J. (2000). *Human communication theory and research: Concepts, contexts, and challenges.* Mahwah, NJ: Lawrence Erlbaum.

Herman, E., & Chomsky, N. (1988). *Manufacturing consent: The political economy of the mass media.* New York: Pantheon

Hudson, M., & Stanier, J. (1997). *War and the media: A random searchlight.* Phoenix, AZ: Sutton Publishing.

Lang, D. (1974, December 14). A reporter at large: The bank drama (Swedish hostages). *New Yorker*, 56–126.

Lewis, J., Threadgold, T., Brookes, R., Mosdell, N., Brander, K., Clifford, S., Bessaiso, E., & Harb, Z. (2003). *The role of embedded reporting during the 2003 Iraq war: Summary report.* Commissioned by the BBC. Cardiff, Wales: Cardiff University.

Project for Excellence in Journalism (PEJ). (2003). *Embedded reporters: What are Americans getting?* [Electronic version]. Washington, DC: Project for Excellence in Journalism. www.journalism.org/resources/research/reports/war/embed/ default.asp

Powell, C. (1990). Department of Defense National Media Pool planning requirements. Washington, DC: Joint Staff Info Service Center. Retrieved March 4, 2004, from www.call.army.mil/products/newsltrs/00-6/00-6app.htm

Rampton, S., & Stauber, J. (2003). *Weapons of mass deception: The uses of propaganda in Bush's war in Iraq.* New York: Jeremy P. Tarcher.

Reyes, L., Samsel, J., Curtis, T., Ulmer, P., & Wilson, C. (2004). *Embedded broadcast journalists: Reporting operation Iraqi freedom from the frontline.* Capstone Project 04A, Department of Defense Joint Course in Communication, University of Oklahoma.

Whitman, B. (2003, October 30). Clarke meeting with bureau chiefs. Retrieved March 4, 2004, from www.dod.mil/news/Nov2002/t11012002_t1030sd.html

15

The Power of Public Reporting: The Independent Media Center's Challenge to Corporate Media

Lisa Brooten

The introduction of each new media technology has sparked debates between those with pessimistic and utopian views of the changes it will usher in, and the introduction of the Internet into the media landscape has been no different. It is important to avoid the "widespread historical amnesia" that obscures our recognition of the exaggerated expectations that have repeatedly greeted each new "history-ending" communication technology, a pattern Vincent Mosco calls the "ever-ending story" (2004, 117). Yet the way people and publics communicate is in some way altered with each new technology, and the Internet, while increasingly shaped by transnational corporate power, also offers a tool for networking on an immediate and global basis for those working to enhance global democratic communication. The Internet offers a decentralized, multimedia platform, "an unprecedentedly tractable technology for network interconnection" (Schiller 1999, 9). As one media activist argues, "Instead of activists having to subvert a centralized media technology, it's the corporations madly trying to subvert a decentralized technology, and so far largely failing" (as cited in Meikle 2002, 95). Central to the effort to keep the Internet decentralized and nonproprietary is the free software movement (also known as the open source movement), which has created tools, such as "open publishing," that allow for immediate feedback and multiuser interaction. These developments have in turn posed a challenge to traditional concepts of objectivity and legitimacy in the presentation of news. In short, the characteristics that make the Internet unique also allow it to operate (at least for now) outside the confines of the centralized structures that make other media profitable but limited in their potential to contribute toward democratic media experiences. Yet the power of the Internet lies not in the technology itself, but in its capacity as a tool for those working to mobilize bodies into action in locally based yet globally networked places, to challenge the corporate media's representations of not only what is happening, but also what is possible.

This chapter focuses on the ways in which the Internet was used by the Independent Media Center (IMC) to challenge the hegemony of corporate media during the war on Iraq, in large part through the development of a collective process of research and critique in which the discussion becomes an integral part of the finished text. The IMC is more of a facilitation mechanism than a news service, and as such is not usefully examined with the lens used to judge traditional journalism. Yet the IMC is challenging the nature of news, how we get it, and how we make it. The IMC disrupts corporate media hegemony by challenging people's passive acceptance of the authority naturalized through corporate media news, by encouraging people to take control of the storytelling; to place current events in their historical, social, and geographic context; and to attend to and challenge the process through which reporting, especially war reporting, dehumanizes victims and trivializes outrage. The IMC presents a small but growing model of democratic communication, important in that it challenges people to work actively to democratize both media representations and the processes of media production, and provides at least those with Internet access the tools to do so.

A BRIEF HISTORY AND DESCRIPTION OF THE IMC

It is often said that the Independent Media Center (IMC) was born during the "Battle in Seattle," the protests against the World Trade Organization that began during the last days of November 1999. Certainly this event fostered the IMC, but its birth wouldn't have been possible without the existing networks of activist groups and media with a long track record of grassroots organizing (Downing 2001; Halleck 2002; Herndon 2003; Kidd 2003a). The Seattle experience clarified the power of an online, multimedia network capable of providing rapid access to information for a global audience. The IMC provided text, photographs, streaming audio and video, and hyperlinks to alternative information sources with few gatekeepers and a turnaround time that often mounted a direct challenge to mainstream media coverage (Downing 2001; Kidd 2003a; Kitaeff 2003). Mainstream news services such as Reuters and CNN linked to the Seattle IMC site, which had received about 1.5 million hits by the time the Seattle scuffle wound down (Kitaeff 2003).

Since then, the network has been has been the primary organizing mechanism and news source for the (misleadingly named) "antiglobalization" protestors, as well as the global antiwar movement, and local IMC chapters worldwide are affiliated with or link virtually to many progressive political and social advocacy groups. The network has also become a source of information for the wire services, especially during meetings of the major international organizations and the street protests that now seem to regularly accompany them.

The IMC grew to include thirty chapters in the first ten months after the Seattle protests (Meikle 2002) to over fifty in 2001 ("Reality" 2001), and to about ninety worldwide in September 2002 (Downing 2003). In early 2003, there were 110 IMC chapters (Herndon 2003), and there are approximately 133 chapters as of this writing in April 2004. There are chapters in North America, Latin America, Europe, Africa, Asia, and Oceania. They are still concentrated primarily in the "West," with fifty in the United States, eleven in Canada, and thirty-six in Europe, but network chapters and regional groupings continue to form in other parts of the world.

Although the IMC is entirely volunteer run, with no headquarters or formal governing structure, its size and reach outstrip even the largest news organizations, both geographically and in terms of labor. Each local chapter is self-governing and does its own fundraising. The network's virtual headquarters is the global website (www.indymedia.org), which links to local chapters. Network decisions are made online in a series of discussion groups linked to the global site and operating through a consensus process. The features found on the IMC's global site are usually culled from local IMC websites worldwide. Local sites generally include a news features column down the center of the page, links to all the other IMC websites running down the left side of the page, and, on the right side, the open publishing newswire, where anyone with Internet access can post their information. In April 2002, a proposal to move the open publishing newswire from the front page of the global site was approved through the global IMC process, because of the immense volume of postings and the regular spamming of the site (Meikle 2003). The global IMC webpage now features a newswire on the right composed of the syndicated features from all local IMC sites, as well as a link to an open publishing newswire off the main page.

According to the global website, the Indymedia network as a whole receives an estimated 500,000 to 2 million hits per day, depending on what is occurring worldwide at the time. One IMC member estimated that the network's coverage of the Democratic and Republican conventions during the summer of 2000 reached at least 30 million households ("Reality" 2001). And during the first few days of the attacks on Iraq in March 2003, some local IMC sites (such as IMC Italy) were receiving about half a million hits a day.

Each local IMC collective has its own policy regarding how features are posted to the central column of its website, and its own newswire policy, but the general agreement is that anyone can post noncommercial information to the newswire without being edited. In many instances, those who post to the newswire forward their stories to an editorial board at one or more IMCs, each of which then works on a consensus basis to determine whether or not a submitted story qualifies to be posted as a feature. While the makeup of the editorial team and the process through which they approve stories are determined by each IMC collective and therefore vary in terms of their openness, each local website also hosts the unedited, open publishing newswire and a comments section after feature articles.

Many of the IMC's local chapters were formed in response to crisis events such as protests against international financial or policymaking institutions, or corporate entities. Their emergence was driven by a desire to document the reasons for the protests, the protest events themselves, and the official reactions to these protests. These chapters therefore developed in such a way as to function best and most flexibly *during and as a response to* crisis events rather than *in spite of* them, and thus from the start contested corporate media versions of these events.

The virtual IMC works in conjunction with physical spaces that function as local nodes of a global network. Global protests occur in local spaces, and the IMC provides a means by which activists from around the world can gather and work together. Naidoo (2003) describes the space housing the South African IMC as more than a gathering place, but "an incredible space in that it removed the often-assumed hierarchies that usually determine how relations between different layers of activists interact and saw 'leaders' and 'luminaries' of the anti-globalization movement speaking as equals with 'ordinary' activists" (21).

Despite the IMC focus on inclusion, those capable of volunteering for the IMC for significant amounts of time tend to represent a small minority of young, white, male North Americans and Europeans (Kidd 2003a). This is combined with unequal global access to the Internet to limit participation in specific gendered, class, and racialized ways. In addition, the IMC's increased visibility has made them a target of not only hate mail and spammers but also national and international security agencies such as the FBI and police forces in many countries (Kidd 2003a, 2003b). Several IMC sites have been shut down and others systematically hacked (Kidd 2003a). While there are those who would dismiss the IMC as a fringe movement, the power of the collective so threatening to the status quo when it appears on the street is translating into a different sort of power online: the power of a public, global process of challenge in which the roles of reader, researcher, and writer blur, made possible through the decentralized nature of the Web.

JOURNALISM AND THE WEB

There is a growing interest in the effects of the Web on journalism and on the creation and presentation of information necessary to support a society more democratic to the extent that it accommodates "interactivity over mere connectivity" (Hacker 1996). Jones (2000), for example, maintains that "public disdain for journalism has fueled use of the Web because news on the Web seems less like the journalism to which we've become accustomed" (172). The Web is used for purposes of information gathering different from the use of traditional print and broadcast media, in that "the Web is *not* a background medium" (Jones 2000, 175) but rather "a medium of predominantly active users" (Blumler and Gurevitch 2001). While Blumler and Gurevitch (2001) warn against idealizing or exaggerating this activity, Burnett and Marshall (2003) find that "the Web has led to a shift in how we recontextualize news around a much larger search for information." As news consumers become researchers, they become comfortable with getting and ranking news from a variety of sources. Web users, as a result, have begun to share the role of searching for information once held by journalists (Jones 2000). Jones (2000) maintains that the Web has also shifted the meaning of news from creating a record of what has already happened to "anticipating what's next by accumulating information and making connections among stories, hearsay, gossip," and other information linked via hypertext, so that "the sum of connections makes a content greater than the sum of the parts" (178).

As Meikle (2003) points out, however, conceptions of news and information gathering are still framed primarily in terms of reception by consumers, rather than in terms of production, and do not address new ways of developing and publishing news. While Burnett and Marshall (2003) do recognize the Web's role in promoting new levels of criticism of the traditional news media through fostering dialogue between reporters and readers, their analysis maintains a producer/consumer binary, and presents the personal webpage and weblog as the primary counterbalance to the commercialization of the Web and the increasing professionalism of online news sites. Others suggest that the Internet's greatest potential for change may lie in its capacity to provide direct communication between citizens and politicians (Blumler & Gurevitch 2001; Hacker 1996). Meikle (2003) maintains, however, that in addition to this type of direct citizen-to-politician communication, and with the shifting nature of news consumption in the online world, "there is also a corresponding ongoing shift in the boundaries of what constitutes newsmakers" (4). The IMC network presents an interesting example of this ongoing shift.

STRUCTURE AND PROCESS IN THE IMC

As a decentralized network, the IMC does not have a single unified voice or policy, but all IMC collectives subscribe to practices of open publishing and consensus-based decision making as part of the network's *Principles of Unity*:

> All IMCs, based upon trust of their contributors and readers, shall utilize open web based publishing, allowing individuals, groups and organizations to express their views, anonymously if desired. . . . All IMCs recognize the importance of process to social change and are committed to the development of nonhierarchical and antiauthoritarian relationships, from interpersonal relationships to group dynamics. (http://docs.indymedia.org/view/Global/AboutUs)

Although the most obvious IMC challenges to the Bush administration and its war aims were the network's documentation of the antiwar sentiment worldwide and its critique of corporate media versions of events, perhaps more important was its offer of an alternative model for media participation. The IMC challenges the hierarchical relationship between producers and audiences, and between business and military "experts" and the person on the street. This challenge is mounted in large part through the system of open publishing, made possible through the efforts of the free software or open source movement. This movement operates on the principle of free exchange of information and cooperative software development, emphasizes freedom from proprietary software, and works to keep software free and source code open for collective development and use (see Stallman 2002). The free software movement is arguably the greatest challenge to the privatization of the Internet (Meikle 2002), and many members of the IMC tech crew are associated with this movement (Kidd 2003a; Arnison 2001). As increasingly larger portions of the Internet become dominated by the "dot-coms," the open source movement is as much a political statement—and an effort to keep the Net open and navigable by as many as possible—as it is a software development effort (Kidd 2003a).

Many IMC activists also openly challenge the concept of "objectivity" in journalism, arguing that it is better to be honest about one's biases, in contrast to corporate media ("Reality" 2001; Hintz 2003; Kitaeff 2003). IMC coverage of events tends to rely heavily on firsthand and eyewitness accounts, eschewing a reliance on the traditional notion of the trained "journalist" in favor of a forum open to a more grassroots and diversified set of viewpoints. As Arne Hintz of Indymedia Germany notes, "The radical subjectivity implied in Open Publishing is a logical evolution of the alternative media approach to criticize journalist standards of allegedly objective reporting by focusing on subjective accounts" (2003, 25). "Be the media," reads the IMC motto, encouraging people to participate in creating the media they want. It's an effort that Downing (2001) has described as conducted with "a fine missionary spirit of demystifying digital dark spaces" (13).

There is an ongoing debate within the network about how to deal with its increasing number of collectives and IMC's growing audience. In response to racist or hate-filled postings, some question the wisdom of a totally open publishing system, as opposed to a system with some control to move hate-filled posts to an easily accessible open posting section. Several local sites have implemented some form of content selection or ranking system (Kidd 2003a). This is the model employed by IMC Germany, and according to one member, it "has generally raised the quality and readability of the site, while keeping a direct Open Posting section which is easily accessible to everyone from the front page" (Hintz 2003, 23). The debate and the search for alternatives are ongoing, and include the idea of using open publishing capabilities to provide an "automated open-editing" process (Arnison 2002a) that could increase standards while involving more people in the collective development and editing of news (Meikle 2003).

THE VIRTUAL IMC AND THE WAR ON/IN JOURNALISM

The discussion presented here is based on an analysis of seventy-three feature stories on the war and war-related topics as presented on the IMC global features page from February through May 2003. This time period includes the buildup to the war, the attacks themselves, and a month of events beyond the official "end" to the military phase of the war on May 1, 2003. The features usually consist of a short summary text with a series of links to a longer feature and usually to additional sources of information. Each feature ends with the option to "add your own comment," and often this discussion section is the lengthiest part of the text. The texts analyzed here include both the features and the discussions that follow them. Although the network uses multiple languages, the global features are in English, and while analysis of IMC content in other languages is a fruitful area for further research, this analysis focuses on these English-language features and discussions. The volume of material prevents a detailed analysis of every document or of all the themes that emerge from inductive analysis. Therefore, while many of these themes pose a direct challenge to the Bush administration and its war aims, I will focus this discussion on those emergent themes that exemplify how the IMC opens new forms of participation that challenge conventional notions of journalism. I quote frequently from online discussions, choosing comments that typify these emergent themes and providing citations for

lengthy quotes. Although a citation for each short quote would prove un-
wieldy, all quotes can be found within the IMC archive (http://indymedia
.org/en/feature/archive.shtml, which unfortunately has no search function)
during the period under analysis.

The rhetoric of IMC content reflects the fact that some chapters explicitly
identify with anarchist philosophy, especially the promotion of nonhierarchi-
cal, nonsexist, nonracist, and anti-imperialist values. These are defined rhetorically in direct contrast to the patriarchal, hypermasculinized, and aggressive
actions of both the U.S. administration and the "corporate media machine" that
supports it. The people who post to the IMC are generally framed (and often
frame themselves) in binary terms: right-wing/left-wing, antiwar/prowar,
those who hate America/love America, true patriots/blind followers, and so on.
Some participants critique binary divisions like this, but the binaries persist.

The IMC is predominantly used by those who share its philosophy, but
there is far from a single perspective represented, and prowar and more conservative voices often enter the dialogue, making for some interesting discussions. A key topic in these discussions is the legitimacy and credibility of
those reporting for the IMC and posting to its discussions, and it is here that
we can gain insight into how conceptions of journalism are being challenged.

JOURNALISM AND LEGITIMACY

While there are still many who lean on the ideal of objectivity, the concept
has been openly challenged by the IMC, which has introduced several
other ideas about what makes for a good and credible writer. Writers gain
legitimacy or credibility in features and discussions in two primary ways:
when they present ample evidence to back up the claims they make, in the
form of links and citations; and when they have had direct experience with
an issue, most often by being an eyewitness. One critique just after the
bombing began, for example, asks the IMC to provide more information
from inside Iraq, including "authentic pictures, video, audio and firsthand
accounts," which would provide the necessary evidence to make the
writer's claims about the disastrous nature of the war "convincing." Reporters writing from the scene are generally represented as more credible
than those sitting in a TV or radio studio back home, and courage is a characteristic regularly attributed by discussants to the reporters, human
shields, and other observers in Iraq. While at times praised, embedded
journalists are more often represented as tainted by the process, such as in
this comment: "When journalists take up a weapon, learn how to help sol-

diers, and drive with them in their vehicles—that's no longer journalism, it's nothing but propaganda."

In addition, the discussions suggest that for many participants in the IMC, reporters gain credibility when they contextualize their stories, providing the "historical perspective that all corporate media avoid." There is also a consistent theme that no single information source should be relied upon exclusively, and that the reader must be aware of both who owns the source and what their ideological assumptions are. One writer, for example, encourages others to "read all of the papers. Find out who owns them. Look deeper." There is also a great deal of attention paid to what does not appear in corporate media, which is exemplified by cynical comments such as "still waiting to see or hear any mention of Iraqi wounded from the mainstream media, like that'll ever happen." A related theme is the lack of attention in corporate media to the "common people." One participant, for example, identifies a "proper journalist" as one in whose reports "the voice of the never-heard ones is raised."

Those who critique the IMC generally call for objectivity, maintaining that firsthand accounts are "biased" or "slanted," especially those that indicate the writer's political position on an issue or display the writer's emotions. These participants challenge the IMC by demanding "impartiality" and "journalistic standards," and by calling on writers to stop editorializing. "Just report what you see," demands one typical comment. In one long discussion after an article by the professional journalist Robert Fisk, linked to the March 22, 2003, "Report from the Frontlines" feature, Fisk is criticized for "the fact that he twists facts," and for prose that "reads like a supermarket tabloid" compared to the "top quality" and "professionalism and objectivism [sic] that is at the heart of the rest of journalism." Another writer suggests that papers that don't agree "with a particular worldview" are most credible, especially "the large, responsible papers."

Responses to those critiques call for a transparency of ideological leaning that is not made explicit in corporate media. In response to the critique of Robert Fisk, for example, one writer notes that Fisk

> is better at separating his editorializing from his reporting of facts, and makes it plain he is doing both. Wouldn't it be nice if all media did this? Including the ones whose ideology you support? A human being standing in the middle of this horror. . . . Wouldn't you find him more at fault for trying to perpetuate the myth of "objectivity" . . . instead, [he is] plainly stating: this is the plain fact of what I see . . . this is what I think of it and how I feel as I see it happening. Make of that what you will. (www.indymedia.org/front.php?article_id=301081)

KEEPING COLLECTIVE WATCH

The IMC network has become a tool for exploring the process of media representation itself, encouraging a collective public process of both textual and visual analysis that not only targets corporate media for public scrutiny, but also allows for a running critique of the IMC itself. The IMC has in essence taken on the watchdog function traditionally associated with mainstream media, arguing that because the mainstream media have become lapdogs for corporate interests, these media now need their own watchdog. The difference between the IMC and media literacy or media watchdog groups is that the IMC encourages its reader/producers to play this role themselves by keeping a critical eye trained on corporate media and writing about it, and includes the open publishing technology to make this possible both on a collective basis and on a global scale.

A fascinating example of this process in action began on March 3, 2003, when the IMC global page featured a story entitled, "US Surveils United Nations, American Media Ignores Story." The summary on the global page is brief, and includes two links: one to the original story that broke in *"The Observer*, Great Britain's oldest newspaper," and the other to the entire IMC feature on the New York City IMC, which broke the story within the network. The story reports that the United States' National Security Agency (NSA) conducted an "extensive spying campaign against members of the U.N. Security Council . . . [which was] according to *The Observer*, 'part of its battle to win votes in favor of war against Iraq.'" The focus of the IMC feature, however, is not so much the actual incident, but rather how the U.S. mainstream media had not yet run the story, especially since the story had broken in London "well over thirty hours ago."

Using the Google News database, the writer had found twenty-three media outlets that had picked up the story, only one of which was a U.S. media outlet. The story notes that of these twenty-three, "six were British, six Australian, six Middle Eastern or Pakistani, two Canadian, one German." Three U.S. sources were carrying the story, but two of these were advocacy or alternative media outlets. The third U.S. source to carry the story was the "right-wing *Washington Times*, which questioned the 'British English' used in the original *Observer* report." *The Observer* responded that they had changed the English spellings in the leaked memo on which the story is based to standardize it for a British audience.

The feature includes multiple links, including to the original story in *The Observer* (which has a link to the actual leaked memo) and the *Democracy Now* interview of the journalist who wrote the story. The feature ends with a call to readers: "Try it yourself . . . click here [the link to the Google search engine used to track the story] to see if and when the American newspapers pick up this story." At the end of the story is a link to "Comment and Report Back," a discussion that is interesting for how the participants maintain an ongoing analysis not only of when and where the story is appearing around the world, but also of how it is framed differently in different papers. Comments posted to this discussion range from dismissals to engagement with the story and its travels through the world's media.

This discussion suggests a new twist to the often-sophisticated attempts by activists to influence the media coverage or framing of events in order to better represent their concerns. The process unfolding in this discussion and others on the IMC exemplifies the use of the electronic resources of the Internet to track the circulation of news and the way that this news is framed. In the process, the attempt to do this tracking as well as what is found become the focus of the collective, unfolding story, which attends to the process of how and why the story gets told in addition to its content.

THE DISCUSSION PROCESS

The attention to process is also apparent in the discussions, but is not shared by all participants. In general, the lengthier the discussion following a feature, the more likely it is to contain at least some hostile or insulting messages. Those posts that are most negative or aggressive quite often elicit passionate responses, often dismissive and insulting in turn. Prowar and antiwar participants alike hurl insults, and those of like mind posting to a discussion do occasionally "gang up" on those expressing different perspectives. This reinforces the notion that online debate is often a matter of "cacophony rather than wisdom" and that the floor often belongs to those who log on most often (Davis 1999). Reading these posts can be depressing, filled as they often are with personal attacks that do little to further dialogue. More hopeful, however, is the significant "middle ground" that conducts dialogue in respectful yet critical terms, and that encourages others to do the same. It is in these exchanges that attention to process is evident in references to the discussion itself, its limitations, and its value beyond the immediate comments being made. One participant writes,

> I don't want you to declare yourself an ideological copy of myself. That would be ridiculous. But exposure to new ideas and differing opinions are how you continually reaffirm to yourself what you believe; where common ground may lie between us; what, therefore, we can work on together; and when we should avoid each other until further information is known. (www.indymedia.org/front .php3?article_id=301255&group=webcast)

Oftentimes, posts expressing views counter to the prevailing ideology of the IMC are answered in great detail, especially when they are not openly hostile, or when they provide specific claims, accusations, or evidence of a writer's knowledge of an issue. In one example that typifies a prevalent pattern, one writer argues that rather than protest the war, activists should provide some "workable alternative to military action." Many responses to this comment address its arguments directly, such as one detailing past U.S. government actions in Iraq and elsewhere, possible alternatives to the war as presented by many in the United States and UN prior to the war, and the writer's take on George W. Bush's lack of concern for those U.S. citizens "who are not very wealthy." The statements are extensively supported by quotes and details of where the sources could be found to confirm them.

It is clear that people actually do follow links and read information that is contrary to their own views, and that they sometimes rethink their opinions and find the conversation fruitful. In one discussion, a comment headed "This discussion is proof . . ." continues in the body of the message, "that diplomacy works! If you were here, I'd shake your hand." The other writer responds, in a very short comment headed "peace," with "Ain't peace grand?" In another discussion, one participant writes, "It's great to see a little exchange going on here!" Others in the same discussion thank those with differing viewpoints for expressing them. In the end, while the opinions of many participants do not seem to change explicitly through these exchanges, there is evidence that for some, the discussion provokes a different way of looking at an issue or event, or a shift from certainty about something to a willingness to withhold judgment while more evidence can be gathered.

BLURRING THE BOUNDARIES: READER/RESEARCHER/WRITER

Many people and groups conduct their own research and use the IMC to post their findings. This research varies in terms of formality and depth, and participants range from individuals to more structured media watch groups. We have seen one example already, in the collective tracking of the *Observer* story about the U.S. surveillance at the UN. A participant in a different discussion responds to another's praise of her detailed posts to the IMC, insisting that she does not write professionally: "I have been prompted to do my own research by the dissatisfaction I felt with mainstream media. . . . There are many good journalists and writers of many different nationalities who publish and I have made extensive use of their work to draw my own conclusions." In another example, a feature details the results of "a non-scientific survey of attendees" at both a prowar rally and a peace rally, and while the number of people surveyed is small (twenty-six people at the "liberate Iraq" rally, and thirty-four at the peace rally), the results are interesting. The surveys show, in response to a query about their "major source for in depth news coverage," that peace rally participants cite a fairly diverse set of sources, including several international sources, a good deal of reliance on the Internet, and very little TV (other than 12 percent C-span), while 35 percent of the "liberate Iraq" rally participants report getting their in-depth news from talk radio and an additional 39 percent from TV. While most of the responses to the article debate various aspects of the rallies themselves, one praises the article as "great reporting. . . . Ideology set to the side, just the facts as you see them." The discussion also includes critique of coverage by a local newscast by one person who thought they had marginalized the protestors, and another who thought they were overly sympathetic.

In an example from before the bombing began, a February 5, 2003, feature on antiwar protests in Michigan during a visit by President Bush includes a link entitled "analysis of local media coverage" posted by a nonprofit media watchdog group, the Grand Rapids Institute for Information Democracy. After a brief description of the protest itself, the article notes that the local media focused its coverage on the arrest of ten people rather than on the fact that there were "between 1-2000 people from all over Michigan" who had demonstrated against the impending war without incident. To back up this claim, the article analyzes the coverage of the event by the local Fox affiliate and two other local TV channels, as well as the press coverage in Grand Rapids, where the protest took place. The article concludes that "much of the reporting was biased and limited. How the demonstration was framed gave wrong impressions. . . . This event was the biggest demonstration that Grand Rapids has seen in over 30 years and it was organized in roughly three days." The story ends with a call to readers to "contact all four news outlets and challenge them on their coverage." The discussion afterwards includes two writers who offer examples of additional coverage they found, one critical of a local paper, the other arguing that another news station had done a good job. The final comment is from a person who found the IMC while looking for coverage on the demonstration she had taken part in, saying that "press coverage was poor and did not reflect my experience." She proceeded to detail her experiences, telling a compelling story of a run-in with an overzealous policeman she described as acting in "unwarranted rage."

While this type of informal research and the discussions it brings about may not lead to statistically significant conclusions, it is a frequent activity on the IMC by both individuals and organizations, and offers a model for others. It supports the claim that Web use can encourage a collective process of critique in which, as Jones (2000) suggests, "the sum of connections makes a content greater than the sum of its parts" (178). It furthers Burnett and Marshall's (2003) claim that Web users are increasingly taking on the role of researchers, but takes it a step further, in that the research being conducted is not carried out exclusively on the Web, but also in the streets or people's homes, stretching the boundaries of what constitutes a newsmaker.

THE VALUE OF A GOOD "CHINWAG"

> Content is not king. . . . Because what does matter is communication, social interaction . . . that process of writing news, publishing it, commenting on it, editing it, that engagement of people in the fundamental task of telling a good story, of sifting through which stories are important, and having a good old chinwag when the storyteller finishes. That process may turn out to be more important than the story itself.
>
> IMC activist Matthew Arnison (2002b)

The IMC presents a process-oriented challenge to corporate media, providing a forum for a collective process in which participants provoke and encourage each other in the creation of the collective text. The IMC's attention to process becomes apparent in the network's content, especially during the discussions that follow features. In offering a tool for media activism characterized by decentralized networks and hyperlinks between multiple information sources, the IMC network opens the kind of "deliberative spaces" required to maintain an active democratic citizenry (Dahlberg 2001). This process in action during the war not only challenged the Bush administration outright, but also reframed normative U.S. concepts of "expert" status and "objectivity," calling into question a profit-driven media that many argue leaves as much out as it reports.

The IMC's rapid growth indicates that it is filling a need, yet it also faces significant challenges. Both in the makeup of its local collectives and in its global content, the IMC will need to continue to reach out, to invite citizen participation, and to involve those without access to or great fluency with computers, especially activists in the global South and marginalized groups in the world's richest nations. In addition, the way many of the IMC features are framed, with a central focus on protest, tends to divert attention from the fact that the reports also provide analyses (albeit of varying depth) of concerns voiced by protestors, police response to the protests, and inconsistencies and unstated assumptions in mainstream media coverage. As Meikle (2002) argues, the challenge for Internet activists is to develop ways of telling their stories that deal with the issues but do not replicate "the conflict-based narrative structures of established media" (99). While it is unfortunate that many of the IMC features do not provide evidence of a move away from such conflict-based narratives, many of the discussions that follow features do show attempts to break down binaries not only between "us" and "them" but also between "reporters" and "readers/viewers."

The IMC presents a small but growing model of democratic communication, important in that it challenges people to work actively to democratize both media representations and the processes of media production, and provides at least those with Internet access the tools to do so. The network challenges the status quo in several ways, not least in its function as a forum for the collective exchanging of, sorting through, and debating of information counter to the official line. In the best IMC discussions, those who participate are treated with respect and held to the same standards, despite their political persuasions. The IMC challenges participants to identify and challenge the types of authority naturalized through corporate media news, by urging them to "Be the Media" and write rather than just consume the news. By questioning standard news practices, the IMC encourages a critical eye, asking that people place current events in their historical, social and geographic context, and urging them to attend to and actively challenge inaccurate or problematic corporate media representations. With the call for eyewitness accounts, links, and citations as the grounds for establishing legitimacy, the collective "chinwag" at times demands a level of accountability that corporate media would find hard to meet.

REFERENCES

Arnison, M. (2001). *Open publishing is the same as free software.* Retrieved April 15, 2004, from www.cat.org.au/maffew/cat/openpub.html

———. (2002a, January). Open editing. In M. Arnison (2001), *Open publishing is the same as free software.* Retrieved April 15, 2004, from www.cat.org.au/maffew/cat/openpub.html

———. (2002b, September). Content is not king. In M. Arnison (2001), *Open publishing is the same as free software.* Retrieved April 15, 2004, from www.cat.org.au/maffew/cat/openpub.html

Blumler, J. G., & Gurevitch, M. (2001). The new media and our political communication discontents: democratizing cyberspace. *Information, Communication & Society* 4 (1), 1–13.

Burnett, R., & Marshall, P. D. (2003). *Web theory: An introduction.* New York: Routledge.

Dahlberg, L. (2001). The Internet and democratic discourse. *Information, Communication & Society* 4 (4), 615–633.

Davis, R. (1999). *The web of politics: The Internet's impact on the American political system*. Oxford: Oxford University Press.

Downing, J. D. (2001). The Seattle IMC and the socialist anarchist tradition. Paper presented at the OURMedia I Conference, Washington, DC. Retrieved March 13, 2004, from www.ourmedia.net.org/general/papers.html

———. (2003). The IMC movement beyond "the west." In A. Opel & D. Pompper (Eds.), *Representing resistance: media, civil disobedience, and the global justice movement* (pp.

Hacker, K. L. (1996). Missing links in the evolution of electronic democratization. *Media, Culture and Society* 18, 213–232.

Halleck, D. (2002). Gathering storm: The open cyber forum of indymedia. Paper presented at the OURMedia II Conference, Barcelona, Spain. Retrieved March 13, 2004, from www.ourmedia.net.org/general/papers.html

Herndon, S. (2003). Indymedia. Paper presented at the OURMedia III Conference, Barranquilla, Colombia. Retrieved March 13, 2004, from www.ourmedianet.org/om2003/om2003.papers_eng.html

Hintz, A. (2003). Indymedia Germany: A local node of the global network. *Media Development* XLX (4), 21–25.

Jones, S. (2000). The bias of the web. In A. Herman & T. Swiss (Eds.), *The World Wide Web and contemporary cultural theory* (pp. 171–182). New York: Routledge.

Kidd, D. (2003a). Become the media: the global IMC network. In A. Opel & D. Pompper (Eds.), *Representing resistance: Media, civil disobedience, and the global justice movement* (pp. 224–240). Westport, CT: Praeger.

———. (2003b). The Independent Media Center: A new model. *Media Development* XLX (4): 7–11.

Kitaeff, L. (2003, January/February). Indymedia. *Utne*, 85–86.

Meikle, G. (2002). *Future active: Media activism and the Internet*. New York: Routledge.

———. (2003). Indymedia and the new net news. *Media Development* XLX (4), 3–6.

Mosco, V. (2004). *The digital sublime: Myth, power, and cyberspace*. Cambridge: MIT Press.

Naidoo, P. (2003). The independent media centre—South Africa. *Media Development* XLX (4), 18–21.

Reality according to www.indymedia.org. (2001, September 28). *CQ Researcher* 11 (33), 775.

Schiller, D. (1999). *Digital capitalism: Networking the global market system*. Cambridge: MIT Press.

Stallman, R.M. (2002). *Free software, free society: Selected essays of Richard M. Stallman*. Boston: GNU Press.

Index

About the Contributors

Lee Artz (Ph.D., University of Iowa) is associate professor in the Department of Communication and Creative Arts at Purdue University Calumet. His most recent books include *The Globalization of Corporate Media Hegemony* (with Yahya Kamalipour, 2003), *Public Media and the Public Interest* (with Michael McCauley, Eric Petersen, and Dee Dee Halleck, 2002), *Communication and Democratic Society* (2001), and *Cultural Hegemony in the United States* (with Bren Murphy, 2000).

Heinz Brandenburg (Ph.D., Trinity, Dublin, 2002) is associate professor in the Department of Sociology and Political Science at the Norwegian University of Science and Technology (NTNU) in Trondheim, Norway. He teaches media sociology and political science. His work has been published in *How Ireland Voted* (2002) and the *Harvard International Journal of Press/Politics*.

Lisa Brooten (Ph.D., Ohio University, 2003) is assistant professor at Southern Illinois University, Carbondale, Department of Radio-Television. Brooten's research interests include militarization and media, gender, human rights, alternative media, social movements, and globalization. Her work has been published in the *Asian Journal of Communication* and in the recent book, *Global Media Go to War*.

Elisia L. Cohen (Ph.D., University of Southern California, 2003) teaches media studies and political communication in the Department of Communication at Saint Louis University. Her recent research has focused on media and public responses to the September 11 tragedies. She has contributed chapters to *Communication and Terrorism* and *Crisis Communications: Lessons from*

September 11, and has published in *Journal of Broadcasting and Electronic Media* and *Prometheus*.

Timothy M. Cole (Ph.D., University of Washington, 1987) teaches international relations and American foreign policy in the Department of Political Science at the University of Maine, where he is the department chair. His research integrates questions of American foreign policy, political communication and rhetoric, media studies, and public opinion. His most recent publication is "Presidential Impeachment and Institutional Dynamics in the Iran-Contra Affair and the Clinton-Lewinsky Scandal" (with Dr. Amy Fried) in the spring 2004 issue of *Congress and the Presidency*.

Christian Fuchs (Ph.D., Vienna, 2002) teaches media studies and information society studies at the Vienna University of Technology and is a research assistant at the Institute of Design and Technology Assessment. His specialist fields are the sociology of technology, social theory, information society, media theory, and self-organization. Recent publications include *Informatics and Society* (with W. Hofkirchner, 2003, in German), *Crisis and Criticism in the Information Society* (2002, in German), and *Causality, Emergence and Self-Organisation* (coeditor, 2003).

Mike Gasher (Ph.D., Concordia, 1999), a former newspaper reporter, teaches critical journalism studies in the Department of Journalism at Concordia University in Montreal. His research focuses on issues of media representation, political economy, the geography of news, and journalism education. His recent publications include *Mass Communication in Canada* (with Rowland Lorimer, 2004), *Hollywood North: The Feature Film Industry in British Columbia* (2002), as well as essays in the *Canadian Journal of Communication and Journalism: Theory, Practice and Criticism*.

William B. Hart II (Ph.D., University of New Mexico, 1999) teaches courses in international communication, intercultural communication, research methods, and rhetorical criticism and a new course on communication and 9/11 at Old Dominion University, Virginia. In addition to his research in intercultural communication, he is conducting a study of the popular music of 9/11 and the portrayal of bin Laden, al Qaeda, and the Taliban in editorial cartoons since 9/11.

Fran Hassencahl (Ph.D., Case Western Reserve University, 1970) was a college debate coach, a Fulbright scholar in Morocco, and exchange faculty in Iraq and Syria. She teaches communication at Old Dominion University and directs the minor in Middle Eastern studies, doing research in rhetoric, media and popular culture, and contemporary politics and culture in the Middle East. Recent publications include "Individuation and Integration in Orhan Pamuk's *The White Castle*" in *Abhath Al Yarmouk* 20 (Jordan, 2002).

Adel Iskandar (M.A., Purdue University Calumet, 2000) is an expert on Middle East media. His research interests include transnational media, globalization, media ethnography, and postcolonial theory. Iskandar is the coauthor of *Al-Jazeera: How the Free Arab News Network Scooped the World and Changed the Middle East* (2003) and coeditor of the forthcoming volume *Edward Said: Emancipation and Representation* (2005). He is completing his doctoral degree at the University of Kentucky.

Liz Jacka is professor of communication studies at the University of Technology Sydney and has published a number of books, including a history of Australian cinema, *The Screening of Australia* (with Susan Dermody); *Australian Television and International Mediascapes* (with Stuart Cunningham); and *New Patterns in Global Television: Peripheral Vision* (with Cunningham and John Sinclair). Jacka is currently working on a major research project looking at the future of public service broadcasting, focusing on the Australian Broadcasting Corporation.

Andrew Jakubowicz (Ph.D., University of New South Wales, 1977), a longtime academic and social activist on issues of racism and social change, currently teaches sociology, new media, and the politics of racism at the University of Technology Sydney, Australia. His research concentrates on new media and social change, and the nature of empire in a globalizing world. Recent work includes two websites, *The Remaking of Multicultural Australia in the 21st Century* (2004) and the *Menorah of Fang Bang Lu* (2002). He has also published in the *International Journal of Communication*, *Gazette*, and *Journal of Intercultural Studies*, and in book chapters in the United States, Indonesia, and the United Kingdom.

Sue Curry Jansen (Ph.D., University of Buffalo) is professor of communication at Muhlenberg College, Allentown, Pennsylvania. She is author of *Critical Communication Theory* (2002) and *Censorship: The Knot that Binds Power and Knowledge* (1988, 1991), and is coauthor of *Humanism in Sociology: Historical Roots and Contemporary Problems* (1978). She has also published in the *Journal of Communication*, *Communication Theory*, *Communication Yearbook*, *Feminist Media Studies*, *Theory and Society*, and the *International Encyclopedia of Communication*.

Robert Jensen (Ph.D., Minnesota, 1992) has taught graduate and undergraduate courses in media law, ethics, and politics at the University of Texas at Austin since 1992. Prior to his academic career, he worked as a professional journalist for a decade. He is the author of *Citizens of the Empire: The Struggle to Claim Our Humanity* (2004) and *Writing Dissent: Taking Radical Ideas from the Margins to the Mainstream* (2002). In addition to his scholarly work, he writes frequently for mainstream and alternative popular media.

Yahya R. Kamalipour (Ph.D., University of Missouri–Columbia) is professor and head of the Department of Communication and Creative Arts, Purdue University Calumet, Hammond, Indiana. He has taught at universities in Ohio, Illinois, Missouri, Indiana, Oxford (England), and Tehran. His most recent books are *War, Media, and Propaganda: A Global Perspective* (with Nancy Snow, 2004), *The Globalization of Corporate Media Hegemony* (with Lee Artz, 2003) and *Global Communication* (2002). He is managing editor of *Global Media Journal* (www.globalmediajournal.com) and editor of *Global Media Monitor* (www.globalmediamonitor.com).

Douglas Kellner is George Kneller Chair in the Philosophy of Education at University of California, Los Angeles, and is author of many books on social theory, politics, history, and culture. Recent books include a study of the 2000 U.S. presidential election, *Grand Theft 2000: Media Spectacle and the Theft of an Election*, and *The Postmodern Adventure: Science, Technology, and Cultural Studies at the Third Millennium* (with Steve Best). He has just published two books, *Media Spectacle* and *September 11, Terror War, and the Dangers of the Bush Legacy*.

Matthew A. Killmeier (Ph.D., University of Iowa, 2003) is assistant professor of communication at Truman State University. His research interests include the cultural history of radio, popular music, critical theory, and political economy of the media.

Debra Merskin (Ph.D., Syracuse, 1994), a former advertising media director, teaches communication studies in the School of Journalism and Communication at the University of Oregon. Her research in cultural studies focuses on media representations of race, ethnicity, and gender. Merskin has published in *Mass Communication & Society*, *Sex Roles*, *Journalism & Mass Communication Quarterly*, and *Journal of Current Issues in Advertising Research*.

Tanja Thomas (Ph.D., Tübingen, 2003) has studied arts and German (University of Saarbrücken), media studies (Eberhard-Karls-University Tübingen), and gender (International Women's University Hannover). She is lecturer in the Institute of Media and Communication Studies, Technical University Ilmenau, Germany. Her research in media studies focuses on cultural studies, gender studies, racism and media, nation/nationalism, and media. Recent publications include *Deutsch-Stunden: Zur Konstruktion nationaler Identität in Fernsehtalks* (German-Hours: The Construction of National Identity on TV Talk Shows; 2003).

Fabian Virchow (Dipl. Soc., Hamburg, 1987) has studied sociology, political sciences, and social history. He teaches at the University of Applied Sciences in Kiel, Germany. His main interests are the sociology of the history of ideas, political culture, social movements, militarism and militarization, and the history, ideology, media, and organizational forms of the far right. Recent publications include *Technologietransformation* (2000), and essays on racial nationalism as a paradigm in international relations (peace and change), on civil war as race war (civil wars), and on the "demonstration-policy" of the far right in Germany.